ALL NIGHT AWAKE

sarah A. HOYT

ACE BOOKS, NEW YORK

This is a work of fiction. Names, characters, places, and incidents either
are the product of the author's imagination or are used fictitiously, and
any resemblance to actual persons, living or dead, business
establishments, events, or locales is entirely coincidental.

ALL NIGHT AWAKE

An Ace Book / published by arrangement with
the author

PRINTING HISTORY
Ace hardcover edition / October 2002
Ace mass-market edition / November 2003

Copyright © 2002 by Sarah A. Hoyt.
Cover art by Judy York.
Cover design by Erika Fusari.

ISBN: 0-441-01112-8

ACE®
Ace Books are published by The Berkley Publishing Group,
a division of Penguin Group (USA) Inc.,
375 Hudson Street, New York, New York 10014.
ACE and the "A" design
are trademarks belonging to Penguin Group (USA) Inc.

PRINTED IN THE UNITED STATES OF AMERICA

10 9 8 7 6 5 4 3 2 1

Praise for
ALL NIGHT AWAKE

Chosen as one of the year's Best Fantasies by *Chronicle*

"The author of *Ill Met by Moonlight* continues her portrayal of the secret life of William Shakespeare with a tale of deception and betrayal that brings to life the raucous world of Elizabethan England. Will have particular appeal to fans of literary fantasy." —*Library Journal*

"Hoyt has a deceptively clear and easy style. [Her work] is finely polished. Her characters, historical and magical, are deftly drawn and completely believable."
—*Chronicle*

"Readers will delight in Hoyt's clever reverse-engineering of Shakespeare's works into her own unique plot."
—*Starlog*

"Hoyt sustains her intriguing premise with a soaring lyrical style. A most enchanting novel." —*Booklist*

"An entertaining blend of historical facts with fantasy lore. Hoyt's prose has a lyrical feel that adds to a wonderful book." —*Midwest Book Review*

"As a historical fantasy, [the book] has much to praise."
—*Mythprint*

continued . . .

This book is dedicated to the participants in the 1999 Oregon Coast Professional Writers Workshop—a.k.a. the Kris and Dean Boot Camp for Writers.

To my fellow students: Rebecca Lickiss, Phaedra Weldon Steele, Terry Hayman, Mike Moscoe, Walter Williamson. "We few, we happy few, we band of brothers" (*Henry V* 4.3.60). In shedding our ink together we cemented friendships I can only hope will be lifelong.

And to instructors K. W. Jeter, Ginjer Buchanan, and, above all, to Kristine Kathryn Rusch and Dean Wesley Smith, "I can no other answer make, but thanks. And thanks" (*Twelfth Night* 3.3.14–15).

Prologue

❧

Scene: *A wooden stage, looking very real and solid, amid swirls of yellow-green smoke or fog. On the stage three women sit on wooden stools, beside a painted hearth. A beautiful maiden spins the thread, a strong matron measures it, and a wrinkled crone cuts it with a pair of golden shears. A man appears at the edge of the stage. He's a middle-aged man who looks insignificant, with his receding hairline and dark curls that brush the shoulders of his cheap russet wool suit. Only his eyes, sharp and intent, golden as a bird of prey's, hint at curiosity and intelligence. He walks to the center of the stage and faces the women.*

Will does not know if he dreams or wakes.

He walks on a creaking stage with hesitant steps and knows not how he got here. Only minutes ago he slept in his own bed, in his rented room in London. By what magic has he been brought hence?

Three strange women face him. Women they look to be, women they seem to be, and yet something about them proclaims them something else.

"All hail Will Shakespeare!" The maiden lifts her head

from her spinning. As her blond hair falls back, it shows that she lacks ears. "Hail to thee, great poet."

Will jumps back, shocked both at deformity and greeting.

Great poet? Did she indeed greet Will thus? He could scant believe it for he knew that his poetical talent was as yet all dreams and none of it survived the harsh light of reality.

"All hail Will, whose verse generations yet unborn shall recite." The matron looks up from the thread she winds and measures. Her smile shows feral, serrated teeth.

"All hail Will," the crone pipes. Lifting her head, she shows no eyes amid the wrinkles on her withered face. "All hail Will, whom death shall not defeat."

Scared, Will takes three steps back. This is a mocking dream that thus torments him with the possibility of his dearest hopes. He takes his hand to his collar and seeks to loosen it, as though by breathing deeply he might regain his footing in real life and the waking world.

"Live you?" he asks. "Are you aught that man ought to question? Do I dream, or am I awake? You look not like the inhabitants of the earth. You should be women, and yet strange women you are. What are you?"

"We are not women but that of which women are spun. We're images of dream, creatures of the mind. Through us do human minds perceive all. Through us, the mold and form of female reality, do human minds see the force like a womb that, within the universe, spins all that's female in the world of men," the maiden says. "We were created before man was man, from the dim minds of brutes in their caves, and since then have we been in human minds and actions and dreams. Our presence the more real for being illusory, our power the more true for being imagined, encompasses all and shapes all. Thus does the imagined mold the real and the real the imagined again."

"By us is all life threaded and measured and cut, ours the weaving of human fate," the matron says.

"But ours will be the undoing and the death, should we not find a champion to defend us." The crone's hair flies wild, framing her face in snow-white tendrils.

"Defend us," the maiden says. "And you shall be the greatest poet born of woman's womb. Your plays will be heard, your verses repeated world without end."

Will clenches his fists. They mock him. Surely they mock him. "Six months I've been in London and no one will listen to my poetry. Six months of starving and spending. Now are all my money and all my hope run out. And yet you mock me."

The maiden shakes her head. "We do not mock, but promise."

"Only do as we wish," the matron says. "And fame and ever-living poetry shall be your reward. For we command that part of the human mind that, dreaming, imagines itself awake and in that same place does poetry reside."

"The kingdom of elves is in turmoil and the disarray of that sphere threatens ours. Sylvanus, who should be the Hunter's slave, plots to rebel against his master, who, like us, is an ancient and powerful invention of humanity, an element and avatar of all that's justice in males," the matron says.

"Sylvanus, who was king of elves, and for his foul deeds was enslaved to the Hunter, the justiciar, the provider," the crone says.

"Sylvanus will destroy us and thus remove both the male and female pillars that hold up the world as human minds have built it. Thus, like a cloak unraveled, the universe shall fall, in tatters and threads with no meaning."

"Into our place Sylvanus shall weave himself, within

the mind's warp," the maiden says. "Like a rotted patch shall he sew himself upon a new cloth of dream, rendering the whole worthless."

"Why do not you stop him yourselves?" Will asks.

The maiden shakes her head. "We can no more stop him than we can stop the tide. We spin the thread, we wind and cut. But our tools must be the human mind, the human heart. We cannot weave our own fate. We do not tie our own knot."

"Stop Sylvanus." The matron smiles, sharp teeth gleaming. "And the reward shall be yours, your poetry remembered, your words echoed through the ages unending."

"Stop Sylvanus," the crone says. "And we shall make you greatest of his kind, for words that burn and spell and bind."

"I am dreaming," the man says. "And in this dream, uneasy, do my fondest hopes mock me."

He vanishes like smoke upon the stage, leaving the three women behind, spinning and cutting and measuring the eery thread that glimmers white in their laps.

Scene 1

∝∂

The nave of St. Paul's Cathedral, or Paul's Walk, as it is called in Elizabethan England. People of all descriptions crowd every corner of the ample space—tailors, factors, lawyers, pickpockets, sellers of racy woodcuts, bawds, and chimney sweeps—all of them do business here, beneath the soaring arched roof and between the lofty columns. The imposing stone tombs of the nobility, the rood loft, even the baptismal font are used as money-changing counters. Dandies stroll aimlessly, displaying their fashionable clothes. An ill-dressed young man in his late twenties, with the beginnings of a receding hairline and long black curls that brush his frayed lace collar, stands by the eastern door, anxiously perusing a confusion of papers glued there, each headed "Si Quis."

Will Shakespeare looked at the Si Quis notices posted on the door. There were so many that one was glued upon the other, till the whole door appeared to be made of paper.

Si Quis meant *if anyone*. *Si Quis would be tailor, Si Quis would be serving man, Si Quis would be fencing master.*

All the jobs in London were spread before Will, like the countries of the earth before the tempting devil.

Yet Will remained unemployed, his stomach empty, his rent long overdue. Only an hour ago, Will's landlord had awakened Will from uneasy, fitful sleep to demand payment for lodging that he'd long occupied but not paid for. Another day, and Will would have no lodging, either.

Si Quis would be chimney sweep. Si Quis would be gardener.

All these professions, though many, were to Will's purpose none.

His head hurt with a thunderous headache, and clotted remains of his dreams haunted his mind.

A great poet, the creatures had said Will would be.

Will. A great poet.

A middle-aged man, with fading looks, a provincial grammar-school education, and next to no friends in London, Will felt as though his fortune were as out at heel as his suit and his frayed lace cuffs.

No one wanted a would-be poet. No one was looking for an aspiring playwright. No one craved to hire even someone with Will's other, meager abilities: a petty schoolteacher, or a glover with little more than apprentice skill.

"Sweep chimney sweep, mistress," a man's baritone boomed just behind Will, deafening him. "With a hey derry from the top to the bottom."

A chimney sweep advertising his services.

The smell of roasting meat, seasoned with nutmeg and ginger, drifted up to Will's nose, tantalizing his stomach with savors of a supper he couldn't afford.

"Well met, Richard, well met," a man said to Will's left, hurrying forward to clasp another man in his arms. "Would you take ale with me? And sup?"

Will dearly wished someone would invite him to sup.

But in his six months in London, he'd formed near to no acquaintance and been befriended by none. He'd been cozened and fooled and stolen from. He'd been duped and mocked and betrayed, but he'd formed no useful connection, no gentle friendship that might ease his penury.

The little money he'd brought to London with him— scraped together from his father's failing business and his wife's selling of homegrown vegetables—had fallen drop by drop into an empty barrel of despair from which the sweet wine of hope had long since evaporated.

Now he had nothing. Not money enough to buy supper, not even enough to return home.

Nothing was left to him but to walk to Stratford, which would take days. Will would starve long before that.

Tears prickled behind Will's eyelids. How confident Will's wife had been, his Nan, when she'd pressed the few coins of their meager savings into Will's sweaty hand before he left home.

She'd kissed Will and told him that with his words and his wit he could pry London open like a treasure coffer, and make his fortune and the fortune of his whole family.

Oh, deceived wife. Oh, poor, way-led woman who— despite having lived with Will for ten years and borne him two daughters and a son—still believed her man to be a Hyperion, a sage, the form and glass of all mankind.

Poor Nan, who would never even know that her husband had starved in London, dead of his own folly and inflated pride.

"Help, help," an old man screamed to Will's right. "Someone has cut my purse. Help. Cozenage and damnation."

Behind Will men swarmed and pushed around the Si Quis door. Some were dressed as poorly as he, others arrayed in fine silks and velvets. All, by Will's side and pressing, shoulder on shoulder against him, read the notices on the door with the kind of hunger for employment that bespeaks the specter of starvation nearby. Each made a little triumphant noise or read the words aloud when he found a likely position and then tore off the sheet and sauntered away.

A man in a sky blue doublet, three finger-widths of creamy lace peeking from beneath his sleeves to shroud his hands, put a well-tended finger on the paper asking for a fencing master, and pushed Will out of the way to tear the sheet off the door.

It was no use, Will thought, jostled and pushed, feeling lost and hopeless. He would go back to his lodgings and dream for his supper while he starved.

In his dreams he'd been a poet, but waking no such matter.

His gaze swept over the yellowed papers and the crisp white ones, perusing the words scrawled upon them with desperate longing.

Si Quis would be smith. Si Quis would be weaver. Si Quis would be horse holder outside the bear garden.

Will's breath arrested. *Wait.* He could do *that.* He put his finger on the paper.

He could look after horses for customers who went inside to watch the bear baiting.

He grasped the corner of the sheet, meaning to tear it out and follow instructions on how to apply for the job.

"Holding horses," a man said, so close to Will that his breath tickled Will's ear. "Well, I could have done that."

Looking over his shoulder, Will saw a blond man as threadbare as himself. He looked back at Will and smiled, disarmingly. "Though, for my money, I'd rather have been an actor." He grimaced as though he'd named the lowest profession he could think of.

Will sighed. "I came to London to be a playwright," he said.

"No." His new acquaintance looked skeptical. "Did you indeed?" He pointed with sudden animation toward a man a few steps from them. "Look, there, in the red doublet and green hose. That's Philip Henslowe, the owner of The Rose, as I live and breathe."

In a moment, Will let go of the paper and turned, the thought of a job vanishing from his mind. The idea of holding horses in front of the bear garden became abhorrent, as did the idea of any job *not* in the theater. As abhorrent as stale beer when fresh wine is offered.

If Philip Henslowe was the owner of The Rose, in Southwark, then Henslowe was the owner of the largest and most successful theater in London. In The Rose were enacted Kit Marlowe's plays, the most acclaimed shows of the age. Even in far-off Stratford-upon-Avon Will had heard of *Tamburlaine the Great* and, with trembling admiration, read its lines printed on the cheap paper of a hastily copied booklet.

All his dreams reviving, Will thought that if only he could meet Henslowe, if he could impress Henslowe— why, Will would conquer the theater and become as great as Marlowe, and perhaps greater. He blushed at the hope, which he would never dare voice, even as it beat madly in his shying heart like a bird imprisoned in a glass dome.

The man in the red doublet and green hose stood in the center of the nave, right in the middle of Paul's Walk, talking to an auburn-haired dandy in a dark velvet doublet slashed through to show flame-colored fabric beneath.

The dandy didn't matter, but Philip Henslowe did. In six months, Will had yet to meet someone as important in the theater. This could be the turning point of his luck that led to the fulfillment of all his hopes.

Now he would brave Henslowe on his own, with no introduction. Or, Will thought, clenching his fists while his lower lip curled in disdain, Will deserved no better work than to hold horses in front of the bear garden.

Will elbowed the surrounding men out of the way, cut through the middle of a group of loudly arguing dandies, and extending his hand, as though to beg, charged toward Henslowe.

His extended fingers touched shabby red velvet and he spoke indistinctly through a mouth that suddenly felt too dry. "Please, Master Henslowe, I am a poet."

At that, all of Will's wit fled him and he stood, mute and frozen, before the theater owner.

Will wanted to say that he would like to write plays, that he was sure he could write plays as fire-woven as Marlowe's, or better. But he could say no more.

Up close, Henslowe looked older than Will had expected, his face as sun-tanned and worry-creased as the face of Will's wife, back in Stratford.

Will's mouth opened, but his tongue could not find the turn of a rounded phrase or even the trick of a single word.

Philip Henslowe looked average: a man with brown eyes and longish, straight brown hair.

His bold-colored doublet and bright green pants showed as much sign of wear as Will's russet suit. At elbows and knees, the fabric had worn old and thin, all the pile gone and nothing but the threadbare weave beneath.

He looked back at Will with lusterless eyes and arched his eyebrows. "A poet?" he said, as though the word were a fantastical sound referring to some obscure occupation or some marvel told by sailors returned from distant lands.

"A poet, Philip," the dandy to whom Henslowe had been talking said, and tittered. He glanced at Will, and his long-lashed grey eyes sparked with humor. "You know them, surely. They grow under rocks and in untended places, and hide in clusters in universities."

The dandy smiled, showing white teeth that went well with his fine-featured, smooth, oval face, his well-clipped beard, and the fine moustache that traced his upper lip like a well-drawn line. He turned to Will and winked. "Tell me, good man, did you go to a university or to an inn of the court and there tend your wit as others tend vegetable patches, with the manure of learning and the heat of argument?"

Henslowe looked at the ceiling, as though beseeching a far-off divinity.

Will's mouth remained dry. He shook his head.

Who could this be, whose clothing looked newly made, whose auburn hair showed the darker roots that indicated art aiding nature, whose every trait and feature betrayed a nobleman? Why would such a one talk to a theater owner, the impious rabble of society? And why would such a one bother to mock Will?

The dandy's grey eyes looked a question, and his eyebrows arched. "Not a university man?"

Will cleared his throat. "I've never gone to university." He bowed slightly. "I went to grammar school and then I taught for a time in the country. Then I helped my father in his shop."

The finely drawn eyebrows of the auburn-haired gentleman arched upon his white brow, a movement more intent and meaning than Henslowe's similar look. "Not gone to university? And your father had a shop? Why, that's fatal."

The dandy pulled from within his sleeve a kerchief edged with lace worth more than all of Will's clothing. He waved this foppery in front of his nose, as though to dispel a bad stench. "A poet should never be a useful kind of person, capable of handling the grosser stuff of life. Tell me, your father is, mayhap, not a butcher, or some such gross occupation?"

Will shook his head, bewildered, "I pray, no. He's a glover, but—"

"Ah, he busies himself with the egg and flour of tanning, does he? And was it at his foot that you learned the fine chervil leather of a couplet, the whiting of poetry?" The gentleman smiled.

"I . . ." Will swallowed nervously. "I've always made poems, pray, to the local girls and . . . And I admire Marlowe's plays much."

The dandy laughed, a delighted cackle that jangled in the air, mingling with the calls of tradespeople, the enticements of bawds. "A good thing to love Marlowe's plays. I sometimes enjoy them myself. Do you not, yourself, enjoy them, Phillip?"

Henslowe rolled his eyes in silence.

The dandy laughed and turned to Will with sudden, giddy enthusiasm, "So, say a poem for us. A poem." He stuffed his handkerchief back into his sleeve and stepped back, as if to make room for Will's expansive wit.

"Declaim," the dandy said, and waved a hand encased in pearly grey chervil gloves with a heavy golden fringe at the end that dangled over a dainty wrist.

Will glanced at Henslowe, who stared not at Will but at the other man, with something like wonder or alarm.

Would Henslowe listen? Could Will earn his place as a playwright this way?

Standing with his feet close, Will cleared his throat.

When he'd dreamed of a moment like this, he'd imagined a tiring room, the air thick with the smell of grease paint, the actors all bespelled by Will's very presence.

A theater owner, or perhaps even a nobleman, would ask Will to recite a poem and all the actors would fall silent, all movement stop, till, in the end, nothing stirred amid props and costumes, nothing moved except Will's voice rising and falling and dazzling all.

But Will's reality always fell short of his dreams, and therefore, he cleared his throat and made to start.

"I have Dutch coins, and German, and French too. Change your coins here, before you set abroad," a money changer yelled near Will's ear.

Will jumped, but his would-be listeners didn't move. The dandy looked attentive, the theater owner bored.

His voice shaking, Will started, in measured cadences, to speak his best sonnet.

It was the one he'd written for Nan when they were courting, the one that ended in *hate from hate away she threw / And saved my life, saying not you.*

When Will had finished, the noise of Paul's had not died down. From somewhere came the high-pitched laughter of a bawd, and somewhere behind Will two gentlemen argued loudly.

"The sad ballad and sorrowful fate of Romeo," a ballad seller called out, just to the right of Henslowe, waving a sheaf of smudged printed sheets just within the theater owner's field of vision. "How he did kill himself for love unrequited."

And the dandy, his eyebrows more arched than ever, looked puzzled. "A fine sonnet, to be sure," he told Will. "A fine sonnet." Despite the man's words, his lips worked in and out, battling some emotion that Will feared was mirth.

With sudden heat, Will attempted to explain, "Your lordship will allow," Will said. "That my lady's name is Hathaway, you see."

The small, neat mouth—whose corners trembled upward, beneath the narrow moustache, when Will addressed its owner as "lordship"—opened in a round "o" of astonishment.

"Ah. Hathaway. Hate from hate away. Why it's marvelous, man. No more than a poet in two would think of such a clever pun, I say. What say you, Henslowe?" He turned to the theater owner.

Suspecting he was being mocked and feeling his heart droop down to consort with his worn-out boots, Will, too, turned toward the theater owner.

But Henslowe never once glanced in his direction. Instead, he looked impatiently at the dandy and flicked him on the shoulder with a shabby glove, as though to call his attention. "I think you have strange amusements, Kit." And before the dandy could more than open his mouth for what promised to be a droll reply, Henslowe added, "And I think your time would be better employed in writing me a play that I could stage. What, with the plague raging over this winter and the playhouses just reopened, we could use a new play to pack the groundlings in. Faustus has run its time upon the stage. Give us something new. I have a new playhouse to pay for."

In Will's brain the given name of *Kit* added to Henslowe's request for a new play, and to the name of *Faustus*, and as Will turned to gaze on the dandy—Will's mouth opening in wonder, his eyes wide—he realized that this creature, with his slashed-through sleeves, his immaculate, white silk hose, his expensive boots, his lace handkerchief, and gold-fringed grey gloves was no other than Kit Marlowe, the leading playwright of the age, the Muses' darling, the light of the London stage.

"Many good simples for all illnesses," a shrunken man in a black cloak called out, walking between them and away, waving a large, dark bottle. "It cures the French Pox, the ague, and the plague."

Kit Marlowe laughed.

"In time, my dear Henslowe, in good time. I'll write another play." Marlowe smiled on the theater owner. "But first I've promised my lord Thomas Walsingham to write a long poem on the sad tragedy and most sorrowful death of Hero and Leander."

Philip Henslowe made a rude noise at the sad tragedy.

"And on their romping, perforce, beneath a silken sheet. No. Don't answer that." He waved away Marlowe's attempt at speech with a hand clad in a glove dark with wearing. "Don't answer that. It doesn't bear discussing. I know why lordlings care about long-dead lovers. More honest, I say, to write for the people."

"And make sure plenty of blood spurts, to make the populus throw its greasy cloaks in the air," Marlowe said softly. "More honest that might be, Henslowe. But not nearly so profitable."

Marlowe swept his hand left to right through the air, describing a perfect arc and as though signifying the futility of human life. "Stay." He held Henslowe's arm as Henslowe made to turn away. "Soon as I'm done, I'll write you something new. A piteous doomed romance, maybe. Or would you prefer a revenge tragedy, like Thomas Kyd's?"

Kit's eyes acquired a faraway look as if he were reading in the entrails of his future for plays not yet written. "Perhaps I could write on the legend of Hamlet, the Dane, and how he avenged the murder of his heroic father."

Henslowe sighed. "Write on what you will, so long as you write. Marlowe's name on a playbill still draws them in."

Marlowe laughed. "For which you pay me enough to buy the buttons for one of my doublets. No. Mind not. I'll write my poem for Walsingham and get my money there. I would be finishing my poem even now at the lord's home of Scagmore, had not urgent business called me to London yesterday." He sighed and grinned. "Be gone with you. When I have my play, I'll come searching."

The playhouse owner patted Marlowe on the shoulder, as if acknowledging a joke or thanking Marlowe for a favor.

"But pray what did you think of my poem?" Will asked.

His voice, strangled and small, did not carry very far and missed Philip Henslowe altogether, as the theater owner turned his back and disappeared amid the throng.

"He didn't listen to your poem," Marlowe said and smiled at Will as though this too were droll.

Will's stomach twisted in hunger. Did Marlowe not understand that this was Will's very life in the balance of the theater owner's attention?

"They never do. Why would you wish him to? They know nothing of poetry, the unfeeling philistines. Theater owners listen only to the soft tinkling of coins, the whisper of gold." Marlowe adjusted the gilded fringe on his gloves, and bent upon Will a look of disarming honesty. "No, do yourself better, friend. Write a long poem. Know you the classics?"

Will's mouth went dry again. Marlowe, who had translated Ovid's *Amores*, asked if Will knew the classics. Even the *Amores*, Will had read in translation. "I have little Latin and small Greek," he stammered.

"Well, then, enough, I say. Write yourself a long poem, say on the subject of Venus and Adonis, and have the lovers disport in the glades of Arcadia and any nobleman will give you coin for it. What, with your clever punning style . . ."

"But my lodging—" Will started, intending to explain that he was already overdue in paying for that and must make some coin or perish.

"Your lodging is not convenient to gentlemen's abodes?" Marlowe asked.

Will shook his head. "I lodge in Shoreditch, at Hog's Lane," he said. "Over the Bonefoy hatters there, and I—"

He would have said more: that he owed money to his landlord, that soon he would be turned out, that he hadn't eaten in a whole day, that he knew no noblemen, no one who might help. He might so far have forgotten himself as to ask for the help of this stranger, of this crowned, gilded king of poets. And Will less than a peasant.

But before he could speak, two men emerged from the crowd, like wrathful gods from stormy waters, pushing aside money changers, ballad makers, and smirking, tightly corseted bawds.

The men flanked Marlowe, one on either side.

Will stepped away from them.

Somberly dressed, in black with no adornments, the two men looked like Puritans.

They were not the sort of men that Will expected to see with a playwright.

Marlowe looked at one, then the other. His whole face contracted, aged, soured, as if he'd tasted bitter gall.

One of the men had narrow-faced, thin looks that reminded Will of a rat in a house with a fast cat. The other one was round, but old, his face wrinkled and his chin sporting only a dismal growth of beard, like grass striving to thrive on poisoned land.

Will expected Marlowe to dismiss them or make fun of them.

Instead, Marlowe turned to face them and gave them his full attention and a weary look. He bowed to each one in turn. "Gentlemen?"

"If you would come with us," the small one said, his voice echoing with an incongruous boom.

Marlowe smiled, an oddly forced smile that lacked the mobility of his amusement and the malicious quickness of his teasing. It looked like the grin of a death mask, like the drawn lips and vacant eyes of a final rictus.

Funny how, when people died like that, their neighbors said they'd gone to their reward smiling. Will would never believe it again.

Marlowe bowed as a statue might bow, all stiff poise

and graceful dignity. "I am, as always, at the council's disposal, am I not?"

The three of them walked off, the two men on either side, hemming in Marlowe. Despite Marlowe's smile, his easy walk, he looked like a prisoner led to the gallows.

Will stared after them, blinking. It couldn't be. What would a playwright be arrested for? His writings?

No. The Queen's censor approved all plays, did he not? So, how could something libelous get on the stage?

No. Those men must be Kit Marlowe's friends, and Will's foreboding the fruit of his own sick thoughts.

Hunger gnawed at his entrails like a sharp-toothed rat, and all dreams of work in the theater had vanished before Will's eyes like a lacy fog that—lifted—uncovers dismal reality.

He rubbed his calloused thumb and forefinger across his eyes, trying to thus remove the veil that tiredness and faintness dropped in front of his vision.

Earlier that afternoon, to evade his hunger, Will had taken a nap. In that sleep, a strange dream had visited him, a dream of womenlike beings, who'd hailed Will as a great poet and forecast such a great future for him.

In this, his dismal waking reality, such dreams must be dismissed with a smile and a shrug. But tears prickled hard behind his eyes at the loss of that dreamed greatness that had never been his.

He retraced his steps through the thronging multitude, past a woman selling grilled chicken meat, to the Si Quis door again.

But the notice for the horse holder job was gone, as was the man who'd pointed Henslowe out to Will.

Will would find no work in London. He was too simple a man for this town. In Stratford, respectable men were honorable and people acted as they seemed. Nothing had prepared Will for the widespread deception he'd found in

the capital. Each day in London, it seemed, Will had been
ill used by someone. His purse had been cut, his meat
begged away from him, his bread shorted, his room over-
charged for.

Yet, he could go nowhere else. He lacked the money.

He'd die in London.

He might as well return to his lodgings. If he were
lucky, his pious Protestant landlord would already have
gone to bed and would not demand the rent that Will could
not pay.

Thus, Will would have a bed for yet another night. A
postponing of the harsh fate he could not avoid forever.

Scene 2

❧

*Arden Woods, near Stratford-upon-Avon. These ancient
trees are all that remain of the primeval forest that once
covered all of the British Isles. As befits their antiquity,
the woods are the run of fairy kind and the abode of
elves. On a clearing, amid the trees, a tall translucent
palace rises, more graceful and perfect than any built by
mankind. And in the gold-and-white-marble throne
room, the King and Queen of Elvenland sit on their
gilded thrones, and receive a centaur ambassador from
the far-off reaches of their realm. Tall, regal-looking,
Quicksilver sits on the throne, his long blond hair combed
over his shoulder. He wears a magnificent suit of dark
blue velvet and pale blue silk stockings. Queen Ariel,
smaller than her husband, and paler, sits next to him,
wearing a white dress that makes her look at once too
innocent and too young for the heavy crown that rests
upon her head.*

Running steps approached the throne room of Fairyland.

"Lord," a breathless voice called. "Lord, our boundary
is breached."

Quicksilver looked away from the ambassador of the centaurs.

The centaur ambassador shrugged his broad human shoulders, while the glossy black legs of his horse half tip-tapped uneasily on the marble floor.

The ambassador had been in the midst of one of the long speeches beloved of his people, mingling Greek and English with artless effusion.

Now he, like all of the court, turned his attention to the broad-arched entrance to the palace, from which a breathless voice called, "Milord, milord, a breach. A breach in our defense."

An elf careened through the marble archway that opened to the outside of the palace.

His eyes wide with fear, his breath ragged, a tall, dark elf male stumbled into the room to collapse, prostrating himself in a panting heap on the red velvet carpet in front of the throne.

The centaur ambassador cantered away from the newcomer, closer to the magnificent lords, the bejeweled ladies of Fairyland that, in two sparkling aisles, lined the room.

The ladies' fans moved nonstop, their lips whispering fast behind those fans, of the shocking alarm and what it might betide.

Quicksilver rose to his feet, recognizing the elf, whose sturdy body betrayed human origins, but who wore the green velvet of Quicksilver's own private guard, and whose black hair sported the golden coronet of a prince of Fairyland. "Malachite?"

This was Lord Malachite, Quicksilver's childhood friend, his milk-brother, raised with the king at the feet of the late fairy queen, Titania. A trusted friend, a keen advisor.

Quicksilver's pulse sped in alarm. Brave Malachite thus

alarmed? What could this bode? Decorous Malachite disrupting a royal audience? It could mean nothing good.

As the whole court recognized Malachite, the elven ladies' fans moved faster. Whispers rose from amid the elven gentlemen. Queen Ariel gasped and leaned forward. Her small, rosebud mouth opened in startled alarm.

Malachite knelt, gasping for breath, and half raised his face, his mouth working, trying to say something for which he had no breath. His great jade-green eyes were full of that speaking force which eyes have when lips lack the strength to utter.

Ariel stood and rested her arm on Quicksilver's. Together, the sovereigns of Elvenland descended the ten marble steps from the platform on which their throne sat. They flanked Malachite, who, still kneeling, managed to draw in full breath that whistled through his words as he spoke.

"If your majesty pleases," he said, turning wide eyes to Quicksilver. "If your majesty pleases." He looked at Ariel. "Our defenses have been breached."

Quicksilver knit his brows. *If your majesty pleases.* What a phrase. He pleased no such thing. Not sure what Malachite meant, yet he was sure it betokened no good. "The defenses?" he said. "What defenses, man? Speak."

For they were not at war, nor were there defenses around the realm that another realm might break through. No. Nor such realm as might wish to do it.

"The defenses to Avalon, milord. The defenses set around this palace, around this forest." Malachite gulped in air like a starving man will devour food. "The living defenses that ever protected our kind from evil beings abroad."

Still kneeling, he straightened so that his knees supported his weight, the rest of him upright. His earnest face, with its too-sharp nose, its jade-green eyes, faced Quicksilver.

"While we were on patrol, we sensed it, Igneous, and I, and Birch and Laurel. And then we ran to the place where right away we saw the breach blooming in our magical defenses, evil resounding through it."

The muttering of the court stopped, every breath suspended.

Quicksilver shook his head. He could not doubt Malachite. Yet the defenses *could not* be broken.

These magical wards and spells and dread enchantments of which Malachite spoke had been placed around the capital of the magical kingdom, time out of mind, by Quicksilver's ancestors.

They protected the source of the hill's magic, the collective strength of hill power, the core and Soul of elvenkind.

Humans and other natural creatures could wander through the defenses, in and out of the forest, and disturb nothing. Most humans, blind, ephemeral creatures that they were, couldn't even see the fairy palace and that great, gilded land that coexisted along the human world like two pages of a book, touching but never mingling.

But any enemy with ill intentions would be kept out by these defenses, unable to come near the ancient, sacred palace of elvenkind, unable to touch the living force of their magic, the fountain of elf power.

There was no record, ever—either in Quicksilver's memory, or in the collective memory of his race which, as a king, Quicksilver held—of the defenses being disturbed, much less broken.

This elven kingdom had fought and won and lost wars against other magical kingdoms. It had suffered encroachment by humanity and dissension within its ranks, and yet those defenses that protected the core of the kingdom had remained inviolate.

Until now.

"You must be wrong," Quicksilver whispered. Yet he trembled with fear that they might not be. For if they were right, then Elvenland met a threat such as it had never encountered.

Malachite shook his head, pale lips compressed into a straight line.

Quicksilver's court fell mute. The ladies blanched so that their cosmetics stood out in vivid relief. The horror-stricken faces of the lords looked like wax above their vivid, colorful garments.

Feeling his hair stand on end, Quicksilver bent down, grasped Malachite's shoulder, and pulled up, forcing his lieutenant to stand. "What force is it, Malachite? What force?"

"Oh, milord, it looks . . ." Malachite swallowed and his Adam's apple bobbed up and down on his long neck. "It looks like the force of the Hunter, milord, like the Hunter's magical power has borne upon this your kingdom with unsheathed malice and, overcoming these ancient wards with his greater might, affixed his cannon against our hill."

The silence of the court broke on a collective gasp from many throats. Looking up, Quicksilver saw alarm, surprise.

But most of all, he saw fear, fear of the Hunter, a dread creature of elven legend, said to punish the wrongdoers and collect the souls of criminals.

The Hunter was older and more magical than elves, a creature of primeval darkness and unbound might. In the old days, elves and humans both had worshiped him as a god. Whether he was such, Quicksilver couldn't hazard.

But Quicksilver had met with the Hunter face to face,

and knew the creature's power to avenge, the creature's strength to do justice upon evildoers.

The Hunter had visited this hill only once in living memory, and that for dread purpose.

Compared to the Hunter's power, all of Quicksilver's might and power and kingdom were as a child's wooden dagger to a man's sword.

Quicksilver pushed his features into a smile and straightened up. "Come, come, you must be mistaken." He forced hearty heat into his voice and looked doubtingly at Malachite. "The Hunter? What would the Hunter, that great lord of justice, want with us?"

His voice fell—hollow—upon the still room.

Quicksilver's father, Oberon, had once said that a quiet court was a sign of danger, that the flutter and gossip of Fairyland were a sign of health as telling in absence as the silencing of a beating heart.

Around the vast hall, nothing moved, and Quicksilver felt the gazes of his subjects resting on him like so many drawn daggers pointed at his chest.

Even the servant fairies—the tiny, winged beings who did all the hard work of Fairyland—seemed to have stopped midflight, the iridescent pattern of light they used for speech stilled.

Malachite shook his head. "I know not, milord. I know not what he wants with us."

He looked away from Quicksilver as if he suspected his king of some crime so foul that only the supernatural vengeance of the Hunter could expiate it. "Not in fulfillment of his natural fate since that would not demand his breeching our defenses. They gave him entrance easily enough when he had business among us."

Malachite spoke *business* with a heavy tongue.

Only ten years ago, the *business* of the Hunter in Fairyland had been the collecting of the king, Sylvanus, Quicksilver's brother. Sylvanus had committed parricide, and thus enslaved himself to the Hunter. In forfeit and payment for his many crimes, he'd been condemned to becoming one of the Hunter's dogs, enslaved for eternity to the dread lord of justice and slaying.

Quicksilver shivered. He was Sylvanus's brother. Could the taint extend to him? But he had committed no crime.

"I must see this breach," Quicksilver said, drawing himself up with regal might he did not feel and drawing a hearty breath.

"Milord, I will go," Ariel said hastily, nervously. Small, slight, she stood beside her lord like a page boy who showed the meaning of courage to mature royalty. "I'll go see what the Hunter seeks."

Quicksilver flinched. Why would she think he needed protection from the Hunter? He spun around, looking at his court, and in every eye he read horrified suspicion which Ariel's gallantry had only encouraged.

Of what crime did they suspect him? Why feared his lady for him?

Quicksilver said, "You dare too much, milady. You dare too much and you're too bold. I am the king, and I need no protection. Not from the Hunter."

And though he shivered, thinking of the dark being and unfathomable power he'd encountered before, he tried to look brave.

In an indecent display of magical power—what he hoped was a reassuring flaunting of his might—Quicksilver frowned down at his clothes, which changed, in that look, from silk to well-cured leather, and from tailored doublet and exquisite hose to crimson leather armor over well-padded tunic and breeches.

Pulling his hair back and knotting it behind his head, he bowed to his alarmed wife, as suede gloves materialized upon his long-fingered hands. "Milady," he said.

"You must do the honors of my court. I, the king, will defend my kingdom."

But Ariel stepped close to him and laid her hand on his leather-gloved arm. "At least let me go with you, milord. At least let me help—"

Quicksilver drew himself up and away from her. "Milady, indeed, I need no help." He shook her hand from his sleeve and turned to Malachite, giving his back to his queen. "Igneous and Laurel and Birch?"

"Waiting outside the palace, milord. But should you . . ." Malachite shot a glance at Ariel, who stood behind Quicksilver, and swallowed. "Is it wise to risk your majesty?"

Was it Quicksilver's fate today to suffer fools? Did every one of his vassals believe Quicksilver a secret criminal?

He exhaled noisily. "My majesty was made for risk and to brave danger that my people might be safe," he said. With a quick eye he spied the incredulous looks of his courtiers, and this tempted him on. "Come, Malachite. We'll go and heal the breach that would undo the peace of this kingdom."

Quicksilver kept one step ahead of Malachite as they jogged out of the broad throne room, and through the arched door of the elven palace to the imposing entrance staircase outside.

On the broad white marble steps, three guards—Igneous, a languid blond, and Birch and Laurel, dark-haired twins—looked awfully young and painfully eager.

They bowed to Quicksilver, their flushed faces and impatient breath like that of a maiden at her first ball. They longed for danger and thought to court her as a fiery and fulfilling mistress.

They knew not the Hunter, Quicksilver thought. They knew nothing of that eternal, immortal darkness nor the danger it engendered.

Scene 3

✺

*St. Paul's Yard, the marketplace of choice for book prin-
ters and booksellers in Elizabethan England. Around the
corners of the yard, houses encroach, shadowing the
space and making it look like the inside of a building,
lacking only the roof to be a cathedral as imposing as
the one beside it. Colorful tents dot the yard proper,
streaming booklets and papers like festive ornaments.
Amid the tents, the well-to-do stroll in their finery and
velvets, and older scholars in dull wool cloaks skulk.
Along the center aisle between the tents, Marlowe walks
toward the outer gate, at a clipped pace imposed by the
two men who flank him.*

Kit would not be scared.

Over the gallop of his heart, he ordered his hands
not to clench one upon the other, as though in prayer to
the God in which Kit no longer believed.

This was the second time in two days that Kit had been
seized by envoys of the Queen's council.

Only the day before, Kit had been dragged from Scagmore—his patron's home—by one of these men, Henry
Mauder, and brought to town in such a great hurry that

he'd not been given the chance to change out of his indoor slippers.

Treason Abroad, a pamphlet pinned to the side of a printer's tent, slapped in the breeze, catching Kit's gaze as he was hurried past. The cover displayed a caricature of the King of Spain.

Yesterday Kit, who had worked covertly for the Queen's council since his days at Cambridge, had invoked names of those he had served as a shield against those who would now arrest him. Blithely, he'd named the late Sir Francis Walsingham and Cecil, the Queen's present secretary.

Yesterday, Kit had been let go.

But look how he'd been apprehended again today. Had those names, then, so quickly lost their power to protect him?

"What do you wish with me, milords?" Kit asked, casting his voice just so, attempting to keep it from showing shaking anxiety, attempting to keep his fear from the sure knowledge of all the men walking past, all those scholars shopping for pamphlets and books, as Kit had done so many times before.

Henry Mauder, on Kit's left, cast Kit a brief, triumphant glare. A messenger for the Queen's chamber, Mauder looked perpetually scared and angry in equal measure. Kit had learned there was none so dangerous as a scared man.

Kit's mind cast about for the cause of today's arrest. What had Henry Mauder found out? What did he know? What did he hold over Kit like the sword of Damocles, precariously suspended?

All of Kit's sins, remembered, danced before his eyes with lewd display. He'd blasphemed and gambled and once, drunk, said a whole lot of nonsense on the subject of boys and tobacco, to see the shocked expressions in the pious faces surrounding him. Could any of these have

come home to him? "Pray, pray," he said, his voice thin
and dismal. "What think you I've done?"

Henry Mauder shrugged. "You are being taken for to
answer some questions."

A trickle of sweat ran from Kit's forehead, past the
ineffective dam of his thin, arched eyebrows, to sting in
his eyes.

His captors enforced a fast step. He saw a friend passing
by, a friend who was also a secret service man.

This friend who had defended Kit in street brawls and
been one of the first critics of Kit's poems now passed by
Kit as though Kit didn't exist, his gaze not answering Kit's
beckoning recognition.

So word was out among secret service people that Kit
was taken, Kit thought, chilled. Word was out that Kit
was lost, caught in the net of official displeasure that
fished him forth from his natural element to a terrible fate.

"What questions can you have that you did not ask yesterday?" he asked the fat man at his right.

The fat man didn't even look at Kit. Swollen and wrinkled at once, like a prune too long forgotten in sugar water, he looked unimportant. A mere secretary. A witness.

Or a nobleman in disguise?

In the secret service, one could never tell. Fair was foul
and foul was fair, each thing turned from its true nature.

Henry Mauder pursed his mouth into close semblance
of a chicken's ass and tilted his head sideways. "I see,
Master Marlowe," he said, "that heavy deeds weigh upon
your conscience."

Kit's throat seemed to close upon his breathing, and his
brain felt as if it had become a single teeny drum echoing
only *What do they know?* Out of his panic, Kit spoke
blindly. "I'll not meddle with a conscience," he said, in
reasonable imitation of his normal teasing tone. He forced
his lips into a smile again. "It makes a man a coward and

it fills a man full of obstacles. It made me once restore a purse of gold that by chance I found. It beggars any man that keeps it. It is turned out of towns and cities for a dangerous thing, and every man that means to live well endeavors to trust himself to live without it."

He took a deep breath and resolved not to show fear. Like rabid dogs, justices and officers of the crown were very like to smell your fear and, smelling it, to react to it like a hungry man to meat and bread.

They were now almost through Paul's Yard. Almost to the outer iron gate. Almost past any hope of rescue.

Passing the tent that displayed the sign of the white greyhound, where John Harrison, printer, should be indebted to Kit for many weighty purchases and many, even weightier profits, Kit found neither recognition nor interest in his plight. The printer and his apprentices glanced past Kit as if he were suddenly invisible.

It was as though Kit were a dead man already, the lid of his tomb closed upon him, cutting him off from the world and his imagined friends.

"So, you had no conscience, then, when you wrote down that Jesus was not truly God's son, and twenty other such blasphemies, that you proclaimed while in college?" Henry frowned again, his lips contracting into their narrowest moue, his eyes no more than slits on his suspicious face.

Kit started and drew sharp breath, turning around to stare at Mauder and needing not to fake surprise. He was astonished. While Kit had been in college? Eight years ago?

Beggar the fools, had they all gone mad?

He stared, his mouth hanging open, while in his mind he reviewed the riot of mad living he'd engaged in at Cambridge: the drinking, the gambling, and the carousing.

With those, like a man given weak ale after strong wine,

Kit had in vain tried to rinse away his memory of his first love, his *elf* love.

Oh, Kit had not been so bad. He'd not stolen, nor killed, nor any other of those offenses that rightly might have brought a man to justice.

As for what he'd said . . . What might he not have said? Those had been years of pain. Years without hope.

The memory of the elf lady, Silver, his lost love, had made Kit mad enough for anything. Even now, he shivered at the thought of Silver: dark silken hair, pale silken skin, and a mouth that tasted of new wine.

He stared at Mauder. "Who told you this?" he asked. "That I wrote any such thing?"

"Never mind who told us," Mauder said. "We have proof enough, in a paper penned by your own hand."

Mauder smiled wider, showing crooked teeth, yellow and savage. A wolf's teeth, which would maul and tear. "Master Marlowe, what we have against you is right enough to see you three times hanged or disemboweled or quartered, or indeed all of them."

Marlowe drew in a quick breath.

Unlike the boy he'd once been, who'd entered Cambridge hoping to be a minister, Kit had lost all hope of paradise beyond. Death meant nothing, save only keeping company with worms. Of his shattered faith no hope at all remained, only the fear of something worse hereafter. Doubting heaven, he kept the suspicious certainty of hell. Therefore death scared him more than it had in his young and pious days.

"Well, then," he said, his voice sounding hollow and yet striving for a note of bravery. "Well, then, you can kill me but once." He took off his gloves and put them on again, to give his hands some occupation. "Are we headed, then, to execution?" Even pronouncing the word made his voice tremble and he bit the inside of his cheek hard, willing pain to steady him.

Outside Paul's Yard, just past the gate to which they hurried, he saw that a dark, boxy carriage with no markings waited. Four dark horses pulled it, driven by a black-attired coachman who might have been the devil himself.

Was this Kit's final conveyance?

Henry Mauder looked gravely at Kit.

"We would prefer if you would do the Queen a service and reveal where you might have heard those foul heresies you then wrote down," Henry Mauder said. "For certainly, you realize, the mouth of so dangerous a member of society must be stopped."

The coachman descended from his perch and opened the door to a spacious but dark interior. Black seats and heavy black curtains seemed all the darker for light of the lantern suspended from the side of the carriage by iron brackets.

Kit took a step back, shying from the carriage like a nervous horse will shy from battle.

"Do you not have friends?" Henry Mauder asked. "Do you not have friends who speak such vile lies, as Christ not being divine?"

Kit could not imagine of whom they spoke. He had very few friends. He took care not to form friendships he might be forced to betray.

Mauder huffed, exasperated at Kit's silence. "Climb on, climb on, Master Marlowe," he said and gestured cordially to the dark maw of the carriage.

With Mauder on one side, Mauder's silent companion on the other, Kit could no more avoid the route thus indicated than he could hide from spiteful fate. These men were not just two but a multitude. Behind them stood, arrayed, law and might. They were the crushing arm, the overreaching might of the Queen's council.

He climbed into the carriage on trembling legs, trying to hold his head high and pretend a light step.

The two men sat together on the bench that faced his, thus both staring at him like unavoidable judges.

Mauder arched his eyebrows. "Come, come, Master Marlowe. Do you not remember? Did someone not read you an atheist lecture, that you have since then repeated to others? Was there not something called a *School of the Night* that mocked the teachings of the Church?"

The words fell like a strong light upon Kit's thoughts. It seemed to him that the sounds around him receded and his head grew faint. He took a deep shuddering breath.

A School of the Night. That was what they'd been aiming for.

By the mass, they were talking about Sir Walter Raleigh. Sir Walter Raleigh, who'd befriended Kit years ago, when Kit was only a penniless student, Sir Walter Raleigh, who had enlarged Kit's perspective of the world a hundredfold. Sir Walter Raleigh, generous enough to speak to Kit as to an equal when Kit was but a poor cobbler's son, attending Cambridge on a scholarship.

These two men wanted Kit to denounce Sir Walter Raleigh for an atheist and thus doom him to death.

The coachman closed the carriage door, and presently, the vehicle moved. Marlowe heard the clopping of hooves on the ground, but through the dark curtains that covered the windows, he could not see where they were headed. His heart told him his destination lay in some prison's oblivion. Cold sweat broke upon Kit's brow.

Once before, while at Cambridge, Kit had been arrested. He'd made friends with Catholic students. At the time innocent, an ardent Protestant, in his missionary zeal he'd thought to talk them out of their grievous errors.

The council had seized him and asked him what incriminatory things he'd heard of them. Kit had refused to answer, all high-minded indignation and strong-worded pride.

But Kit's bravery had earned him naught.

Alone, friendless, with no powerful connections, Kit had thought all lost and the pit of the grave had yawned at his feet.

Where his actions had not, his fear made him a traitor. He had given the names of those students who, in the heat of theological argument, had admitted their beliefs to him. He'd betrayed their dreams, their hopes, their not-quite plots.

He'd watched his friends die on the gallows, and he felt happy enough to have escaped. Since then had the secret service men known his limits and had tapped them again and again, sending him to parties where he would listen for the traitorous joke, the incautious remark, watch for the impolitic friendships.

Thus had Kit been seduced to working for the Crown and that first misstep, caused by fear and rewarded with gold, had gained him other secret offices till Kit's conscience, blunted like an ill-used knife, troubled him no more, or only a little sometimes, late at night, when the ghosts of betrayed friends seemed to gather round his solitary bed.

And yet, Kit must have felt put upon. Something in him, some secret stirring, must have censored him.

Six months ago, when Thomas Walsingham, an old schoolfellow newly ascended to family honors, had offered Kit lavish patronage, Kit had shed the coils of secret like a snake that sheds its skin. He'd told Cecil he was done with it. From that moment on, he'd be a poet. A poet, nothing more.

And yet, the business would not leave Kit be. Like a sleeper returning to the same nightmare, Kit now found himself at the starting point of all his treasons. They wanted him to denounce a friend again. They wanted him to denounce Raleigh.

He looked from one man to the other and found nothing encouraging in those countenances.

This must be a plot of Essex's, Kit thought. Essex was Raleigh's rival for the Queen's attention and her affections.

Two noble cocks strutted for an aging hen, and Kit would be caught in the middle of their bloody fight.

If Kit denounced Raleigh, the council would let Kit go. But if Essex's plot failed, Raleigh could avenge himself on Kit in a more terrible way than Essex could, for Raleigh was an imaginative man, as Essex was not.

And besides, even Kit's ill-awakened conscience yet rebelled from his being called again to the office of traitor.

He took a deep breath. "If I'm guilty of atheism, then it's my own guilt," he said. "I will name no other."

Mauder chuckled. "A fine stand, Master Marlowe. A fine stand." He grinned, showing yellowed teeth.

The carriage smelled of wet wool and sweat.

The curtains were closed. An oil lamp fixed on a bracket lit the carriage and gave off a greasy, burnt smell.

Mauder rapped on the wood near his head, and the carriage slowed to a funeral pace.

"Have you heard of Master Topcliff?" Mauder asked. "Master Topcliff, now." Mauder shook his head and smiled with admiration. "He's the Queen's own torturer and he can break a man on the rack in an instant. Or make him sweat with all his weight suspended from manacles. Or other things, some of them so secret only he knows them. Why, it is said he can cut into a man for days, and take one sense at a time from him, all without killing him, while, little by little, crippling him forever. What think you, Master Marlowe?

"Hard to hold a quill when you have no fingers, hard

to write when your eyes are gone, hard to court ladies when you have lost that which makes you a man.

"You'd be advised, Master Marlowe, to confess now, before you're put to the torture, while you might yet *walk* away free."

Kit felt cold, yet sweat dripped down his back and soaked through his fine velvet suit. He smelled it, rank and sharp.

He could see himself, a shapeless cripple, crawling on the filthy street, a begging bowl clutched between his few remaining teeth. *Alms for the cripple.* What good then his wit, his fine grey eyes, his Cambridge education?

He shivered.

Removing his right glove, he clenched both hands tight upon it, as if by squeezing it he could throttle his vile tormentors. "I have nothing to confess that could be said after torture—or before," Kit said. He meant it as a courageous scream, but instead his voice echoed the cringing, begging tones of his cobbler father.

To Kit's surprise, Henry Mauder sat back as though conceding the point.

"It was at your lodgings that they told us you'd gone to Paul's," Mauder said softly.

"At my lodgings?"

Into Kit's mind, unbidden, came an image of the modest house where he lodged in Southwark and, with it, an image of Imp, whose real name was Richard.

Save that Imp was barely seven and that his hair yet retained a natural trace of red without need for the artifice of henna, it could have been Kit's own face. And a good reason for that, as Kit had long suspected that Imp, the son of Kit's landlady, was the result of his desperate attempt to put off paying his rent long ago. A miraculous result of so base an act.

These men *would* have asked *Imp* where Kit was. That

was sure, or they'd never have found Kit. Only Imp always knew or cared where Kit went.

Henry smiled, showing his bent teeth. "That is a fine boy your landlady has, Master Marlowe."

Kit flinched. Imp was Kit's religion. At the innocent's foot he worshiped and for that small creature had he such hopes that they beggared heaven.

Kit wished Imp away from these unhallowed plots and trembled to know him so close to them, so near the sprung trap.

"A fine boy. A shame if something were to happen to him, but a high-spirited boy might do such things—steal an apple, say—as would render him fit only to be hanged," Mauder said.

Kit's hands trembled. He'd sacrifice anything, anyone, give anything up. Anyone but Imp.

In his life, he'd loved but twice. The first time, when he'd been barely more than a boy himself and he'd fallen in love with a dark-haired elven maiden. And the second time—quite a different love—Imp, the result of Kit's pleasing sin.

Yet Marlowe could not betray Raleigh. Raleigh was powerful and rich enough to take revenge and to avenge himself on Imp as well as Kit.

Kit's head felt as dizzy as if he had worked long on a hot summer's day. Shapes lay on either side of him. He took a deep breath. It did not steady him.

"Are you ready to talk now, Master Marlowe?" Henry Mauder asked, his gaze steady upon Kit. "Are you ready to talk and tell us who taught you vile disrespect of religion?"

Scene 4

ꙮ

The place where Arden Woods and the town of Stratford-upon-Avon meet. It is a warm summer night, and the few noises of the town—the distant singing of a drunkard, the voice of a man calling an errant dog—mingle with the sounds of the woods—the hooting of an owl, the shriek of a scared mouse. To the human eye, it all looks calm, but the elven eyes can see a blight like a blot of darkness spreading at the very edge of the woodland. There, no owl hoots and no creature moves, as though everything alive knows the presence of a predator.

"I'll met by moonlight, my proud brother."

At the voice in front of them, Quicksilver and his guards stopped.

A chill ran down Quicksilver's back like a cold finger dragged along his spine. The voice he heard was the voice of his brother. Changed and disembodied, but his brother's voice, nonetheless.

The voice issued from the tendrils of light that, to elven eyes, marked the boundary between the human village and the sacred forest.

There, a blot of darkness marred the pure light, the

shimmering strands of Fairyland's protective enchantments.

The words themselves seemed to pulse through with the very essence of distilled darkness.

The younger elves shied back from it.

Only Quicksilver advanced, with Malachite close by.

"Sylvanus?" Quicksilver said. The word dropped from between his lips, unmeant, as a coin will drop through the tear in a rent purse.

"Quicksilver, wait," Malachite said, and, a step behind Quicksilver, he laid a hand on the king's shoulder.

"Aye, wait, Quicksilver, wait."

The darkness throbbed with laughter that bespoke no mirth, but only a cold amusement, a distant mocking.

Then the dark node parted, like an eggshell cracking, and birthed a creature: an elf, goodly built, with dark hair and beard and features that resembled Quicksilver's, from oval face to pulpy lips.

Though this elf looked half-transparent, like a painting on glass, like a cloud passing in front of the moon, his cold blue eyes appraised Quicksilver with amusement.

"Fares it then so badly with my brother?" the elf asked. "That he must thus consort with changelings?" He spared a cold, calculating eye to Malachite. "Is this your leeman, Quicksilver, that he thus calls you by your given name and lays hands on you?"

Quicksilver felt hot blood ascend his cheeks in shameful heat, and wrenched his shoulder away from Malachite's clasping hand.

Yet Malachite reached, yet he persisted, yet he said, in a strangled voice, "Milord!"

Quicksilver gave Malachite a withering glance, over his shoulder. "Go, Malachite, I order you. I'm man enough to handle this villain alone."

As Malachite stepped back, the transparent elf grinned,

showing teeth larger and sharper than elf's teeth. "Aye, brother, man enough and woman enough, too, I grant you. How fares my sister, Silver?"

The blood on Quicksilver's cheeks flared and burned, the color of a red rose, hot as a poker fresh from the fire.

Now had Sylvanus's ghost, Sylvanus's emanation, touched the secret shame that had dogged Quicksilver ever from his birth.

Quicksilver had been born a shape changer, with the capacity—the need—to become a dark lady, with midnight black hair, the Lady Silver.

On Ariel's request he'd forsaken the aspect, and forbore to change if he could control it. Yet, the Lady Silver was still within him, and he would change, sooner or later, meant or not.

This ability, more suitable to a lowly woodland spirit than to a royal elf, had almost cost Quicksilver the throne. He often feared his vassals still mocked him for it.

Quicksilver glanced over his shoulder, half expecting to see his young guards fleering at him.

Instead, he saw them staring at Sylvanus, their faces stripped of all their cocky self-confidence, and infused with the pale strained look of fear.

Their fear lit a rage within Quicksilver. Looking back at the flickering elf amid the dark core that floated near the houses of Stratford, Quicksilver squared his shoulders, and made his face stern. "What want you, Sylvanus? Speak fast, for I'll be done with you."

The grin died upon the transparent face, like a candle blown out.

Sylvanus's eyebrows gathered, his mouth pulled in a rictus of pain. "You were done with me, brother. Or so you thought. Done with me when you turned me out of Fairyland and stole my throne."

A hunting horn sounded in the distance.

Sylvanus's transparent shape wavered and trembled with each note, as though the sound injured him.

Quicksilver looked up at the sound, because he knew that horn well. Louder and clearer than any human instrument, it was the call of the Hunter, a being who had existed before the elves, a being whom the elves themselves believed embodied a fundamental thread in the fabric of the Universe. God or demon he might be. But powerful he was. Years ago Sylvanus had been made the Hunter's dog, the Hunter's slave.

Up on the horizon, in the purpled sky where thunderclouds began massing, a dark shape showed, looking like a hunter on horseback, his silver horn at his lips, calling to his dogs that clustered, growling and threatening, around his horse's legs.

Twice before had Quicksilver met the Hunter, twice before, once in sorrow and once in joy.

But neither time had he escaped unscathed. The terror of the Hunter, the knowledge of something that, beyond elf and man, judged both and cared for neither, had chilled some core of Quicksilver's innocence and forever ended his prolonged elven childhood.

Now, feeling the hair rise at the back of his neck, Quicksilver looked over his shoulder at Malachite and the three younger elves, all of them terrified looking, all pale, all trembling.

"Go," Quicksilver said. "Go, all of you. Stand back. Take refuge."

The three younger elves ran madly toward the trees, but Malachite stayed, stubbornly, rooted to the spot, staring at his king.

"You, too, Malachite. Go."

Malachite shook his head slowly. "No, milord. There's something you must know—"

Sylvanus, in the center of the darkness, screamed, his

voice changing from elven speech to a wide baying.

Quicksilver turned. Sylvanus transformed.

He transformed as if he were being burned, as though his substance had ignited in the hottest breath of a blazing furnace.

Twisting and writhing like a bit of hair that, caught in a candle flame, curls and twirls and is finally consumed by heat, Sylvanus dropped to all fours and trembled, and changed, and transformed, until in his place there was only a squat, square-headed, heavy-jawed dog.

One of the Hunter's own dogs, which Sylvanus had become, in punishment of his many crimes.

In that shape, a form neither wolf nor dog but something predating both—a creature that had rounded and nipped at man in his cave and howled around the mountain holds of the elves when the world was young—Sylvanus turned baleful eyes to the Hunter.

The Hunter had stopped, amid the thunderclouds, and with outstretched arm, incited his dogs forth.

The dogs ran down from the sky, seemingly descending a staircase woven of darkness and steps made of roiling purple clouds.

As they neared, Quicksilver trembled. Panic closed his throat and ice gripped his stomach. What dread creatures, these, square and squat, broad of head and shoulder, low of legs, creatures made to hunt in ice eternal and eternal night.

How would it be to be hounded by them?

Sylvanus trembled and looked as piteous, as forlorn as a deer faced with the baying dogs that would tear it apart.

Whining, he backed away from the other dogs, his belly close to the ground, his tail tucked between his legs.

His squat body trembled, his hirsute fur ruffled at the neck, and his piteous eyes, Sylvanus's incongruously blue eyes, turned to gaze at Quicksilver as the dog slid and shied away from the Hunter's mastiffs.

"Brother," Sylvanus said, his voice composed of growls and low baying, which yet formed intelligible words. "Brother, they've come and they'll rend me limb from limb, or yet worse, they'll take me with them. They'll take me with them forever, to be one of them."

He had time for the words—no more—as the dogs closed around him, screaming, nipping, baying, a pile of fur and open maws, of claws and blood-lapping tongues.

Quicksilver gaped at the mayhem of fur, the melee of furious canine bodies. His heart contracted in horror as fur covered fur and jaws snapped, and teeth met teeth in ferocious clash.

This was his brother there, he thought. His brother, turned to such a low, demeaning form. Sylvanus, Quicksilver's brother, born of the same noble Titania, sired by the same majestic Oberon, once Queen and King of Fairyland. Sylvanus's birth had been welcomed, celebrated through the hilltops of many lands. Sylvanus had been a pampered prince, once.

And now this—this pile of fur, this bestial strife.

Quicksilver heard Malachite draw breath behind him.

With scant breath, Quicksilver asked, "How does he not come to us? How not run this way?"

"I've tried to tell you, lord," Malachite said. "The barrier hasn't really been breached. Your brother has projected the illusion of it being so. But it remains whole. Whole enough that he can't crawl onto our side."

"An illusion?" Quicksilver asked, and yet dared not look away from the giant figure of shadow, with glimmering red eyes and a shining silver horn, who climbed down from his horse and strode down the same stairway his dogs had used, toward them, toward cowering, pitiable Sylvanus.

"How an illusion?"

"How I don't know, Quicksilver." Malachite spoke in a whisper. "But that is all. It is all delusion. He has no power such as would breech our defenses. Yet he fooled us, and me first of all. What a trick to master! I think it was that he knew the defenses so well, having once been . . . our king."

Once the King of Fairyland and now a cur.

Quicksilver shivered.

Why had his brother wished him to see this? Had he meant Quicksilver to have nightmares over it, all his life long?

"Come," the Hunter said, and his speaking rustled the leaves of the trees like an icy wind, freezing Quicksilver's mind and heart. "Come."

At this word, the dogs parted and heeled to him, gamboling and frisking like happy puppies on seeing their master.

On the ground lay a pile of fur, wet with blood, stained with the iridescent saliva of the creatures. Nothing more.

The Hunter took the horn to his lips and blew upon it. The cold, silvery sound wove itself into the surrounding trees like a mist of ice, bringing a reminder of winter to the summer night.

"Come," the Hunter said.

At that one word, the pathetic remains quivered.

At that one word, the bloodied piece of fur moved.

Legs grew on it, and a muzzle. A cowed, shivering dog stood on uncertain paws, bleeding from myriad wounds.

You see how it is, Quicksilver heard in his mind. *Neither death nor eternity will free me. I was greedy, brother, but I meant no harm. I thought you not able to rule the land, and so I tried to rule in your stead. Does this deserve punishment eternal?*

The voice was not a voice, but a thought, whispered

close into the ventricle of Quicksilver's brain. But that thought was Sylvanus's. The voice of a scared elf.

It echoed a voice Quicksilver remembered from when Sylvanus had been but a young prince and faced with the monumental sky-cracking rages of their father, Oberon.

And though Quicksilver knew that his brother had done more than enough to deserve this fate, though he knew Sylvanus's crimes mounted to the sky and raised bloody hands to the heavens, craving the gods' revenge, yet in his heart Quicksilver pitied the vile thing.

Sylvanus had once reigned in Fairyland.

Now Quicksilver was the king of elves.

In vain he told himself that a king must be impervious to the hurts and lacerations of his subjects.

Yet if Sylvanus was his subject, then couldn't Quicksilver decide to stop Sylvanus's punishment?

Ten years, Sylvanus had endured near the heart and center of a vengeful force, his elven body consumed away, his elven nature distorted. Was that not enough?

Behind Quicksilver, Malachite withdrew his hand and whispered, "I'm sorry, milord. I—"

Raising his hand, Quicksilver spoke, his voice small against the gathering thunder, the baying of the dogs that clustered around their master, Sylvanus's whimpers of desolate pain.

"Stop, Great One," Quicksilver said. "Stop, I beg you."

The Hunter turned to Quicksilver a face that looked almost human or elven, save that no human, no elf, could even envision the perfection of the Hunter's noble look, from curly dark hair to chiseled features. As he turned, the Hunter exposed his chest where—in the place a human heart would lodge—an empty darkness, an absence of all, reigned.

"You beg?" the Hunter asked. Laughter poured out, as cold as ice, as chilled as winter fog. "You beg me to stop?

Who are you to beg and to demand how I should punish this cur, and when I should stay?"

"But justice—" Quicksilver said.

Again the Hunter laughed. "Justice is a word you don't understand, oh king, who judge everyone according to your changeable measure. This is true evil, and this I will punish."

The Hunter's arm rose. Upon it something crackled, a whip of light, a cord of lightning.

He raised it and let it fall upon Sylvanus's canine form.

Sylvanus howled and fell, bleeding again, yet rose again as the Hunter called, "Come."

Quicksilver could not endure it.

He could neither watch it nor turn away. His heart pounding, his blood raging through his head like a fever, he raised his hand.

"No," the Hunter yelled. "No. Give way. I'll take what's mine."

Sylvanus, the dog, whimpered, belly to the dirt.

Before Quicksilver knew it, he lifted his hand. He summoned to him his magic and the gathered strength of his hill, that gathering of elven souls and bodies and magic over which Quicksilver reigned, his to command. He aimed a bolt of destruction at the Hunter's feet and threw it and felt the burn of power leave his hand.

The power of the hill, in a form like the thunderbolt, flew from his open palm.

Quicksilver meant only to let the ball of fire land between Sylvanus and the Hunter, and thus call the Hunter's attention and give his brother respite.

But as the fire crackled, bright, from his hand, it flew past the dog and the dog, somehow, reached out a hand that looked like Sylvanus's and caught the fire and spun it off again—toward the thatched roofs of Stratford.

Fairy lights burned in the mortal night, a trail of power

splitting the mundane peace of mortal repose.

Fire hit the roofs of the nearby houses.

The thatch blazed.

Dogs howled, men screamed, babies cried.

"Milord," Malachite whispered.

"Stop," the Hunter yelled. "Stop."

Quicksilver took a deep breath, tainted with the smoke from the burning houses. One breath to realize he was alive.

Another breath as the smoke grew worse.

Another breath and Quicksilver saw Sylvanus writhe to human shape and grow and smile, a smile of satisfaction such as babes show after milk and men after love.

"He's feeding on the deaths," the Hunter yelled. "He's feeding on the life force of dead mortals. From me he learned that, but I refrain unless the life comes from evil-doers."

Sylvanus's almond-shaped eyes narrowed in satisfaction, his small, pulpy lips widened in a broader smile, and he waved a hand that looked more solid than before, in the direction of the fire that spread, from roof to roof and from thatch to thatch, like vermin that jump from one body to the other and consume all.

"Thank you, brother. Thank you. I would have lived my whole life as the Hunter's dog, but for you. By setting this fire have you given me lives that, in the manner of the Hunter, I can collect to grow my own, and increase my force."

As Sylvanus twisted and writhed in his obscene plea-sure, he grew. The dark mist around him overspread, darker and darker, like a killing frost, its tendrils reaching out to the burning houses and by them growing in strength and force, like a dark octopus that grows and spreads over the floor of a blighted sea.

There was plague in that wicked mist, Quicksilver

thought, the pestilent touch and evil humor of illness.

And other things, other dark things that would bring death to most and feed Sylvanus's swollen appetite.

What was this creature Sylvanus was becoming? What powers would it have?

Never in the collective memory of Fairyland had something like this happened.

Never had an elf been king and slave to the Hunter and then . . . what?

Quicksilver broke into a sweat of shame and fear.

Never had a king been so weak as to help free his mortal enemy.

Quicksilver wished he could hide, wished he could crawl away in shame.

Screams echoed from everywhere in Stratford. Women and children and men woke to find themselves engulfed in flame.

Some ran out of the houses, flaming like living torches, to burn and die on the street. Others ran here and there, with buckets of water, throwing these at the flames, which mockingly grew despite all.

Quicksilver, unable to breathe, unable to think, looking at his brother grow in power, looking at Stratford being consumed, sank to his knees and screamed, "What have I done?"

"No time for that, no time," Malachite said. "No time for that, milord. These your vassals await orders. Should we not fight the fire?" He gestured to the elven youths who stood behind Quicksilver and waited.

"Listen to him, listen, brother," Sylvanus said before Malachite was even fully done. His words echoed of amusement and mockery. "Listen to him, for he's a man, his wit greater than your womanly wiles."

Quicksilver wanted to scream, he wanted to rage. He wished he could throw fire again, this time the fire that consumed his heart and burned his soul. But instead he nodded to Malachite and said, "Aye. Go. Help them."

Aware of what he must look like to the young people he commanded, he stood up and, trembling, tried to brush the knees of his breeches.

Sylvanus's power still grew and Quicksilver must do something.

Steeling himself, knowing he gazed on his own death, knowing nothing would come of this but his own destruction, he stepped forward.

The Hunter stepped forward also, in giant steps, approaching Sylvanus. "There will be an end to this, cur," the Hunter said. "You cannot thus break your bond."

Once more, Sylvanus changed, as if the sound compelled him, his well-formed humanlike form compacting and shrinking into the shape of a square-headed, squat dog.

Only the dog was bigger than he'd ever been, almost as big as a dog as he'd been as a man.

The Hunter looked puzzled for a moment, then his voice sounded so loud that it seemed to make both earth and sky tremble, and almost obscured the screams of the dying humans. "Come to heel, you *creature*."

He advanced on Sylvanus, like a displeased master calling his puppy. "What? You dare defy me?"

Sylvanus hunkered down and showed his glowing teeth as the Hunter approached.

Suddenly, Sylvanus leapt. His glowing teeth pierced the darkness of the Hunter's arm.

The Hunter screamed, a sound such as had never been heard before. Reality wavered and turned and reeled, like a windblown paper dancing in the whirlwind that announces a storm. What light there was, amid the smoke of the fires and the darkness of the Hunter and his dogs, seemed to waver also, the very moon growing pale as if in distress.

Drops of glowing blood fell to the earth, withering and blighting the very weeds it touched.

Around them, as if this were a contagion-infested breath, Quicksilver could feel crops withering and dying in the fields.

Time was out of joint and the mechanisms of the world jangled off-key.

The dog charged again, this time sinking its teeth into the Hunter's leg. He pulled, seeking to bring the Hunter down.

The Hunter wrenched away and turned, his misty shape looking sickly green where it had been pitch black and alive before. "This is your fault, oh Quicksilver, king of elves. And I will come for you in judgment," the Hunter screamed.

With his scream he vanished, like a fog upon the air. With him vanished his waiting horse, and the pack of his cowering dogs.

"My first victory is won," Sylvanus crowed, his voice changing from a low growl to a smooth human voice as he shifted and unfolded into his elven form once more. "Now for the others."

Quicksilver realized he was covered in a sweat of fear, as he hadn't been in many a year, not since acquiring the rule of Fairyland and all the power that came with it.

Trembling, he watched as Sylvanus grew and seemingly called to him every tendril of darkness that touched on every one of the burned houses. He changed and shifted to a dark miasma and transported himself somewhere.

To London. Quicksilver felt it both as a word and an image impressed upon his fevered brain. Sylvanus had gone to London, the largest city in the land. It wasn't so much knowledge but a deeper certainty, born of blood, of sinew, of Elvenland magic.

Sylvanus had transported to London, capital of this human realm whose boundaries overlapped sacred, elven Avalon—like two pages in a book will share a leaf, each taking up a different face, the two touching but never mingling.

What would Sylvanus want with London? What would he do there?

Quicksilver looked at the charred ruin around him, heard the lamentations of those who'd lost loved ones, and trembled.

What would Sylvanus *not* do there, in that London of packed multitudes?

More than half of Stratford had burned. Only a few houses stood amid the destruction caused by magical fire. Quicksilver's magical fire.

Where the town had been silent, now it echoed the screams of widows and the inconsolable cries of orphans.

And all because of Quicksilver.

The Hunter said he would come for him. Come for Quicksilver he would, doubtless, as soon as the Hunter had recovered.

If the Hunter recovered. Quicksilver shivered and wrapped his arms around himself, feeling small and young and foolish. Oh, curse the day he'd become king, he who was so naive, so dumb, so frail, so divided.

What if the Hunter didn't recover? Quicksilver would willingly suffer any punishment to be assured of the Hunter's recovery.

For what would happen if the Hunter did not recover? What would become of the workings of the world?

Quicksilver hadn't even known that such creatures as the Hunter could be hurt. He'd never suspected it. And now the Hunter was injured. With the Hunter's scream of pain something seemed to have changed about the very nature of reality, the truths that held everything in its place.

He watched through the smoke his elves, like unseen angels, smothering the last magical fires.

What did it matter, this belated charity? The damage was done.

Done through Quicksilver's hand.

Quicksilver had set the fire, and Sylvanus had fed upon it.

Distracted, Quicksilver stared at the house closest to the forest, the double wattle-and-daub house of the Shakespeares. It still stood, undamaged.

Will's wife, Nan, had organized her in-laws and her own three children—the older girl, Susannah, and the twins, Judith and Hamnet—to carry buckets of water from the river and thus soak all before flame ever touched it.

Quicksilver thought of Will, who was in London. Once upon a time, the Lady Silver, Quicksilver's female aspect, had loved Will with all-consuming passion.

Even now, thinking of that young man with the golden falcon-like eyes made Quicksilver's heart quiver.

Will was in London. Quicksilver remembered hearing elven gossip from one of Ariel's maids, Peaseblossom, who'd seduced a mortal youth.

Will was in London and Sylvanus had gone there.

Quicksilver realized he was trembling again.

He must go to London and stop Sylvanus. He must keep the evil creature from wreaking havoc upon the unprepared humans.

Quicksilver must, if nothing else, keep Sylvanus from hurting Will.

And Quicksilver should stop Sylvanus, rein him in, atone for his crime against Stratford by keeping Sylvanus from destroying London.

He, Quicksilver, was the king of elves, and responsible for all other elves, even those who had ceased to be of elvenkind.

It fell to him to protect London from Sylvanus.

"Malachite," he called, and his friend approached. "Go to your mistress. Tell her I've gone to London, and whatever you do, do not disclose this sad fray here. No reason she should fear."

No reason fair Ariel, who loved Quicksilver enough to imagine him a good king, should know that he had brought doom on innocent humans and loosed plague and danger upon both fairy and mortal.

Scene 5

✢

A road running along the Thames River. On the other side of the river, the impressive mansions of the nobility line up in impressive display, their stone facades vying to outdo each other in grandeur and architectural ornament. On the nearer side, only a few houses, hovels, and decaying warehouses cluster. Amid them, a small shop remains open, a lantern burning over the sign that advertises used clothes for resale. Will Shakespeare enters the shop, where clothes hang from the ceiling and lie in neat piles upon the two tables that take up most of the scant interior space. An old man sits at the back, by a small table at which a wavering oil lamp burns. Two other, younger men argue with him.

"Not worth three pennies." The old man turned a dark red velvet doublet over and over in his dried-up clawlike hands. He squinted at the fabric and squeezed his lips together, multiplying the wrinkles on his already wrinkled face.

"I need five pennies, please, master," a tall man in his twenties, obviously the owner of the doublet, said. "I must have five pennies to pay my gaming debt."

"Three pennies," the man said. "And I'm being too generous. I'll ruin myself this way."

He waved the tall man aside, saying, "Think it over."

The blond youth, no more than sixteen or so, pushed a folded dark suit at the man.

The boy looked scared and his anxiety mounted as the old man picked at seams, and turned sleeves, and made smacking sounds with his mouth.

Will Shakespeare held on tightly to his best suit, of much-washed black velvet, and waited his turn.

His suit had been new ten years ago when he'd married Nan. It was not, Will knew, nearly as well made as the tall man's wine-colored doublet.

And yet Will had to have ten pence for the suit.

It wouldn't pay Will's rent, but it would—if he husbanded it right—feed Will through the days it would take him to walk home.

But what were his chances of getting that much when the much-better doublet was held so cheap?

Will watched the old man purse his lips with finality and look at the young man. "Poor quality," he told the boy. "Poor quality. I don't think I can—"

On those words he checked and arrested.

The young man had started quivering, like a leaf upon a tree in high wind.

He stumbled, gave a strangled cry, and fell toward Will.

"What's this, what's this?" the shopkeeper said.

To save himself from being toppled, Will dropped his suit and put his hands out, easing the tall, thick-boned youth onto the beaten-dirt floor of the shop.

"He'll be drunk," the tall man said. "Drunk or hungry. It's hard days in the country and many young bucks come to town searching for work and food. As if we had it to give."

Will shook his head. He'd come to town in search of

work, but no one would call him a young buck.

He knelt beside the young man on the floor. He looked like a farmhand and he smelled neither of ale nor wine. Will lay his hand on the youth's forehead, as he would have on Hamnet's, back in Stratford. It was hot enough to feel burning to the touch.

"He's ill," Will said. He fumbled with the man's shirt, trying to open it, to give him air.

But as Will pulled, the worn-through shirt ripped, exposing the man's underarm, and the huge, pulsing growth beneath it.

"Jesu," the seller said. He got up and bent over the youth, staring at the growth. "Jesu. It's the plague." The old man's lips quivered. His hand went to his forehead, tracing the papist sign of the cross in atavistic exorcism. "My shop will be closed now. What will become of my grandchildren?"

"How long have you been ill, good man?" Will asked. He wanted to ask where the man had been, where he might have contracted this illness, whether in London or the countryside.

For a moment he thought the man was too far gone to answer. His pale blue country-boy eyes looked at Will uncomprehending.

But then he cleared his throat and coughed, and whispered, "Faith, I've not been ill. It was just now, this pain. . . . I've not been ill. Tell my mother—" He stopped, and coughed again, and his body convulsed, in a long shudder. "Mother," he said and he was still.

Will saw that breath didn't rise in the broad chest.

Dead, the boy was dead. And he'd said he was well till just now, till that pain beneath his arm.

It could not be true. It could not be true. Even the plague took time to kill people.

Yet something told Will that this was true. He remembered the boy walking down the street, ahead of Will. He'd walked like a healthy man.

Trembling, Will stood up. Trembling, he wiped his hands to his pants.

Mercy, let him not catch the plague. Oh, mercy, not so far from his wife and children. How horrible it would be, dying here all alone and being buried without name or care. His sense of his mortality, awakened, beat afraid and agitated wings against his reason. Oh, fool he was to have left those he loved and for the sake of an illusory dream of poetry to have come so far to so dangerous a city.

"Out," the old man said. "Out. I'll not be buying any clothes for a long time." With fumbling urgency, he pushed Will and the tall man with the wine red doublet from his shop.

Will could but stop and pick up his suit on the way, as he was being pushed out.

Outside, the cold air allowed Will to think more clearly, despite the bitter complaints of his empty stomach.

The plague. In truth, it was that—the growth beneath the arm that sapped a man's vital humors.

But the plague came on slowly, took days to come on.

What strange plague was this that killed so quickly?

A strange plague, like a curse, like a supernatural miasma.

Will wiped his hands on his breeches again, one at a time, and he shoved his suit under his arm.

Oh, let him not catch the plague.

And yet, he thought, his despair mounting as he looked back at the closed shop, let him catch it, for the plague, this fast plague, would kill Will faster than starvation, and starvation was his only other choice now. He knew there were other used clothing shops in London, but this had been the most accessible, the one that catered to the poorer people who might indeed wish to buy Will's cast-offs. All other shops would sneer at Will's velvet suit.

Outside the shop, Will stood on the narrow road beside the Thames, with his nose full of the stink of the great river that served London as well, sink and sewer.

The Thames looked oily dark in the moonlight, like the River Styx flowing through a realm of the dead.

Along its dark waters, barges slid.

On the nearest barge, upon a chair like a throne, a creature sat, who, as the barge neared, Will discerned to be the golden majesty of the Queen of England: Elizabeth, just over sixty years old and still ruling the country with unfaltering hand.

From this far away, she looked young and majestic, easily as young as twenty years ago, when Will had seen her in Coventry, where she'd come for a pageant put on by the Duke of Leicester.

Will frowned at the barge and at the Queen, and at the gentlemen in attendance to them, all of them unaware of, uncaring about the starving English subjects, threatened by the plague.

How much of this majesty was true? It was said that the Queen wore makeup thick with lead, hard with egg white, glazed with the perfumes and lacquers of Araby.

The Queen and London were one, the Queen and London alike. This glistening London to which Will had come in search of fame and fortune had proved itself a pit full of villains, into which Will's energy and fortune vanished.

London was naught, Will thought, like the Queen might be naught beneath her grand clothes, her makeup.

A plague-eaten naught where he would die alone.

Will's dream had died. He'd never be a poet.

That had been a dream. A dream and nothing more.

Scene 6

ॐ

The fairy palace, rising amid the trees of the Forest of Arden. Queen Ariel, in her room, sits at her vanity, before her silver brushes, her unguent bottles, attended by her maids, who comb her hair and lay out her nightclothes.

Sitting in front of her crystal mirror, Ariel, Queen of Fairyland, King Quicksilver's wife, found herself more restless and more fearful than ever before.

So many times she'd sat at this table, late at night. So many times had her maids, Peaseblossom and Cobweb and Cowslip, tended to her needs. And how often had Quicksilver, himself, been standing behind her, watching her nightly preparations with a smile.

But this night Quicksilver wasn't there. This night, Quicksilver had left, to face some threat, some evil on the boundary of elven Avalon—a threat that bid to be more monstrous than anything Fairyland had ever faced. And Ariel must wait here, in the false safety of the palace.

Oh, she knew she had upset Quicksilver with her offer of help. But why could her lord not understand that Ariel would rather be there, beside him or instead of him, facing whatever danger threatened to swallow the land, than here, in the palace, slowly driven mad by waiting anguish.

Oh, the traditional lot of females, human and elf alike, was much crueler than that of males. Females must wait and seem to smile while out on the field of battle their loves might be breathing their last.

Ariel could not endure it. With a gesture—raised hands, exasperated expression—she bid Peaseblossom stop running the soft brush down Ariel's pale blond hair. "Stop, Peaseblossom. Stop. I cannot endure touch. Only tell me if there's word . . . any word of my lord?"

Peaseblossom shook her head. She was one of Ariel's prettiest maids and today looked tired and out of humor. But she'd looked thus before the boundary breech had been announced. What ailed her was the absence of her human lover, a Stratford weaver named Nick Bottom, who'd gone to London on guild business.

Ariel wondered if the silly thing even knew that the whole hill was threatened and that Ariel's lord and king might be dead at this moment.

And yet, he couldn't be dead, could he, truly?

For Ariel, besides being queen, was the seeress and prophet of Fairyland, her powers acquired through having been born at summer solstice, the blessed night for her kind.

If Quicksilver were dead, surely she would have felt it.

And yet she couldn't be sure of it, and yet she sighed, and yet she frowned at her maids and wondered what could be delaying her lord and why her lord tarried so.

A knock sounded upon the door, a sharp knock, almost martial.

Quicksilver.

"Peaseblossom," Ariel said, gesturing toward the door.

But the door, opening, revealed no more than the long face, the dark hair of Malachite, his features pinched into worry such as Ariel had never seen.

Ariel rose hastily, breathlessly, her heart at her mouth, her fear in her face, not knowing what she feared until she should hear it, refusing to fear that her lord was dead, for fear the confirmation of it should slay her.

Would she not know Quicksilver was dead? Would she not? Was she not queen and the seer of Fairyland, and were their hearts not united?

"Milord Malachite," she said, hurrying toward him in a flying flurry of her nightgown's lace. "Milord Malachite? What of my lord and husband that you come here, thus, without him?"

Malachite, pale of cheek, wide of eye, showing fear on his face and smelling of smoke and death, shook his head.

"Milord—" Malachite shook his head and looked at his feet. "Milord bid me to tell you guard his kingdom and look after his subjects as he would himself, and in all obey his will, as though were you him, milady."

Oh, was Quicksilver dead? Why else would Quicksilver bid her to watch over his subjects as though she were himself?

Hand to her chest, as if seeking to still her heart from beating through the slight ribs and the skin that covered them, Ariel gasped. "What happened to my lord? Oh, tell me and be done with it. Is he then dead?"

Malachite shook his head. "No, milady. No." His denial had no joy. "The breach of the wards was an illusion, an effect of . . ." He visibly hesitated. "Of an ancient curse. That is all solved." His eyes, dark with worry and small with sadness, would not meet her gaze. "Only . . . only . . . only some urgent business calls my lord to London and he might be some days upon returning. He begged me to tell you from him that you should watch for his return and meanwhile guard his kingdom with your heart and govern it with your own solid mind."

Ariel breathed fast as she stood staring at Malachite,

torn between relief and doubt. She could not believe the breach had been of so little account, after such an alarm. And why would Quicksilver so hasten to London? What had he to do in London?

What could be the truth? Was Malachite lying to hide Quicksilver's death?

No, that could not be. Quicksilver could not be dead, or else would Ariel have felt it. As King of Fairyland, Quicksilver held in his own the power and the souls of all his subjects.

Quicksilver's death would have thrown all that power and might on Ariel, the Queen of Fairyland, and she would have felt it, felt it through and through, the loss of her lord, as strongly as the loss of her own life.

No, Quicksilver wasn't dead. But then Malachite must speak truthfully and Quicksilver must have gone to London. Why to London? Why would the King of Fairyland go to that land of dirt and iron and massed humanity?

She wished Malachite would give her an explanation of this sudden departure.

The cold upon her chest, the horror trembling through her limbs, all of it bespoke what she feared, perhaps more than death.

Her attempt at protecting Quicksilver had offended him. It had been too much. Humiliated, fearing that she loved him not enough, Quicksilver had returned to a former love—that human whom the Lady Silver had loved so dearly, that William Shakespeare, who had taken himself to London six months ago.

Ariel had loved Quicksilver ever since she could remember, since they'd been toddlers together in the vast palace hall.

For Ariel, Quicksilver's love was more important than life, or hill, or indeed the whole world entire and filled with all wonder. For without his love, neither life nor hill nor world could exist for Ariel.

Was his love for her threatened? Had he left for London just because he resented her offering to help with defending the boundaries?

Was his love for her so frail? A firefly in a summer evening, the inconsequential dust of Fairyland?

Ariel shook her head. She felt tears heavy beneath her eyelids, like threatening grey clouds hanging over a fair day. "Thank you, Malachite. No. I need no more. Thou hast comforted me marvelous much."

She returned to her vanity and to her mirror, and contemplated her features in the mirror. An unexceptional face, oval and pale.

Did her lord still love her? Would he ever come back?

And if not, what would become of the hill without him?

What of poor Ariel, without his love?

She'd be a shadow, no more. A captive spirit doing his bidding and devoid of all self-worth.

Scene 7

✸

A narrow street on the outskirts of London. It is obviously a not-too-prosperous but respectable-enough area, the lowest floor of each of the five-floor houses a modest shop. Hatters and glovers, printers and bakers. By a dark brown building, with a ramshackle outside staircase that climbs, crookedly, to a door on the fifth floor, a dark-haired lady in silk appears, as if birthed out of the air itself. No one else is on the street, save for Will, who approaches the woman cautiously.

The Lady Silver stood at the foot of Will's stairs.

Will's heart raced. His breath caught. Was this an illusion spun off from hunger?

Or was the elf lady truly here, so far from her green glades?

The dark, silken hair of Lady Silver fell, unfettered, down to her waist, over a white silk dress that Will knew could scarcely be lighter or silkier than the skin it hid. Will felt dizzy.

Suddenly, he was once more nineteen, and tramping unawares the paths of Arden Woods, only to be seduced by the Lady Silver in all her splendor.

Silver's tiny waist emphasized her abundant womanly charms that overspilled from her tight white bodice. Will felt as though he were falling, headfirst, into a dream of love.

He smiled. He hurried toward Silver.

She smiled at him, her dark red lips promising velvet touch and the sweetness of newly pressed wine.

In Will's mind, Nan's face rose in remembrance.

Nan, Will's wife, was not as beautiful as Lady Silver. Mortal and ill used by fate—hard worn by life and children and husband—Nan had aged in the last ten years, as Silver hadn't.

Nan's hands felt calloused and rough compared to the Lady Silver's soft, smooth silk skin.

Yet, when night came, and when old age robbed food of its flavor and the sky of color, Will knew it was Nan he wanted by his side. And if he died before that, it would be only because of Nan that he regretted it.

He hesitated. His steps slowed.

This fine lady was no more than a passing fancy, a diversion. A fleeting pleasure, fleetingly enjoyed and ever afterward bitterly regretted. Like fairy gold, the love of elven kind turned to dust and nothing all too quickly.

Such momentary joy bred months of pain. This hot desire converted to cold disdain.

The last time the lady had seduced him and made him break his vow to Nan, Will had promised it would not happen again.

He would not break this second vow, not while starving and with death so near.

Oh, he could ask the elf for money or food, but what would that Fairyland aid not oblige him to do in return?

Making his face hard, he stopped and spoke from steps away. "What do you want?"

Silver laughed. Her musical laugh, sweet and soft, rose

over the shabby neighborhood, like wine-filled cups tin-kling in a golden afternoon pouring mirth over a perfect assembly. "Will, Will," she said. "Is that the way you greet an old friend?"

Her laughter moved Will. Again, in his mind there rose a younger man he'd been, full of hopes and dreams never yet tried and with a good opinion of himself never yet tested and therefore never proven futile.

But the older Will, this Will who had lost his hopes of being a poet and eaten his fill of failure and frustration, shook his head. "We are not friends," he said.

Silver looked confused, lonely, like a child who enters a familiar home and finds it changed and a friendly door barred to her access. She blinked. "Not friends?" Her large, silver eyes glimmered with the moisture of tears. "How can you say that, Will? We are friends, aye, if we are nothing else."

She walked toward him, and he stepped back. She arched her eyebrows in sharp surprise, and advanced still, holding on to his arm, her hand hot and firm even through the bulk of his doublet and shirt. "Oh, come, Will, be not that way. I must talk to you, must have your help. I came to London sensing your sweet soul, and on your sweet soul did I home as a bee onto freshly distilled honey."

His soul?

Will had never understood elves. Old legends heard when he was young had said elves were ghosts or demons or a long-lost people.

Did Silver truly want Will's *soul*? Oh, he'd lost much, but he'd not give that up.

Were elves, then, the demons some legends claimed they were? Or the unquiet dead seeking revenge on life?

Will pulled his arm away from her, and stepped back. He remembered the lying dream that spoke of elves, but he could not remember the details.

It had been a mad dream, a dream that promised Will greatness, only to let waking reality disappoint him.

He remembered the time he'd fallen into the tangled affairs of elves and how Silver's seduction then had been naught but an attempt to involve him in killing the fairy king, her brother, and stealing the throne from him.

Had Silver succeeded, indeed, Will would have been dead long ago.

Would not her plots now be similar to her traps and schemes then? Self-serving plans that bode Will no good.

And did Will believe this immortal creature would have shed a tear for him, had he died in fulfilling her plans?

He looked at the reflective, shining silver eyes that, overshadowed by a rich canopy of black lashes, stared so enticingly into his own eyes.

His body's weak senses longed to be overwhelmed by all her beauty and to lay complyingly within her enticing arms. But his mind knew better and whispered to him of treason and mistrust.

He stepped away from her. The movement wrenched at his own heart. He shrank away from the reach of her soft, white hand, though he needed that touch more than he needed the air he breathed.

He stepped back till he found, behind him, the decaying wooden wall of the house where he lodged. "When has elf been friend to man, milady? When have you been my friend? You would use me for your purposes, nothing more."

Silver shook her head, the silken sheaf of her hair rustling in the too hot, too still, too humid night air that was as bad breath, tainted with the odors of London and its wastes.

"You use me ill," she said.

Her face, frantic with some passion, her eyes narrowed and blinking to keep tears away, she looked human and frail and without cunning. "You use me ill and you should not use me thus. For I come in great important business, not just for me, but for mankind entire."

The thought of Silver caring about humanity seemed incongruous enough, unlikely enough to keep Will from the depths of desire and awaken in him a shocked interest. "Mankind?" he asked.

She nodded.

Will shook his head and swallowed hard. Her beauty had its effect upon his heart, like the flame of a candle that, shining upon wax, will soften it. Yet he could resist the melting warmth and the molten beauty that gazed upon him from those shimmering metallic eyes. But the thought of Silver concerned with low, ephemeral humans puzzled him so that he could not walk away from *that*. If she lied not, then here was wonder indeed.

"Please, lady," he said, both voice and words less resolute than he'd hoped. He wanted to know why she cared for humans, and yet he wanted her to leave him alone. "Please, lady. I am but a fool, but not such a fool who doesn't know the havoc your kind can wreak. Please go. Be gone. For you must mock. You, care for humans?"

The lady trembled. From the melting eyes, two tears dropped, rolling down her curved cheek like twin crystalline globules, upon which Will saw all his future.

He'd die in London, a lonely, desperate man. He'd never again see a glimmer of magical beauty. Never again would he touch something like the silk of Silver's skin. Never.

"Humans and elvenkind, in this conjoined," she said. "Will meet twin dooms if you help me not."

This was fantastical and unbelievable. "Lady, you have to go."

Silver looked down at him, her eyes like a wet day, all

rainy where it was wont to be bright. "I have nowhere else to go," she said. "I cannot—

"I cannot go," she screamed. She covered her face with her pale hands and the whole of her slim body trembled.

She reached for his arm, and encircled his wrist with her small hand. The touch of her hand, soft upon his skin, made her seem human, frail, in need of protection. It made her seem like the Silver he remembered.

"To whom will I go if you don't let me abide?" Tears chased each other down her face. "I've *had* to come to London." She stomped her foot and bit her lip, but resolution crumpled upon her face and her eyes filled with tears. "In London I have to remain till I find my brother Sylvanus."

"Your brother?" Mention of the deposed King of Fairyland, the same mention that the three creatures had made upon his dream, riveted Will's attention. He remembered Sylvanus as even more scheming than the run of elves. Sylvanus had tried to steal Nan before the Hunter took Sylvanus. Sylvanus would have had Will killed to leave Sylvanus's path free to wooing Nan.

"Your brother? Is your brother in London? Why would he be?" Creatures of glade and dale, elves both good and bad, did not belong in London's reek, in London's crowded, teeming streets, with their tall houses that obscured the daylight.

"My brother . . ." Silver sighed and cried, tears chasing each other down her little rounded cheeks to drip upon her bosom, where they ran down in rivulets between the twin globules of her breasts like a mountain stream disappearing into a deep crevice. "My brother has . . . He attacked the Hunter. He . . ."

"But your brother is in *thrall* of the Hunter," Will said. His astonishment made him forget his hunger, his fear of Silver, his desperate straits. "The Hunter's slave. The

Hunter's dog. Can a slave thus attack his master?"

He tried to keep his eyes away from the destination of those drops of water that left her eyes only to travel to more intimate locations, and yet his eyes traced their path down her cheeks, to her velvety bosom, and imagined the course beyond, beneath her perfumed garments.

He forced his gaze up as one who forces an errant child back to his books. He made himself meet her gaze. "When last we met, you told me that the Hunter was stronger even than elf and that no elf could escape his thralldom. Now you tell me Sylvanus has escaped?"

Silver trembled, and could do no more than multiply the soft progression of her tears.

She nodded, though, and sighed, her sighs like a gentle spring breeze.

This close to her, with her body touching him, Will didn't smell the rot and garbage of London's least fashionable district, but the warm scent of lilac from Silver's skin.

It reminded Will of spring in Stratford, that hometown he despaired of ever seeing again.

He marshaled all his power to resist her, but all his power broke like a dam, carried away by her flood of tears. How could he be her enemy when she was thus, soft and broken and defenseless? How could he call on the iron of his will against an enemy whose weapons were gentle words and desperate pleas? How could he turn harsh and savage when she cried and begged his help?

Yet she was no more, no less than the other aspect of the king of elves and that Quicksilver was neither soft nor defenseless. But knowing this didn't help. What Will saw overwhelmed what he knew, his eyes reaching for his heart and past his mind.

It didn't matter what Will's reason said, when argued against the persuasive argument of his vision.

What mattered it if Quicksilver's muscles lay hidden beneath this silky skin, these tender charms? It was the Lady Silver whom Will beheld. It was she who cried.

He found his arm, as though of its own accord, encircling those shoulders that felt so frail.

And all the while—while Will's mind censured him his easy giving in and what would be yet another betrayal of Nan—Silver's hair tickled his cheek, her perfume filled his nostrils and her beauty dazzled his mind.

He felt giddy. Giddier than hunger alone could make him.

This wasn't love. Oh, Will knew that.

He knew what love was—Nan's companionship, her loyalty, her sleeping form warming him through the night.

That was love. That, and the respect that came from knowing and believing in another's mind and reason as in his own—that alliance of two beings against the madding world.

But this quickening of the blood, the sudden pulses that thrilled upon his veins like perdition; this whispering of a reason older than man that spoke not to the brain but to the eyes—this was much like being drunk, like being crazed, like being a babe, innocent, and led here and there in the arms of a loved nurse.

It was like iron pulled by a magnet, like rain falling helplessly to earth, like a boat drifting on a current, like praying and trusting a higher power.

Will let his body act and let it go, arm over Silver's up the rickety steps to the door to his room.

Standing on the tiny platform, outside his door, his arm around Silver to balance her, Will slipped the key in the lock and opened it.

And all the while his hands trembled, and it was like an ague, like a fever—like anything which mere man can't help.

He knew what he wanted, what he craved, the longing for her that drove all his senses. But even to himself he could not confess it, lest removing his denial would render him her too easy prey.

In his room, he wrapped his arms around the immortal creature that trembled and sobbed within his embrace.

His sagging, small bed, with its worn blankets, the lopsided old table that served him as a desk, even his better suit which he threw down as he came in, all looked shabbier, older in her presence.

His room smelled of old meals, of dirty clothes, of dust. The taper he lit smelled of burnt bacon and smoked, casting only a timid and dismal light.

Her perfume filled his nostrils, and his mouth ached to feel the soft caress of her skin, to taste the exquisite wine of her tongue.

He closed his eyes and pulled her tight. He lowered his mouth to hers.

Her mouth tasted like wine, her skin felt like madness, his heart beat like the rhythm of a youthful dance.

The knock upon the door startled them both. They sprang apart. She laughed, a high silvery laugh.

But the knocking had awakened Will's reason.

With no money, he couldn't even afford to pay his back rent, much less the standard fine for adultery, which would be levied should his pious landlord denounce him to the Church.

And Will's landlord, who was bound to be at the door, having been awakened by their movement, their talk, would want the back rent and, finding this dazzling lady here, in Will's quarters unchaperoned, *would* denounce Will for adultery.

Trembling with fear now, all lust dispersed, Will shoved Silver into a corner of the room, where she couldn't be seen from the door. He whispered fiercely,

"Hush, milady. Don't move and not a sound, if you ever prized my friendship."

On such flimsy warranty, and fearing very much what she might not do, Will ran his hand back through his hair, smoothing the imagined mark of her hand.

And he opened his door.

Scene 8

❧

The tall, closed carriage trundles by, not far from Will's lodgings. Inside it, Kit Marlowe looks rumpled, sweaty, and very scared. He stares from Henry Mauder to the other man, his eyes twin mirrors of despair.

Kit Marlowe was scared.

From outside the carriage, the softer fall of the horses' hooves told him that they'd left behind the paved area of town and moved now at the outskirts of London.

Were they headed to the tower?

Kit almost smiled at the thought.

Kit was but the son of a Canterbury cobbler, with neither title, nor connections, nor fortune. How could he be taken to the tower like a nobleman? It would almost be an honor in itself, were it true.

Yet the death that would find him in the tower's stony rooms would be as silent, as worm-eaten, as perpetual, as a humble death in a cottage.

The smile faded from Kit's lips.

Dark prospects loomed before him as he stared at Henry Mauder's yellow teeth, Mauder's disdainful smile. He could see himself dead, and worse, he could see Imp dead beside him.

From the racing river of his fear, words issued, spoken in a cringing, lost voice that reminded Kit of his own father talking to an important customer.

"Your honors, I am a playwright. This is a gift that I have, simple, simple; a foolish extravagant spirit, full of forms, figures, shapes, objects, ideas, apprehensions, motions, evolutions."

As always with Kit, panic betrayed itself in a running of the mouth in incessant, high-sounding, little-meaning words. He tried to check the words but he couldn't, they would go on flowing from his mouth—a river of incontinent explanation.

"These are begot in the ventricle of memory, nourished in the womb of *pia mater*, and delivered upon the mellowing of occasion. But the gift is good in those in whom it is acute, and I am thankful for it." By an effort of will, he managed to arrest the flow, his words checking upon a deep breath, something like a ghostly sigh.

Mauder and the other man look puzzled.

Kit bit his lip, and found his Cambridge diction once more. "That's all I am, all. Just a playwright and a poet. Nothing more. Too much for me these intrigues, too high for me these philosophical opinions. How can you accuse me of being an atheist? Atheist, I? I studied divinity, your honors. Would an atheist undertake such study?"

"You studied divinity before someone corrupted you. It is the name of the corrupter we want, and you may go, if you promise to reform," Mauder said with the careful certainty of the self-righteous.

If only it were that simple. If only, indeed, Kit told all and were allowed to go. Even turning in kindly, learned Sir Walter might be worth it, to keep Imp safe.

But it wouldn't be so. Kit would not be allowed to go that easily. Imp would be in danger, either way. For like a wolf, ravenous and confined, these intriguers, once fed the morsel they craved, would demand more and more until they'd devoured Kit and Imp also.

Yet even through Kit's despair, a plan formed in his mind. Or if not a plan, a shadow of it, the bare bones and architrave of a plan as like onto a plan as the painted scenery on stage was like the place the playwright hoped to evoke.

He was a playwright, a maker of illusions.

If he couldn't turn in Sir Walter Raleigh, then Marlowe must be able to turn in someone else and, with that someone else, buy time, until Raleigh turned the plot away from himself, or until Marlowe could find something else with which to hold doom at bay.

"I do know something," he said, his voice low and hesitant and fraught with thought, as though he couldn't quite bring himself to speak.

"Ah," Mauder said, and sat back. "I knew you would be reasonable, Master Marlowe."

"Yes. I meant to be, but . . ." He shook his head. "What I know is more complicated than what you meant. After all, what would it be to you, if I said that this person or that taught me heresy and atheism?" He waved his hand in the air. "It can no more than give the Queen momentary displeasure, but she will not be likely to take action against one highly placed for such a simple offense, will she now?" He flicked the fingers of his naked hand dismissively. His gloved hand still gripped the other glove tightly. "She cares not a fig for religion, does she, sires, when the heretic can defend her realm or . . ." He forced a smile. "Or bring home ships overflowing with gold."

In his mind he cast about for a likely victim, around whom to weave his web of deception.

Outside, the horses raced, their hoof-falls muffled against soft ground.

Will Shakespeare. Was that not the name of the would-be poet at Paul's? He'd seemed unprotected, unconnected. A country boy just come to London, full of fire and ambition and little else.

Will. Yes, he might do very well.

"But there is a conspiracy I know. Indeed, I've been following it for weeks. It touches the highest heads of the kingdom." Kit wove his intrigue with facile speech. "I need but a few more days to be sure," he spoke on, improvising, like an actor upon the stage, spinning seeming truth from his lying words.

From the quickening of Mauder's eye, the sharp look of Mauder's silent friend, Kit could tell indeed that the trout came to the tickling hand. He spoke fast and persuasively, as if this were a speech declaimed on the stage.

As it happened, they were so enthralled that they didn't stop Kit when he twitched the curtain aside and saw that they trundled along a narrow street. From the signs on the shops, Kit recognized Hog's Lane in Shoreditch. Did Shakespeare not live here?

"Would you let me out, gentlemen?" he asked. "I'll look for you anon with more information."

And unbelievably, Mauder gave his signal and the carriage stopped. The door opened, and on trembling legs, Kit stepped onto a muddy street in Shoreditch.

The carriage splattered Kit with mud and filth as it started up again.

He didn't mind. It took him two breaths of the dank air, tainted with smoke and cooking smells, to realize he was still alive. Surely, no after-death smell could be that bad.

He was alive, but at what cost?

Could he run now? But run where? If it were only himself, he would escape this instant, board a ship to France or Spain, and there live by his wits and his work. But he could not leave Imp behind, to suffer the revenge of Kit's enemies.

Nor could Kit take Imp with him without being sure they'd have lodging and food and ready friends on the other side.

Kit looked at the retreating carriage and thought he would have to concoct a plan now, a plot as elaborate as any ever discovered, a plot that would implicate Essex and thus let Raleigh, and Kit, and Imp go free.

He walked down an alley, and up another, to where his memory told him a hatter's should be.

Across the street from him stood a tall, narrow, dark building with a hatter's sign. Two people climbed a precarious staircase to the fifth floor, over the shop.

The man was Will Shakespeare. The woman, dark-haired, beautiful, wore cloth of silver and was . . .

Kit stopped. It couldn't be the Lady Silver.

What would an elf do in London?

Kit stared as the couple disappeared through a door into the fifth floor the shabby building.

What could Will be doing with such a woman? Would this be Will's wife?

Kit smiled at the thought. How could Will, with his much-mended wool suit, his receding hairline, his meek look, procure a wife like that exquisite creature?

How lovely she'd looked, even from the back, with her dark silky hair, her gown of silver cloth, her steps like a soft, hypnotic dance.

She reminded Kit of his first love, that elf lady that he'd loved perhaps not wisely, but too well.

Again, the thought of someone like Will winning the hand of one such as she made Kit smile.

But why would a woman have Will for a lover, who wouldn't have him for a husband? And if not his lover, why would she go into his room alone with him?

Or was there some conspiracy already here?

Did this woman—by her looks, a great noble lady, or a great whore—seek Will for something other than his looks and his homely charms?

More likely she sought him for secret messages, secret plotting, secret maneuvering. London was as rotten with plots as a stray dog with fleas.

Relief washed over Kit like a breath of fresh air. The conscience he'd not been aware of disturbing ceased troubling him.

Maybe he was not concocting a plot unaided. Perhaps Will was not the sweet innocent he appeared to be.

Perhaps Kit would find true guilt where he'd thought to find gullible innocence.

Maybe Will's involvement with this court lady spelled doom for Essex—deserved doom—relieving Kit of the dread guilt of entrapping someone as innocent and unsullied as Imp himself.

Kit climbed the rickety wooden stairs with a light step. Every step creaked beneath his boots and the banister shook like an unsound tooth.

Kit would find out what the good burgher was up to.

Knocking on the door, Kit waited. He could hear rustling on the other side of the door, then an urgent whisper.

He'd just raised his hand to knock again when the door opened.

A flushed Will stood in the doorway, raking his scant hair back from his domed forehead with the gloved fingers of one hand, and wiping his mouth on the back of his other glove.

Shakespeare looked as embarrassed and surprised as a cat caught at the cream.

Kit smiled at him, his slow, practiced smile. "Good eve, good Shakestaff."

Kit couldn't, of course, just ask Shakespeare who the

woman was that Will had hidden in his room.

Shakespeare would lie or, worse, not answer, not even giving Kit the benefit of guessing the truth behind a lie.

No. Kit would use other bait to work his way into the house, to work his way into Will's confidence, to find out all there was to know about this man that he might more easily entrap him.

The man was desperate for a job, any job. Kit remembered seeing Will in St. Paul's standing in front of the Si Quis door. A job in the theater would seem to him his heart's desire, a very dream come true.

"I thought on your plight," Kit said, and smiled at Shakespeare, who looked more than a little bewildered. "I thought on your plight, good Wigglestick, friendless and jobless in London, and I thought on your poem and your excellent taste in playwrights.

"If I were to give you a note for Philip Henslowe, he would surely hire you to play odd parts in the theater. Not big parts, mind, only this man's servant, that man's mute friend. Yet you'd be paid from the common take."

As Kit spoke, he leaned in, to look at Will's room. He leaned now this way and now that, discerning the inside of very poor lodgings.

The wooden floor was strewn with rushes, in the old-fashioned country way. But these rushes looked old and dusty. The table, upon which an inkstone, pens, and paper rested, was old and sagged upon one leg shorter than the others.

Nowhere could Kit see a trace of the fair stranger, the woman with the dark hair, the body of an angel, that he'd glimpsed all too briefly.

Had his mind played tricks on him? Did the memory of his elven love, coming upon the shocks of the last hour, make him suffer illusions?

It couldn't be. Kit had done much in the way of madness, but never yet dreamed a woman out of the whole cloth of his mind.

Were he ever to do that, they might as well come and take him to Bedlam.

Yet, as if to tantalize him with his own possible madness, a smell of lilac wafted to his nostrils—the smell of the magical fairykind, the smell of Kit's lady love in that distant summer, the memory of which still quickened his blood and sped his thought.

He shook his head to clear it.

Will Shakespeare, who'd done no more than open his mouth as if to make some answer, closed it again.

Trust the clod to think the head shake applied to him.

"Speak, good Shakestaff, speak," Kit said.

Will took a deep breath and inclined his head briefly. "I thank you, good Master Marlowe, I thank you. To own the truth . . . I dare not lie to you, as I could use a job and the coin it brings. But I had just latterly . . . that is, today, on the way home, I saw a man. . . . I believe there's plague in the city, and I believe the theater might close again."

Oh. Plague.

Plague again, after the plagued winter. The plague, a summer disease, had ravaged all through the cold winter in London and seemed to have vanished early spring. Let it not be back again. Kit hated the plague, the stench of death wafting through the narrow streets, the miasma of rotting bodies blanketing London as it were a vast, open graveyard.

Yet, plague or not, Kit must make sure that Imp was safe of the stalking danger of the secret service, that other plague that moved through this twilight of the Queen's realm plucking at will the innocent and the guilty alike.

And to save Imp, Kit must sacrifice Will Shakespeare.

To sacrifice Will, Kit must know him better. Every play

necessitated research. Yes. Kit would make himself Will's friend.

"You must not fear," he heard himself say, and with eager hand he clutched at the rough stuff of Will's sleeve. "There will be no plague. You must try the theater. You have talent for poetry—talent such as the gods give, such as must be used for the good of all humanity. Trust not vile fate. Make your fate. Take your destiny in your own hands and mold it. Here, Will Shakespeare, let me give you that note of which I spoke. Let me get paper." Saying this, he tried to push his way past Will and into the room, toward the table, where pens and papers lay in disarray. From that room wafted the smell of lilac, the smell of elvenkind, the smell of the only woman Kit had ever loved. The only woman and, aye—Kit remembered as the blood rose, bold, to his cheeks—the only man. The elf of Kit's worship had been both by turns, now Quicksilver of the moonlight-bright hair, the broad shoulders, and the moss green eyes, now Silver with her rounded body and her metallic eyes.

Could it be Silver, now within that room? Kit pushed forward.

"No," Will yelled, his face contorted in anguish, even as his solid, country-boy body blocked Kit's access to Will's rooms. "No. I pray, wait. I'll get the paper myself." And taking a deep breath, Will flung the door closed.

Hearing the latch slide to, Kit blinked.

Will would lock the door? Why?

After all the good Kit had done to Shakespeare—well, all the good Shakespeare thought Kit intended to do for him—Shakespeare would shut the door?

Was Shakespeare perhaps not what he seemed? Was he so sophisticated that he saw through Kit's deception?

Or had he decided that Kit was insane or drunk and took this opportunity to thus rid himself of an inopportune visitor? Or was Will's visitor that important that Will must hide her at all costs? Oh, Kit must devise a watch upon Will's house, to wait for this woman's return.

Imp might do it. Anything to get Imp away from that house where the councilmen might seek him out.

Kit stared at Will's unpainted, splintered door rancorously, wishing to know the secrets it hid.

Would Will ever come out again?

But the latch slid back, and Will handed Kit two sheets of rough paper and a quill, and held an ink horn in his hand, ready for the dipping.

"I thank you, Master Marlowe, for your pains. Indeed, I find not the words to express my gratitude."

Kit forced a smile to form upon his face, a smile that hurt his muscles with forcing it—like aching legs will hurt with one further step, like an aching head will rebel at the prospect of one more thought.

If so grateful, why not innocently honest? If not honest, then why did he look it and torment Kit's conscience thus?

Did Will conspire? Indeed, it seemed so.

Oh, that Kit could uncover this plot. Tomorrow night, he must get Imp to watch Will's door. One more urchin wouldn't be noticeable in the melee of Shoreditch at night and Imp was ever good at escaping his bed and his mother's vigilance.

Kit struggled to think, struggled to speak, in his honeyed tones, in his most polite patter. "Good Shakesstick, I treasure your gratitude, but this . . ." He lifted the quill and the paper in his hand. "This will hardly do for writing, and I would more appreciate if your gratitude were translated into a ready table upon which to write."

Kit thought he heard a muffled giggle answer his words and again tried to walk in past Will, who without seeming to do it, adroitly blocked Kit's path with simple stubbornness and wide countryman shoulders.

"Dear Wigglespear," Kit started.

"No, please, Master Marlowe, do me the honor of not stepping into my abode, for like onto the abode of the Roman centurion, it is unfit for your presence."

Kit blinked, stopped by such a heavy metaphor. "I'm neither God in man, nor are you. . . . No, Master Wigglestaff. I thought to do you a kindness, but I will not write on mine own knee while perched on this unsteady platform of yours." His hand that held the pen gestured toward the precipice, unguarded and deep, on the side of the stairs that didn't lean against the house.

"No." He handed Will both quill and paper. "If this is how you treat your benefactors, Master Tremblelance, I can see well enough that you wish for no benefice. I shall be gone."

A flush, like a dark red tide, climbed Shakespeare's thick neck to tinge his cheeks. He swallowed, his prominent Adam's apple rising and falling above the frayed, dingy lace collar of his shirt.

"If that's how you see it. . . . If that's how you must do, Master Marlowe, I understand. Though I, myself, appreciate the attempt at helping me and wish you'd not take offense so easily. But I see . . . I see it's useless and I thank you for the good deed you would have done, even if averted."

Kit turned his back and took two steps down the narrow stairs. Two steps, and he stopped, looking down at the smelly, muddy alley below. He expected Will to change his mind, to beg him to come back, to beg him to come in.

Then Kit would see the woman Will hid, and maybe learn what plot lurked behind Will's innocent look.

But looking up, he saw that Will had started shutting the door slowly and reluctantly, as a man that sees opportunity vanish down the staircase of misfortune.

"Wait," Kit yelled. "Wait. God's death, man, you're more stubborn than I."

He forced a grin upon the creases of anger and frustration that plied his skin. "You're more stubborn than I and that has to be good. That has to bode well for your chances to make a living in this madhouse we call London, in this plague-infested bedlam we call the theater. Here, man, here, here." Climbing the steps in a hurry, Kit stood on the narrow perch at the top, and pulled paper and quill from Will's hands.

"Stand not amazed," Kit said as he squatted and set the paper on his knee, half closing one eye against the precipitous drop on one side of him. "Stand not amazed. Reach me that ink horn." And yet, as he sat there, uncomfortable and dangerously balanced, he cast an eager eye inside the room, at the comfortless bed, the draggled stool, the precarious table.

But nowhere did he catch another fleeting glimpse of skin like cream, of hair like midnight spun, entire, from the dreams of man. Or yet of golden hair and broad shoulder and the regal bearing of the elf prince that was the Lady Silver's other aspect.

Will knelt and offered the ink horn.

Kit dipped his quill in it and wrote quickly, with the practice and ease of one accustomed to such task. *And to none other,* he thought, making a face at remembering how clumsy he had been with his father's cobbler tools, in his far-off, despised childhood. He remembered his father's frustrated rage at what he viewed as Kit's intentional clumsiness, and Kit's mind skittered away from further memory.

Philip Henslowe, he wrote. *I beg you as a favor and a consideration, if you wish me to bring you my next play first, that you look upon my friend, Will Shakespeare, of Warwickshire for a role in the play you currently present.*

It need not be a great part. A mute servant, a silent friend will do, provided he gets paid at the end of the day.

He underlined the last line three times, well acquainted with Henslowe's occasional lapses from honesty, with the actors that never got paid until they cornered the theater owner and, by the force of fists and daggers, demanded their share of the day's take.

But if you would, of your kind heart, do my friend a favor, this poor playwright would feel indebted enough not to show his next play to milord of Pembroke's men first.

He signed it with a flourish, writing his name with the same spelling he'd used at Cambridge, *Christopher Merlin.*

The more ancient spelling of his patronymic appealed to Kit's sense of being a wizard, a supernatural being, in control of his destiny. Of being other than a poor cobbler's son, circled by plotters, a long way from home and terrified.

He remembered the dark, swaying carriage, the threatening voices all the more threatening for rarely rising above a whisper. Sweat sprang upon his brow.

Fearful that his fear, his sudden recoil, would show in his face, he handed the paper to Will and started, quickly, down the steps, not waiting for thanks, not trying to force his way into the room again.

It was not until he was on firm ground that he realized, by the thin light of the distant moon, that he'd stained his fine new gloves with ink. The left one had a spot of ink near the index finger.

He rubbed at it to no avail as he hurried home through darkened streets.

Home to Imp, whose life depended on the cunning of his undeserving, unknowledged father.

Will would do for baiting Kit's trap, but now the trap remained to be built.

And could Will indeed be made to appear the mastermind of a great plot?

Kit shook his head. Hard to tell. For who knew what hid in the hearts of men? Kit had always been good with words and the building of fiery illusions with his rhetoric. And he'd ever been bad—bad indeed—at guessing what other people knew or felt.

What if Will was truly a mastermind? What if he had secret contacts of his own?

Scene 9

Will's room. Amazed, Will closes the door and turns to Silver, who stands at the farthest corner of the room, leaning on the dingy wall.

"Will?" she asked, and her voice trembled in asking it. Silver bit her lip, but it didn't help. It would not keep the tremor at bay, and her voice trembled again as she piped uncertainly, "Was that Kit Marlowe? Was it Kit Marlowe at the door?"

Through her mind ran memories she thought long forgotten, memories of Kit Marlowe as a shy, demure divinity student.

At least half the fun of seducing him had come from that shy way of his, his uncertainty about how to act, how to behave, his conviction that he was doing something horribly wicked and out of bounds for a Christian soul.

Which—Silver knowing precious little of mortal souls, Christian or else—he might very well have been.

But she remembered Kit's eager enthusiasm, once his hesitation had vanished.

Silver remembered Kit's lips searching, seeking, attempting to drink her very soul, his lust such as only a young man can feel in the early spring of his years.

She remembered their bodies entwined beneath the ancient copse of trees in the abandoned monastery at the outskirts of Canterbury.

Once he'd lost his reserve, how he had loved, and how the love of elvenkind had maddened him, beating upon his heated blood like the smith's hammer upon red-hot iron.

Kit had loved Silver and Quicksilver both, the elf in both aspects, not caring under which form the elf embraced him, so long as the elf did.

Silver herself hadn't loved Kit, couldn't pretend to. As for Quicksilver, as much as Silver could understand that side of her nature, Quicksilver had nurtured for Kit a tender infatuation that yet fell as short of true love as the light cast by a firefly fell short of the shine of a star.

But she remembered that fevered love of Kit's, that adoration that had perfumed her nights like incense.

Remembering it, her heart beat faster, her heart beat kindly for the man she'd just seen—his face pinched by some unnamed worry, his smiles all cynical pretending and his generosity a strange, imposing one that made no sense and seemed to strike against the normal way of courtesy.

"Was that Kit Marlowe?" she demanded, grabbing Will's sleeve and holding it until the man, seemingly waking, blinked at her.

"Kit? Yes, it was Kit," he said. "And look you here, he has given me an introduction to the theater owner and told me if I go early, I'll surely get a job. Look, and he signed it with his own hand."

Looking over Will's shoulder, Silver read the signature and felt a sick turn in her stomach.

Merlin.

Oh, Kit was of that race well enough. It had been the

unused elven magic burning in him, the unaware icy power hidden beneath the eager human fire that first had called her to him. But his being of Merlin's race meant not that he had Merlin's power. With Sylvanus raging free, Kit's heritage was a dangerous flag that he should not wave.

She wished Kit would not blazon forth that name as a shield, when it would shield him from precious little.

When it could well call the attention of Sylvanus, Sylvanus who fed on death and suffering, Sylvanus. . . .

Silver felt as though she'd swallowed a lump of ice whole and it had nestled in her stomach, leeching her limbs of strength. She'd thought she cared not for Kit and yet, at the thought of what might happen to the man should Sylvanus find him, both her heart and Quicksilver's outraged feelings rose in alarm.

She had thought she cared not for Kit, but still something in her did care for him or for that memory of their joint youth so conjoined with the tender memory of his love for her.

Once more, Silver fell short of true elven ice and detachment. Sylvanus would have laughed at her.

But she'd thought Kit away from London. She'd thought him safe. She'd kept track of his movements over the years. Some protective quality remained after the lust had burned out.

And she'd thought Kit away from London. She'd thought him safe. She'd never thought to worry for him as she worried for Will.

Now panic quickened and outraged dormant affection. It was as though her youth itself were threatened and her tender memories under siege.

"Why is he in London? What brought him here?" She felt something like a premonition, though her power didn't run to prophecy. She felt a cold despondent fear, a thing somewhat like what humans talked about when they said as if someone walked over their grave.

Will waved her away. "It matters not. Look here, it gives me the power, it gives me a chance to get a job in the theater. Look here, it gives me a chance to learn how to write plays by watching them acted and how the audience reacts. And you heard what Kit Marlowe said, about my talent. You heard what he said, he who is the very Muses' darling."

"What *did* he say?" Silver asked, not caring, feeling only that though elves had no graves, their stuff melting into the magic and fire that had first created the universe, something had touched her and foretold . . . *death*. For her or for whom? For Kit? For Will? For the whole cursed world?

Though Kit was vain and shallow, though Kit had grown older and pinched, yet Silver remembered him in the warm heat of his youth. And though there was to Will that meanness which tightened his eyes and focused him only on his wife and brood, yet Silver had loved him once, loved him truly. Perhaps—she thought, as she looked on those golden falcon eyes, the intensity of the emotions that showed on his face—perhaps she loved him yet with some corner of her being, some particle of her magical might.

As for the world, she would fain save that, too, if for nothing else because human and elven worlds were linked and a blight on one was a blight on the other. And because Quicksilver had loosened this doom upon the world.

She thought of the withering crops, the mist of magical plague spreading as Sylvanus's dark might swept over the fields toward London. The plague had been birthed by Sylvanus's monstrous corruption of his state.

What was the equivalent of that withering, in the elven world?

She couldn't contact Ariel with her mind. Not without

Ariel's finding out more about Silver than Silver wished Ariel to know. She hoped the hill was well.

Will was telling her about what Kit had said, and what he had implied, about Will's wish to succeed.

"Listen, listen, Will, you must listen to me," she said, possessed of renewed energy and attempting to make the mortal hear her as he had not before. "You are in danger. That is why I came here. I didn't know that Kit was in danger also. But he is, and you must listen. My ill-begotten brother has hurt the Hunter and thus made the world rock upon its foundations—the plague, you mentioned it to Kit—the plague is the effect of what my brother did to the Hunter."

Will looked up from his paper and swept her with an unattending, uncaring gaze. "The Hunter? What am I to the Hunter or the Hunter to me? Why come you to London to tell me that woodland divinities are threatened?"

"The Hunter is not a woodland divinity. The Hunter is . . ." Silver's words failed her. She put both of her hands on Will, one on each shoulder.

She looked intently into his eyes. "The Hunter is ancient and important and I did not know he could be injured, and he says, he says if—"

She shook her head, stopped. She did not wish to tell Will about the fire in Stratford.

She could well imagine how he would react to such a threat to his family.

Even less did she wish to acknowledge Quicksilver's guilt in what had transpired.

What Will would think of this, she also knew well. That she was a temptress, a danger, and that he must get well away from her. No. Warn him of the immediate danger and be done.

"My brother has learned to feed on human suffering, on human pain, on human death, as the gods of old did.

He has no true body and yet, incorporeal, he can feed and gain power from death. I'm sure he's come to London to feed on the deaths from this plague. We cannot afford to let him do so."

Will's eyes narrowed when she mentioned the plague, but he shook his head stubbornly. "Milady," he said, and his voice had gone all cold, dripping with icicles and fore-telling separation. "Milady, what is your *brother* to me? What is his power? Why should I be the arbiter and judge of elven disputes?" His eyes narrowed further, but with suspicion. "Do you think to make me your dupe once more? To make me commit your crimes for you?"

Silver gasped at the surprise of this accusation.

Her crimes? What did he think of her?

Her eyes filled with tears, and while she stomped her foot at the humiliation of being thus reduced to tears by a mortal, she heard her voice issue through her lips, shaky and high, "Oh, that you dare. Oh, that you say such things. Will, I would never . . . That was before I loved you."

She stretched her hands for him, and he pushed them back, his hands firm and unfeeling.

"Lady, you never loved me."

And before she could protest, he added, "Lady, I care not."

"You *must* care," she said.

Didn't the fool man see that his own world depended upon that other shadowy, supernatural world, like a tennis ball tethered to a paddle, which can no more go than the string will let it, and which must burn if the paddle burns? Did he not understand that Sylvanus would grow with his feeding, and need more death to feed him anew?

Did he not know that whatever Sylvanus meant, surely he meant to destroy the world?

All this she flung at him in desperate shrilling.

Will shook his head. He set the paper on his desk, and

looked up at her. "No more. I care not for you nor for your world. I care for my family, for my wife and children, for my poems that I might perfect and which might bring me fortune and the ability to make my son Hamnet a fine gentleman, and to buy fine clothes for my daughters and give them a dowry that will make them gentlemen's wives." He crossed his arms upon his chest. "I care not for you nor for your kingdom, nor for your shadowy plots that always bring me misfortune and blight what I hold dear. It is my wife I love, Lady Silver, not you."

The words hurt. Being compared with Anne Shakespeare, with her coarse hands, her coarser figure, nettled the Lady Silver like a well-applied bur will nettle the body of a sleeper.

She heard her voice, shrill, a fishwife demanding accounting for her husband's misdeeds. "You mean that not. How can you mean it? Your wife more than I? Have you forgotten?" And on an unconsidered, reckless impulse that swept over her as if come out of elsewhere to overwhelm her reason, she advanced toward him, arms extended.

Will put his hands forward, and pushed her away. "No. Be gone. I have no time for your mad games. I must be at the theater early morning."

Checked in her advance, Silver trembled. She stepped back, trying to recover what of her dignity subsisted. What had she been going to do? Kiss Will? Make love to him?

Hadn't Quicksilver promised Ariel never more to change to Silver? Never more to let Silver have her way with Will?

Bad enough he'd broken the first promise. Bad enough, though perhaps justified by his need to seek Will's help. Will was as much more likely to give in to Lady Silver than to Quicksilver.

But that was not working, and besides, what justification could Silver have for seducing Will?

Double adultery it would be. And a breach of promise and honor. No.

She must go. She must control herself and go, as Will wished her to go.

She must go out into the streets of London. She would get no help here, no rational word from Will. And she must find what had brought Sylvanus to London.

Without knowing how or why, Silver knew that Sylvanus meant to dethrone her—him—meant to destroy all that she had ever held dear, even Will and Kit.

But she wasn't sure how Sylvanus could hope to do that, could hope to prevail against the might of the fairy hill, or the strength of mortal reality.

And not knowing it, she knew not how to battle it.

Scene 10

❧

A neighborhood in Southwark. Amid the muddy fields, the reeking, unpaved lanes, some poor houses stand, tall but graceless and looking like slums anywhere and any when—as though built by children, hastily, with the poorest materials available. Down the narrow, dark street, Kit walks, his clothes strangely out of place in this poor working neighborhood.

Kit walked blindly. The memory of the elf lady he'd once loved overpowered him—the dark lady who could also be a fair youth—took over his senses. He remembered hair of black silk and pale golden hair like moonlight overspilled through a dark night. He remembered hands now soft and small and now large and weapon-calloused. But both hands had been, alike, knowing and daring, both full of arts that humans had never learned, of pleasing vices and gentle sins, of sweetness and tempting older than any human.

Kit remembered the scent of lilac permeating all and making him drunk.

Walking, Kit found, unbidden upon his lips, the simple poem he'd written for Silver—and Quicksilver—in the too brief flowering of his youth.

"Come live with me and be my love," he sang. "And I will give you beds of roses and a thousand fragrant posies."

Somewhere, in the darkened upper floors of the nearby houses, someone cursed loudly.

"It's that creature, Marlowe," a louder, shriller female voice answered. "He's drunk again."

Marlowe smiled and, drunk on nothing but memory, lifted his voice that had once been famous in the Canterbury Cathedral choir, "Our fair swains will—"

A dog barked, and another, shrill voice rose from a window, far above the street, this one saying, "Oh, not again."

"Kit, Kit, Kit." Someone small and looking, in the distant moonlight, like little more than a dark shadow, came running down the center of the street and threw himself at Kit's midbody.

Hit, Kit shut up, jumped back to regain his balance, and reaching forward, grabbed his small attacker around the waist.

"What is this?" he said, recognizing Imp full well, but pretending not to. "What is this? Pray, do footpads come this small?"

He lifted the squealing boy up, till Imp's face was at a level with his. "Speak, sirrah, want you my purse?"

A small image of Kit's own face looked at him—the grey eyes the same, cut in the same almond shape and surrounded by the same dark lashes. The child wore his hair long, tied back with a leather strap, and his clothes were much too fine for this poor area of town.

For years now, Kit had formed the habit of giving his old clothes to his landlady, Madeleine, who, with great cunning and ability, cut them down and took the best portions to make perfect clothing for Imp. So Imp wore a velvet doublet and hose in the best style of two years ago, with a fine lawn shirt whose collar showed, clean and unpatched, around his small neck.

"Ah, a well-dressed footpad," Kit said, marking how much more the boy weighed in his hands than a month ago.

Imp would be what . . . seven, for it had been almost eight years ago that Kit, first come to London and penniless, had succumbed to the blandishments of his landlady, then so newly a widow that the ensuing product of their brief, unloving tryst was taken by all to be her husband's get.

By all who had no eyes, Kit thought, marveling once more that every neighbor didn't point a finger at him and name him Imp's father, when Imp's paternity was written all over his son's guileless face.

He shook the child with mock fierceness. "Tell me, rogue, are you one of these scions of nobility who go around robbing poor people for their fun?" he asked.

Imp opened his eyes very wide. As always, he seemed none too sure that Kit was joking. "I am Richard. Richard Courcy, as you well know, you fool." He kicked his legs. "Put me down. Put me down. You were making the fool of yourself again, Kit. And you are drunk."

It was Kit's turn to laugh as he set the child down. "Peace, Lord Morality. I am not drunk, haven't drunk anything since I took dinner, much too long ago. And that was but a vile ale, milord, as you would not give your dogs, and certainly not enough to make my spirits soar." He tugged on the child's ponytail. "It must be the joy of your presence, milord."

Imp looked up, and frowned slightly. He had this trick of narrowing his eyes, of lowering his eyebrows upon them, while pinching his mouth in something not quite a smile.

It reminded Kit of his own mother, and of the loving,

patient way in which she'd endured his childish follies.

Unlike Kit's father, who usually made his leather strap speak and loudly, too, being convinced that sparing the strap would spoil the child.

Kit put his hand on Imp's shoulder, very gently, almost as an apology to that other Kit long ago, who'd endured not so gentle a father.

But who had a father who acknowledged him, Kit's conscience reminded him. A father willing to call him son, as Imp lacked.

"Mock not, Kit," Imp said. He looked grave and something sparked in the grey eyes, something that made Kit think of tears. "Mock me not, for I must tell you something serious."

Kit picked the child up again, carefully—Imp's legs on either side of his waist, his hands supporting the boy. Kit did not care if Imp's muddy shoes ruined his fine clothing.

"What, child?" he asked. This was the closest he'd ever get to calling his boy son. "What? What is so serious that you must look at me like a preacher displeased with sinners?"

"A man came by," Imp said, and his voice trembled. "An evil man, with dark hair and a nasty face. And he told Mother that you . . . He told Mother he must speak to you, or else all was up with us."

Tears formed in the child's eyes.

A man with an evil smile?

Oh, curse Henry Mauder, curse the creature. He'd been scaring Imp, too. Not content with making Kit himself ill with fright for Imp's sake, he'd frightened Imp.

Kit felt a murderous rage, such as, had Henry Mauder been to hand, Kit would gladly have broken Mauder's skinny neck with the legs of Mauder's clerical black hose.

Imp put his forehead against Kit's shoulder, while Kit walked home along the darkened street.

His steps resounded, lonely, off the facades of surrounding buildings, and each whisper seemed magnified by the darkness.

"Mother says if you bring danger to us, you must go," Imp said. "She says you're a dangerous man and I should not let you . . ." A long silence. "She says you're not a man like other men and that you've spent too much time around the theater and got confused by boys who dress like women."

Oh, by the devils and the eternal fire, Kit thought, and tightened his hold on Imp. "Your mother is scared and knows not what she says," he said. Which was true enough, though Madeleine had come up with this explanation long ago, to excuse Kit's not wishing to repeat their clumsy coupling.

She could never understand that it was other arms he longed for, nor could he tell her that her love paled when compared to that of elvenkind, like coarse bread paled next to the dainties of kings.

No, he couldn't tell her that, and Madeleine Courcy had first conjectured then decided that Kit must prefer embraces of another kind, and finally told one and all that Kit sought this illicit love in alleys and darkened places.

At first it had amused Kit who, relieved that Madeleine no longer pursued him, had taken her ready explanation for his tastes and even let her spread it, thinking that illicit dealing of this kind—rarely persecuted and mostly winked at—would mask other illicit dealing, his presence and his actions in other places as his majesty's courier, or as a secret service man.

And then, in a way, Kit felt as though he could not deny it. In the memory of his one love there commingled Silver's soft charms and Quicksilver's broad back, Silver's silken midnight hair and Quicksilver's golden hair for which the youth of Greece would surely have risked much more than for the golden vellum.

Oh, true, it was Silver who had first attracted him, when he was young and innocent. He'd endured Quicksilver for Silver's sake. But in small steps, so small that Kit wasn't himself sure how he'd got there, Kit had found that he loved Quicksilver as much as Silver and, when his love affair ended, missed them both equally. And sometimes, to dull his longing, he'd taken consolation of that kind, as fleeting and unsatisfying a consolation as his encounter with Madeleine had proven—as futile and as far short of his elf love.

So, he'd not contradicted Madeleine, feeling she was justified in at least a part of her mad suspicions.

But that she'd tell Imp to be wary of Kit, as though Kit's cravings would run to children, as though Kit could be so unnatural and accursed—*that* shocked Kit to his core.

"Your mother knows not what she says, Imp. I love you as though you were my own son." His voice caught in saying the words, and it hurt, as if in speaking he had torn the skin of his throat, the restraint of his truth.

"What about the man?" Imp asked. "The man who came? Mother said he was dangerous and you are dangerous and you must give up your rooms."

Kit shook his head, and swallowed hard. This time as other times past, the two times Kit had got arrested for being caught amid street brawls, the third time, a year ago, when Kit had been arrested for counterfeit coining undertaken as part of a project for the secret service—every time Madeleine protested and threatened to throw him out, it was but a plea for Kit's money, maybe for Kit's love.

His love he couldn't give her, but money he could and aplenty.

Long ago he could have traded these threadbare lodgings, which he'd once shared with Tom Kyd, another play-wright, for better lodgings in a better part of town.

Thomas Walsingham's patronage assured Kit of that ability.

But Kit liked these lodgings, and needed to be near Imp, even if under the pretense of a renter and a family friend.

He shook his head. "Fear not, my Lord Despair. Your mother is a mother and she worries and in her worry she says who knows what."

Imp was Kit's well-loved son, and Kit would stay nearby and would protect him, and would ensure the boy went to university when the time came.

Imp would be a great philosopher, a great master, greater than his father by that much as Kit was than his cobbler sire.

"What about the man with the teeth like a wolf?" Imp asked, and sitting up straight, held his two fingers in front of his mouth, as prefiguring cruel fangs.

"Teeth like a wolf, had he?" Kit laughed, thinking of Henry Mauder. "I rather thought him more like a dog who craves a bone and has none. A wolf's teeth would be like this." Giving low growls, Kit pretended to ravage Imp's shoulder.

The child smelled of herbs and rosewater.

It made Kit wish he could be a child again, running free in the abandoned orchards of the monastery in Canterbury. It would almost be worth enduring again his father's beat-ings for that.

Imp laughed loudly as Kit, who'd kept walking, carry-ing the child, arrived at the door to his lodgings.

Before he could open it, the door was thrown open, by Madeleine Courcy.

Imp's mother had never been beautiful. Or never since Kit had known her.

At least ten years older than Kit, when he had met her

she had already shown a severe face, a closed, hardened expression, probably acquired from living for years under the thumb of a ponderous Puritan husband.

One beautiful feature she'd had then which had drawn Kit like a magnet. Her waist-long hair had been midnight black and silky, so that if Kit put his face in it, he could pretend to himself that this was his love, the elf lady Silver.

But Madeleine's hair had coarsened and turned white and her figure, once good enough to pretend it might be Silver's, had thickened, leaving her with an immense, shapeless bosom that overshadowed a body where no waist emphasized the broader hips.

"What is this?" she asked in the sharp French accent she hadn't lost after fifteen years in England. "What is this? You debauch my son? Why is he not abed?"

Kit swallowed. Lifting Imp, Kit handed him to Imp's mother. "He came to meet me," Kit said, feeling like he'd committed some crime. "He came to meet me, and I brought him back."

Madeleine's black eyes, which he'd never been able to convince himself were just like Silver's shiny metallic ones, narrowed and looked at him with unabated suspicion.

She took her child in her arms, and pushed Imp's face against her shoulder, as if to cover his eyes.

Kit cleared his throat. "I hear you've had an unpleasant visit."

"One? We've had them all day and they haven't ceased yet," Madeleine said, and compressed her lips as she glared at Kit. "It is time you should be quitting your rooms, Master Marlowe. You pay me not enough to endure the thread of constant feet, the suspicions of countless officers, the danger to my child. If my husband were alive, he'd have thrown you out long ago."

If her husband were alive, likely Imp would never have existed, and Kit would have no reason to be here.

"Nothing will happen to Imp, madam," he said. "And as for paying you, tell me how much you want, and like enough, I can find it."

She glared at him over Imp's shoulder.

Imp turned to look back at Kit, his pale little face anxious and drawn, visibly resenting the harsh words flying around him.

Kit remembered when he was very young and his parents argued, how it made him hide under the bed, how it made him wish he could stop existing.

Later, when he'd been scarcely older than Imp, he'd stood in front of his mother, protecting her from his father's rages.

Madeleine opened her mouth and Kit drew breath, ready to counter imputations and insinuations, fearing she'd air, in front of Imp, what she thought she knew of Kit's interests and amusements.

But instead, her mouth, which had learned her severity too early to be able to soften now, said, "His name is Richard, and I wish you'd stop calling him the name of a kind of demon. His name is Richard, after my sainted husband, his father."

And as if she could rewrite Imp's origins with her short words, she turned her back on Kit and vanished, down the long narrow hallway, to where her room and Imp's lay.

Kit sighed and took his way up the stairs, to his own rented room.

That night, carefully watched, Imp would never dare climb the stairs in the dark and beg Kit for a story, as he did almost nightly.

So, Kit had time to plot the snare that would catch Essex and hold him at bay and thus allow Kit and Imp to go free.

First he must make sure Will voiced treacherous opinions and had contacts beyond his sphere with noblemen in Essex's field.

Then it remained for Kit to invent a goal for this conspiracy—killing the Queen would always serve. Everyone feared the death of the childless monarch. It had become a national nightmare. And then Kit would denounce Will.

He paused for a moment, staring at the ceiling over his bed, remembering Will's innocent look, his effusive gratitude.

How could Kit ensnare such a lamb?

He closed his eyes.

It must be.

If the noose thus designed to keep Imp alive and safe must catch in it that poor fool, Will Shakespeare, then so be it.

For one Imp, would Kit sacrifice the world.

Scene 11

❧

The fairy palace. Queen Ariel sleeps on her high, gilded bed, beneath a green silk cover embroidered in gold thread. Suddenly, the darkness above sparkles with pinpoints of light that, like falling stars, burn for only a moment and then are gone. They leave behind a sulphurous stench of waning magic, and objects rain down on Ariel's bedspread like large hailstones.

Ariel dreamed that Quicksilver was a child again, fourteen or fifteen no more and barely into the prolonged elven adolescence that would last till he was fifty.

They played together under a mighty oak, Quicksilver trying to steal a kiss and Ariel avoiding his advances and laughing.

Rain started pattering on them, heavy rain that quickly turned into gigantic rocks, which cut through leaves and broke the branches, and shred the wood of the wondrous overarching oak.

The air smelled of waning magic, of magic gone wrong.

"Beware, milord," Ariel screamed. "Someone attacks us."

But when she turned to look at him, Quicksilver was

not beside her. He was away, at the edge of the human town, talking to a young man with dark curls and the golden eyes of a hawk.

Ariel woke with a muffled scream.

In her dark room, flashes of light showed her bed, her bedspread, all of it unreally lit, too white, too bright.

Something fell on her bed, something small and heavy. The smell in the air was real, not dreamed.

The smell of magic gone wrong.

Ariel reached for her bedside table where, at her word, a tall, never-consuming candle lit up, bringing cool, sane lighting to the room.

On her bed lay the countless bodies of many servant fairies, some lifeless, others yet twitching. Dying of some plague, some curse.

Ariel screamed. People ran down the hallway toward her room.

First arrived her maids, Cobweb, Peaseblossom, Cowslip, in their nightly finery of silk lace and embroidered caps. They put their hands over their mouths and joined their screaming to their mistress's.

After them came Malachite, who threw the door open and ran in, dagger at the ready. He didn't scream, but sheathed his dagger, made a sound like a man drowning, and went pale, his legs visibly buckling beneath his long, white nightshirt.

He approached the bed and, with horror, poked his finger at a lifeless dragon-fly-fine wing, a small, perfect, humanlike body.

"They're dead," he said. He looked at Ariel with horrified green eyes, grown unusually large and scared upon his pale face. He swallowed. "They're dead."

He gaped at Ariel as though he expected her to explain the mystery of the servant fairies' deaths. The dread wonder of death in deathless Fairyland.

His lips trembled.

Other people had come into the room, by twos, by threes, by trembling loneliness.

All of them, including Hyllas, the centaur ambassador, wore their nightclothes, which for Hyllas seemed to be a cap all askew on his dark curls.

And all of them looked horrified.

Ariel recovered her senses first.

"Stop screaming," Ariel snapped at her maids, while yet servant fairies glowed and—their magic burned out—fell to writhing on the bed. "Stop screaming and fetch me my wrap."

Peaseblossom, the quickest to recover, handed Ariel her gauzy wrap—though the maid's gaze remained on the bed, her eyes yet wide and wondering. Ariel wrapped herself and stood up.

"Lords, ladies," she said. "There's nothing here to see, nothing. Our servants are suffering and I must minister to them, but for that I must have silence and peace."

As she spoke, she noticed that several of the servant fairies, seemingly untouched, still flew amid the crowd. She stared at them, wondering what made them different from their stricken fellows, while the ladies and lords, muttering, withdrew to the door of the room.

They walked out but went no farther, collecting in little nervous groups and gossiping crowds in the hallway.

Ariel closed the door in their faces unceremoniously, and left alone with her servants, she walked back to the bed.

It didn't take Ariel's gift of second sight, acquired by being born on summer solstice, to allow her to see that what had killed the winged fairies was lack of magic. Their magic had failed somehow. That power that had come to elvenkind from the very first formation of the Universe had now deserted these small beings.

And not all of her gift could show her why the fairies' magic had failed.

While Ariel watched, several of the dead fairies winked out, returning to the nothing that had birthed them, their bodies disappearing as their magic had.

"Milady, what is wrong?" Peaseblossom asked. The maid held her hands in front of her mouth and spoke through her fingers, as though afraid that her words would give yet more force to dread reality.

Ariel shook her head and, with imperious thought, sent for the leader of the servant fairies, a prim and proper small creature called Marmalade.

Marmalade had tawny hair and a bronze-colored body. Today, her tiny features looked as sick, as bleached of color, as Malachite's had.

Winking her light in the speech of the winged ones, she told Ariel that the servant fairies who were dying were the least powerful of them and that power blight and death seemed to be escalating, climbing the ranks of power.

A mysterious illness, Marmalade said.

Soon, Marmalade said, all servant fairies would be dead. And who after them? As she spoke, tiny Marmalade cast a frightened eye to the bed, where fairies still dropped and writhed and vanished.

See, she winked and blinked her light in fear. *See, oh, lady, how they came to you for help in their extremity. Who will be next to feel this blight?*

Changelings, Ariel thought, though she didn't say it. Changelings—though given elven power and elven nature at their adoption—never completely lost their mortal dross, nor did they ever acquire as much power as those elven born.

They were the members of the hill who had the lowest magic, after the servants.

She thought of Malachite's color, wan and pale, turned

from its normal on seeing the dying fairies.

He'd looked like he knew what was wrong and that he'd be next.

Faith, Malachite, Lord Malachite, Quicksilver's right hand, Quicksilver's friend, knew more about this blight and its likely course than anyone in the palace.

And Malachite alone had been with Quicksilver when they'd met whatever the menace was at the boundary of Fairyland, near Stratford-upon-Avon.

Thus thinking, Ariel opened her door, and ignoring the many high lords and dazzling ladies of Fairyland who crowded around her and pressed her with questions and comments and condolences, she searched for Malachite.

Not finding him, she grabbed the arm of Igneous, Malachite's friend and also a changeling.

Igneous was as blond as Malachite was dark, but his features also showed that blurring of perfection, that inexactitude that denoted a human-born elf.

However, unlike Malachite, he looked unconcerned by the fairy blight, or no more concerned than the true-born elves to whom he spoke. Resplendent in a bloodred nightshirt, he talked and gossiped with the crowding lords, venting opinions about foreign attack, or friendly fire, or perhaps a civil war amid servant fairies.

Ariel grabbed his arm and said, "Milord Igneous."

Sobriety and seriousness came ill to Igneous's face, with its small nose and broad, mobile mouth, but he strived for it, facing her. "Milady."

"Have you seen Milord Malachite?"

"Nay, milady. Or rather, even before you asked, er, ordered us out of your room, Malachite walked out and, I thought, as far as I could discern, back to his room."

"Thank you, milord," Ariel said, and though knowing that her manner had startled the elf, she knew he would resume his peacock-bright preening as soon as she turned her back.

"Ariel, what's this? And where is Quicksilver?" An elf of imposing presence pushed in front of Ariel. He looked not like Quicksilver but much like Sylvanus used to look: dark hair and beard, dark eyes, oval face, small pulpy mouth.

This was Vargmar, older brother to the late Oberon, Quicksilver's uncle.

"I don't know what *this* is, milord," Ariel said, all cold disdain. "But milord the king, I wager, is attempting to remedy it."

"Bah, king!" Vargmar said. "The impudent brat. A bastard of Puck's, a low shape changer. Too young to reign. Too unstable to control even himself, less this mighty kingdom."

Ariel would not argue with Quicksilver's uncle. She turned her back on him and, aware that—around him—a small group of malcontents had started to gather, she headed for Malachite's room.

Malachite's bedroom door was down the hallway from Quicksilver's, where he could be ever ready to run errands at the whim of his inconstant lord.

She knocked on it once, twice, knowing that she was watched by the entire court of Elvenland and a sleep-befuddled centaur in a night cap.

Twice more, and a faint answer came. "Yes?"

"Lord Malachite, I would fain speak with you," she yelled.

Malachite opened the door. His pale face looked draggled and tearstained, his eyes swollen, his lips thickened with prolonged crying. His hands trembled, and his lips, too.

Ariel heard questions fly through the crowd, and fictions, too, about Malachite having done magic that caused the servants' death.

Malachite raised lachrymose eyes to her, "You wish to speak to me *here*?"

Ariel shook her head. "In your room," she said. *"Milord."*

From his scared looks she imagined that he thought she believed the crowd. She pushed him into his room, where he went reluctantly, like a lamb to the slaughter.

The room was small and Spartanly furnished: a narrow oaken bed, covered in green silk, a narrow desk, a small trunk where Malachite, no doubt, kept his personal effects.

Only a large, whole-body mirror in a corner distinguished Malachite and the room as receivers of the king's favor.

Yet, the view of green trees through the large, sparkling glass window, the warmth and cleanliness of the room, all these were what Malachite might never have aspired to, had the elves not kidnaped him from his cradle in Stratford so many years ago, leaving in his place a charmed piece of oak that to mortal eyes had looked like a sickly babe who had, presently, died.

"Milord, tell me why this is happening," Ariel said.

He trembled worse, and gasped. "Lady, what is happening?"

"Do not mock me, milord, you know well. The servants are dying and a plague, a lack of power, clutches at the heart of Fairyland. Why, milord?"

Trembling and pale, Malachite shook his head. "I have done naught," he said. "Naught with magic."

Ariel felt her own lips press into a tight, tight line. "I never believed *you* had."

And on those words Malachite paled yet more, when he should have been relieved. Ariel noted the change and sighed. "Milord, I cannot protect the hill as my lord ordered me if you do not tell me what's causing this."

"I promised not to tell you," Malachite said.

"Promised? To whom could you have promised such?"

"The king," Malachite said. "The king," and his body trembled like a leaf in a storm.

Ariel stared at him, uncomprehending. "Why would the king exact such a promise?"

But he only threw himself on the floor and, pressing his face to the cool tiles, murmured, "Lady, I cannot tell you. Lady, the king made me swear. . . . I'm not to tell you."

"Swear? Swear silence? What would you keep from me? What would *he* keep from me?"

But Malachite answered not, and in Ariel's mind, a monstrous idea bloomed, like a poisonous flower upon an unsuspecting night.

"If your lord were here," Ariel said, "would then magic be whole?"

Malachite gave her a sideways look, a small, surprised look, as if this thought had only now come to his own mind, as if he'd never thought it else.

"If he were here, then would all be well," he said in a whisper.

Ariel took in breath. The air smelled still and dusty, as though the servant fairies, in dying, had tainted the very atmosphere with the mustiness of death, the dust of the tomb.

This was all caused by Quicksilver's absence? But then why had Quicksilver gone to London? Why?

She remembered Malachite, pale and drawn, coming back from the confrontation at the boundary. How nervous he'd looked. How equivocal.

The menace had not been what they'd expected, he'd said. They'd taken care of it, he'd said.

But he looked like he lied, with his face tense and his eyes darting here and there, firefly afraid.

And Ariel had believed the expression and not the words. Fool Ariel.

Malachite, truthful Malachite, a changeling with hardly any power of his own, had told the truth while appearing to lie, and thus had he lied to his queen, while proclaiming verities.

They'd taken care of the menace indeed, which meant that Quicksilver must have gone to London upon his own pursuit. But what pursuit of his could cause this blight?

Malachite had lied with his hands and his eyes, and his sharp, timorous glances.

Quicksilver, irked at Ariel's resistence, smarting from her offer to help him, which had insulted his insecure pride, Quicksilver had rushed to London, like a fool to soothe his offended love with . . . what?

Ariel was not such an innocent nor did she live as retired from the gossip of the hill as Quicksilver thought. She knew well enough who was in London. Will Shakespeare. Will. Shakespeare. Will on whom Silver had doted and for whom Quicksilver, himself, had borne quite an unseemly love.

That explained the blight and the crops withering in the fields, and this strange, humid heat that seemed to suffocate even as it warmed.

Ariel remembered well enough, from her childhood, the epic fights that had shaken the palace.

Unlike herself and Quicksilver, Quicksilver's parents, Queen Titania and the great Oberon, had made no vow of fidelity to each other, nor would they have kept it if they had.

Yet, their jealousy was as furnace-hot as their mutual love was fierce, and their separate affairs and joint raging had shaken the foundations of the palace, the roots of Arden Woods.

And when they argued thus, ever, the disturbed magic

had put a chill in the air, brought unseasonable warmth or cold upon the nearby humans, threw the spheres into inharmonious clashing.

Nothing like the blight had happened, but then Oberon and Titania had never separated. He'd never stopped loving her, nor she him till death had overtaken them together one night, in a sacred glade.

Ariel remembered the cold glare of Quicksilver's moss green eyes, and his quick, impatient step as he left her that night.

Not there, any longer, the soft touch of their honeymoon. Not there, any longer, his eye pliant to love and quick to find favor.

No.

Quicksilver had *left* her. He cared no more. His love was dead and would not return.

And from the death of that love—from the divided powers of the hill—there came the blight that killed the weaker members of the elven realm.

"It is Will Shakespeare, is it not?" Ariel asked. "My lord has gone to him, has he not?"

Malachite scrambled up from the floor, and stared at her with uncomprehending eyes. "He homed in on the thought pattern of Will Shakespeare, sure," Malachite said. "But only as a beacon to be found in a stormy sea."

Or as a light of love, a taper, to light his way bedward. "This is a blight of unlove, a cursed blight. My lord has left us, has he not?" Ariel asked.

Malachite looked scared, but it was an odd fear, filled with a quickening of understanding behind the bold green eyes.

Something like hope? Or simply understanding?

Perhaps Malachite, himself, hadn't understood what happened till now.

"My lord loves only you. Sure, he might stray but—"

Malachite said, his voice low. "But I'm sure my lady . . ." He hesitated, and his voice broke.

Truthful Malachite, Ariel thought, who could tell no untruth, found lies coming oily and evasive to his mouth. He looked away from his queen, and like a child who knows he's lying and doesn't expect to convince, he said, "He loves you only, mistress. Beware, oh, beware jealousy, milady, for it is the green-eyed monster that mocks the meat upon which it feeds."

Too late came his warning, too late his halfhearted assurance, for—already imagining Quicksilver changing to Lady Silver, imagining Silver or Quicksilver himself cavorting with a human in some shady London purlieu—Ariel could feel jealousy tearing at her heart like a hungry beast.

Outside, in the hallway, the centaur waited, tapping his hooves nervously upon the marble floor. He leaned in close to Ariel as she left Malachite's room.

His hair smelled of olive oil and strange perfumes.

"It is a curse, is it not?" he asked. "This kingdom is cursed."

Ariel nodded, not knowing what she did.

Scene 12

෨෨

A street in Shoreditch, dark and narrow, hemmed by old buildings in dire need of painting. The street is deserted in the early morning hours, before sunrise. Many of the houses are boarded and bear the plague seal. Quicksilver walks in front of the sign for a hostelry: The Golden Lion. His light blue cloak billows in the early morning breeze, but his hair falls limp from the unnatural warmth and humidity of this unhealthy summer.

Quicksilver followed Sylvanus's magical pattern here. The pattern and marks of Sylvanus's dark power, which were to an elf's soul like a signature to men: indelible and unmistakable.

He'd followed it through the dark night of men—the day of elves, feeling and sensing his way, darkly, amid the confusion of human souls and human minds, some vile enough to rival Sylvanus's.

But he had it now. It was here.

Sylvanus lodged here, or hid here, in the upper floor of this ramshackle building.

Quicksilver pounded on the door. "Holla," he called. "Awake within."

For a while nothing answered him, then there was the rumble and knocking of furniture being pushed out of the way, and a low voice that approached while muttering.

"Here's a knocking indeed! If a man were porter of hell-gate, he should have old turning the key. Knock, knock, knock! Who's there, i' the name of Beelzebub? Here's a farmer, that hanged himself on the expectation of plenty: come in time; have napkins enow about you; here you'll sweat for't."

Quicksilver knocked again, impatient.

"Knock, knock! Who's there, in the other devil's name?" The voice on the other side of the door neared very slowly, as if the speaker walked erratically. "Faith, here's an equivocator, that could swear in both the scales against either scale; who committed treason enough for God's sake, yet could not equivocate to heaven: O, come in, equivocator," the voice within muttered.

Quicksilver knocked in earnest.

"Knock, knock; never at quiet!" The voice was now right on the other side of the door, and Quicksilver could hear, with it, the sliding and thumping of locks and dead-bolts.

The voice muttered still, "What are you? But this place is too cold for hell. I'll devil-porter it no further: I had thought to have let in some of all professions that go the primrose way to the everlasting bonfire."

The door started to open, but before it could, a voice called, "Quicksilver."

Quicksilver looked up at a face that appeared on the window, in the second floor.

It was a face Quicksilver knew and had seen, at Arden revels in the green forest. It was the man from Stratford, the mortal who courted Peaseblossom and often came to join the fairy dance.

He looked like a man of Stratford, and open enough,

with a round face and round, pale blue eyes.

But now, superimposed on those familiar features, another face moved, another set of features held sway: sharp, features, lupine in hunger and elongated with ill desire.

"Quicksilver," Sylvanus said, speaking through the mortal's mouth.

Quicksilver's hair stood on end. What was here? What evil was this?

"Milord," the tavern owner called, finally having thrown open the door. "Milord." He was a big man, as wide as tall, with a scraggle of red hair on his amiable face. "You'll pardon me, I didn't know it was your highness knocking. I thought it would be a ruffian, a cutpurse." As he spoke, he wiped his hands on the front of his white nightshirt, as no doubt he would wipe them on his apron during the day.

Quicksilver looked at him for a moment.

"Trouble you not about my intent," Sylvanus's voice yelled from the window above. "For soon nothing will matter to you."

And on those words, energy—a bolt, a searing flame of magic—flew past Quicksilver's face, to singe the door post.

The hosteller stepped back, shocked, while Quicksilver wheeled upon his heels to look up.

Where had Sylvanus got so much power? And if he had it, why misspend it so? Sylvanus could not fail to aim well.

"Canker blossom, dog, bastard," Sylvanus's voice yelled from above.

The face retreated within, and beyond the window, a man's shape twisted and writhed, as if fighting something invisible. He looked like a puppet, ill-commanded by an inexperienced puppeteer.

Quicksilver stepped back, ready to hold the power of

the hill as a shield between himself and imminent attack. But no attack came.

"He's drunk, milord. Just drunk," the hosteller said. "You there," he shouted, looking up at the window. "Stop that, and do not defile my premises."

"You will do as I command," Sylvanus yelled.

The man at the window turned. His face emerged again. Then, with a violent, writhing twist, he fell from the window.

Quicksilver jumped back as the body hit the hard-packed dirt of the lane with a sickening sound.

Quicksilver's heart pounding fast, he thought the man would be dead, would he not?

Had Sylvanus killed this man?

But even as he thought it, he heard Sylvanus's voice, no longer coming from the man's throat, "It failed this once, little brother. But triumph not, I will be back. And then will you rue the day you were born."

"Sylvanus?" Quicksilver asked, stepping forward. Charity dictated that Quicksilver see if the man was still alive, that Quicksilver lend what help he could. But what if this was, again, Sylvanus's trap, as the one back in Arden Woods?

As he neared, the man's eyes fluttered open. Pale blue eyes, guileless and round.

"I got rid of him, didn't I?" he asked in a thread of voice.

Quicksilver nodded, amazed, yet shying away from the still body.

"You're the king," the man said. He spoke slowly, in a voice little more than breath. His body lay twisted on the pavement, and he moved nothing save his eyes and lips. "The king of my lady's queen."

Quicksilver nodded.

"Tell her, tell Peaseblossom that Nick Bottom didn't

kill himself. He jumped from a window, aye, but to kill the bastard who had taken control of his body. Will you tell her that, lord?"

Quicksilver nodded, swallowed. "He took control of you? Sylvanus did?"

"Aye, if that's his name. If that's his name, he did. Last night, while I was drunk he approached me and then—he wore me like a doublet, milord.

"But an ill-fitting doublet I proved. I surprised him. I threw myself down. But I didn't kill him. He ran off. I will die for it."

Nick Bottom's words came further spaced, and his eyes had acquired a stillness not likely to be dispelled by reviving life.

When Quicksilver thought he was dead, Nick Bottom yet revived, and taking a noisy breath, he said, "Only tell Peaseblossom, would you, lord?"

"I will tell her," Quicksilver said.

"And would you have, milord, a bard set my story to music, the story of a weaver who loved an elf lady?" The blue eyes seemed to look onto the distant yonder, a distance even Quicksilver's immortal eyes couldn't penetrate. "And it shall be called Bottom's dream, for it has no bottom."

A last breath whispered through Nick Bottom's lips and he lay still.

Quicksilver remained, horror-stricken.

So Sylvanus had learned to take over the bodies of men.

Oh, elven legend spoke of that, of dark elves who did so. The humans called it possession and blamed it on demons.

But it had not been done in millennia, and it had come to be doubted.

Why had Sylvanus chosen this man? How had Bottom managed to rid himself of Sylvanus?

"And now he's dead," the hosteller said, wringing his hands upon his nightshirt. "He was drunk and now he's dead and what am I to do with him?"

Numbly, Quicksilver reached into his belt purse and handed the man coins. "Here is for burial," he said. "And to send word to his family."

"Thank you, milord. But will you not stay?"

The last question the hosteller yelled at Quicksilver's retreating back as the king of elves walked down the street.

Here was an enigma, for which Quicksilver had no answer.

Why would Sylvanus need to take over the bodies of humans to drink the life force of other dying humans?

None of it made sense.

Scene 13

୨୧

*Kit Marlowe's room, where he shaves at a basin set in
an ornate iron stand, in front of a polished metal round,
nailed to the wall. Imp, squeezed between the wall and
the stand, beneath the improvised mirror, holds an empty
ceramic jar of water, and stares at the movements of the
blade with utter fascination.*

Kit shaved.

His troubles whirled around in his mind, while his
hand, unfailingly, scraped the blade against his cheek.

He must get to The Rose and intercept Will. He must
get to know Will better and introduce the man to high
personages.

Kit rinsed the hair from his dagger in the basin of water
in front of him.

A twelve-penny dagger and it wouldn't last him long,
at this rate.

He remembered, when he'd been at Cambridge, where
a barber attended to the students' shaving needs daily, the
barber complained that Kit's red-tipped beard, light and
downy-looking, did more damage to his blade than the
hirsute cheek of the most black-haired of villains.

"Will my beard come in soon?" Imp asked. His large, almond-shaped grey eyes watched the dagger, fascinated.

"Aye," Kit said, and dipped the dagger in the water of the basin, to rid it of the tips of hairs and of soap. "Aye, soon enough."

Imp ran a long, thin finger along his smooth, pale cheek. "And will I have to do that every day, then?"

Kit paused in his shaving because his face insisted on flourishing a smile, and how could he shave himself while grinning like a lunatic?

"Ah, no. You need not shave, Milord Laziness. You may go about unshaven and hirsute like a savage."

He dipped the tips of his fingers in the cold water of the basin and flicked the droplets at Imp. "I tell you what, Milord Adventurer, I shall speak to Lord Raleigh for you and he can take you to his lands in Virginia, where you may join with the savage tribes of men there, and not only need not shave, but run about naked and barefoot, if you well please."

Imp giggled as the droplets of water hit him and he squeezed away from his perch, but only to return again, to watch Kit.

He ran his hand, wishfully, down both his cheeks. "My mother says that my father had a big black beard." He sighed and squirmed and stared at Kit, as though expecting from Kit a confirmation of his paternity.

Or else, perhaps the child suspected. . . . He looked at Imp's features, a mirror of his own, and wondered how Imp could *not* suspect. But the human eye was thus, in thrall to the heart and ever ready to see only what it wished to see.

Besides, Imp had never known his mother's husband. For all the child knew, Master Richard Courcy had looked exactly like Kit, but with a black beard.

Kit made a sound in his throat, neither assent nor denial, more of an invitation to proceed.

"My mother says he was a man like no man," Imp continued in a needling voice, prodding like a butcher that searches the tenderest part from which to cut the steak.

He blinked at Kit and almost smiled. "And that she could never find his like." He paused, and shifted his feet, rustling the rushes on the floor. "Kit, why don't you marry Mother?"

The words so surprised Kit that he cut himself and, feeling the bite of the dagger upon his cheek, cursed, and reached for his handkerchief from within his sleeve.

Kit hated pain, even so small a pain as this.

He remembered his sisters mocking him when he was a child and cried at having skinned his knee. They said he made as much fuss over that small injury as soldiers wouldn't make over battlefield wounds.

He thought of the threat of torture that hung over his head and shuddered. How could he take torture when he couldn't even take this?

Staring at the small flower of blood on his handkerchief, Kit gave Imp a wary eye. Had Madeleine put her son up to this?

No. Kit shook his head to his own question. No. From the anxiety in Imp's look, the mock-relaxed posture of his body, the idea was Imp's entire.

"If you married her, she wouldn't turn you out," Imp said. "And then you'd be my father."

Kit swallowed. Oh, to be extended such a bait on such an enticing hook and by such an unwary fisherman.

A day ago, two, Kit might well have been fool enough to take it.

Marrying the dour Madeleine would be worth it, so long as he could stand up and announce to the world, full voice, "I am responsible for this Imp. I am his father."

Yes, twenty-four hours ago, had Imp said these very words, Kit might well have sent him to his mother, as a pleasing Cupid, to press Kit's suit.

But in twenty-four hours, all had changed.

Kit's admission of fatherhood would do no more for Imp than bring the knife nearer him, tighten the noose of conspiracy closer round Imp's unsuspecting neck.

Torture and prison rode at Kit's back, and death not far behind.

And Kit had seen someone uncommonly like his Lady Silver. Silver, that dream that Kit had given up but not forgotten, that dream that made the reality of any human love pale and shrink in Kit's mind.

Kit had seen someone like Lady Silver with Will Shakespeare.

Kit closed his eyes, and behind his eyelids as on a stage, he saw the Lady Silver—graceful beauty, ethereal grace—and he could almost smell her lilac perfume making him dizzy and drunk.

He opened his eyes and saw, beyond the opened door of the room, beyond Imp's anxious glance, a fine gentleman in green velvet pants and doublet.

A gentleman with blondish hair and a fine, open face, which added bonhomie to his sparkling blue eyes and seemed to announce to the world that here stood a man who liked all men, a man who'd never betray any, a man full of the milk of human kindness.

With a chill down his spine and a burning acid at the back of his throat, Kit recognized Robert Poley—Sweet Robin Poley—master spy, the uncoverer—many said the engineer—of the Babington conspiracy, which had sent fifteen hapless men to the gallows.

It was said that these men had tried to kill the Queen, that they planned to install Mary, Queen of Scots, in Elizabeth's place, but Kit, who'd been close enough to the

apprehension to hear the behind-the-scenes stage setting—
even if he'd taken no real part—had long suspected the
plot had been no plot.

Kit thought that Cecil and this, his minion, Robin Poley,
had hatched the whole thing entire from their heads, Zeus
giving birth to Athena. Without them there would have
been no plot, only the stray words of foolish young men.
Without them, Mary Stuart would still be alive in her captivity. Without them, the Crown would be no shakier than
it was and Queen Elizabeth no more threatened.

Babington himself had been in Robin Poley's room,
supping, when he'd been arrested and so deceived that
he'd sent Poley a letter from jail, begging for help from
Poley's true affection.

Since then, Kit had never been able to face Poley without feeling a sick pang to his stomach and a strange,
shrinking fear, like that of a rabbit scenting fox.

Now he felt all that, added to the heart-tightening sense
that he was no better than Poley. He was, after all, plan-
ning to involve Will Shakespeare in a plot like the Babington plot, wasn't he?

Kit's knife clattered into the wash basin.

He reached blindly for the much-worn towel that hung
beside the wash stand, and wiped his hands and the remaining soap from his face.

Kit dared not tell Imp to go away.

He didn't want to call attention to the child, but he
frowned ponderously at Imp who, not seeing Poley, stared
back with wide open, uncomprehending eyes.

"Well met, Kit," Poley said from the hallway. "You do
not seem happy to see me."

"Surprised," Kit said, and forced a smile. "Surprised."
Robin Poley was not someone he would want to show a
sour face to. Not a courtier or a fine gentleman, yet Poley's displeasure would have more material consequences

than a royal frown or a lost benefit. The first consequence would be a whisper in the night, the second a misstep in the dark, and the third a dagger in your bosom.

"Glad that you were only surprised, Kit." Poley walked into the room with a stealthy, feline confidence which suggested that he had spent too much time in dark alleys, too much time following traitors, real or counterfeit, with his cat step, the claws and fangs of his cruel intent. "Glad that you were only surprised." Poley smiled, in good nature. "I wouldn't want our friendship marred."

Kit retrieved his dagger from the water and dried it carefully, glad of its weight in his hand.

He wouldn't use it, nor would it be of much effect against Poley's kind of stealthy menace, and yet Kit felt better for having a weapon in his hand, and an excuse to hold it so.

Poley's gaze flickered to the dagger. He smiled. "Wouldn't play with that too much, Kit. Lest someone use it on yourself. The strangest accidents happen. . . ." Poley turned, his gaze fell on Imp, and he smiled, putting his small hand, covered in pearly suede gloves, on the boy's bright hair. "Such a beautiful child, is he not? Harry Mauder told me of him and how much he looks like his father."

"You knew my father?" Imp asked.

"Exceedingly well, child. Exceedingly well," Poley said and smiled, a smile full of paternal encouragement, avuncular tenderness.

"And had he a great big black beard?" Imp asked.

"No. More a small, reddish, well-trimmed one," Poley said, and stared at Kit.

Though the laugh wrinkles remained, cozy and comforting like a nest around Poley's bright blue, innocent-looking eyes, the glint in those eyes, the intenseness in that gaze, shone like a naked blade, like a drawn dagger.

Kit grasped his own dagger harder, and took a deep breath. "Go, Imp. Go to your mother, child."

Imp blinked. "But he says—"

"Go, child. God's death. Your mother will be wondering where you are. I don't want her plaguing me. Go, child."

Imp started and jumped. Never before had Kit raised his voice thus to him. Never before had Kit cursed at him.

"But—" he said.

"Go, damn it," Kit yelled, fierce and dark and full of thunder. "Go. Plaguing me day and night. Impossible brat. What time have I for you? Do I look like the sort that consoles the orphan and talks to the widow? God's death, if that were my vocation, I'd have taken orders. Go, curse you, and do not come back."

Something like pain showed in the squint of the little boy's almond-shaped eyes—a shine of tears, a startle at finding disapproval where he'd met only caresses and praise before.

He opened his mouth. He swallowed.

And Kit, longing to apologize, longing to take the small child in his arms and console him for that wounding so necessarily inflicted, maintained his face in a thunderous disapproval, as strong as Jove's own before flinging the bolt.

Oh, only let Poley believe in this display. Oh, only let him believe in this and not in the fleeting resemblance, the tenderness of Kit's gaze when it rested on Imp.

Imp stared and, finding no comfort, grabbed the empty water jar from beside the washstand and ran down the hallway, and down the stairs, the too-large empty jar of water clattering.

"He is his father's glass, is he not?" Poley asked, turning to Kit with a smile of friendship, a seeming open smile of cajoling.

"I don't know," Kit said and felt dark red blood flower beneath his cheeks. "I didn't know his father."

"Ah." Poley's eyebrows rose. "I daresay you still don't. And yet, what was that proverb that the Greeks had . . . Know thyself?"

"Poley, be done with it," Kit said sharply, his irritation having the best of his determination to remain impassive and civil. "You did not come to me to discuss the child, did you?"

Poley smiled. "I came to ask what story you spun to that fool, Henry Mauder, that he let you go so quietly yesterday."

He opened his eyes, palm outward, spread wide.

"No story," Kit said. "No story." His heart had started, fast, fast, like a trapped bird flinging itself on the bars of a cage. "No story but the truth. I know of a conspiracy. I know, and I thought you'd like to know."

Poley laughed, his big, hearty laugh. "A conspiracy. No. True? Kit, you amaze me. You—Kit Marlowe. A conspiracy. How would you come by it?"

"I heard it in my circles," Kit said.

"In your circles?" Poley laughed. "The circles of penniless poets? Or the circle of foolish actors? Maybe perhaps the circle of those who seek illicit love in bawdy taverns?" He made a moue. "Oh, how the council should fear those . . ."

"You forget, milord," Kit said, drawing himself up to his full height, regretting for the first time in his life that his gracile, agile body owed more to his mother's side of the family than to his father's thundering, majestic brutishness. "You forget that I live in other circles. I have a patron—Milord Thomas Walsingham. And before him I courted the favor of Milord Southampton."

Poley chuckled. "Courted *Southampton*, more like. Not that, from what I heard, he'd have made himself a hard catch. And what manner of conspiracy do your circles cross that you could use it to gain your freedom and that child's safety?"

Now the heart that had beaten madly in Kit's chest felt as though it had won passage to his throat and beat there, suffocating him, making him dizzy. Through his heart he spoke, hearing nothing but the rush of blood in his own ears. "A plot against the Queen's very life. A plot to put another upon her throne."

"Another?" Poley's eyebrows climbed up his forehead, in disbelief. "Who?"

Kit shook his head. "I don't know that much yet. I've heard whispers, nothing clear yet. But I know there's something there and I mean to find it."

Poley narrowed his eyes at Kit. "If you're lying, God's death, Kit . . ."

"Would I lie?" Kit asked.

"If you're lying," Poley repeated, ignoring him. "Remember that last year we plucked you entire from that counterfeiting charge, but you'll wish we'd let them disembowel you then.

"If you're lying, you'll beg to die in that manner. You'll beg to see your entrails burned before your eyes. But first you'll see that child of yours maimed and his dam dead. Do you hear me?"

Kit, hands trembling, forced himself to sheathe his dagger, forced his voice through his constricting throat with what he hoped was a semblance of strength, a timbre of certainty. "I am not lying."

Sweat dripped from his forehead. Fool that he was, fool. In this foolish life he led, always in danger of being arrested, always at risk from the secret service work that had fed him for so many years, always nourishing upon that which destroyed him, Kit had no business living near Imp, no cause to bring their relationship to the attention of these vultures that, in the dark, moved behind the Queen's court, using the Queen's age, the growing mistrust of an older woman.

Save he'd no more been able to stay away from Imp's joyous innocence than a bee could stay away from nectar.

"If you're not lying then, surely you can name us someone—someone whom we can question, who will reveal this grand conspiracy?"

Kit looked up, startled. "I don't know the all of it yet," he said. "I don't know the all of it, and what I know is unprovable."

Poley stepped closer. He was not much taller than Kit, just enough that he could look down upon the poet, sneer down his menace upon Kit's upturned gaze. "Some of it has to be provable, Kit Marlowe. And someone there should be whom we can take and make sing. You'd be amazed how men sing on the rack." He looked down at Kit as he walked round the poet.

Kit turned round and round, keeping his eye on Poley. Robin Poley was not one on whom you'd turn your back. Round and round they went, in a lethal dance. Poley circled and Kit turned, like inimical planets locked in opposing aspects.

"Give us a name, Kit Marlowe, so we know you truly do have something. Just one name. An earnest of your faith."

Round and round, and the sick, despairing feeling gnawed at Kit's belly.

He had to turn someone in? He had to stain his hands yet again? An earnest of good faith for his bad faith?

Will Shakespeare? But no, unprepared and unconnected, Will would never pass for a conspirator, nor could they, no matter how they tortured him, exact anything incriminating from that man.

Either that or they'd extract too much.

No.

Will Shakespeare was the main actor in this tragedy that Kit was creating. He could not be sacrificed so early in the game and for so small profit.

Who then?

His mind ran over the ranks of his college friends, searching the vulnerable—just connected enough to be a credible conspirator, just unconnected enough to be harmless; just eccentric enough to have something incriminating to say; just normal enough to pass.

The mind alighted on John Penry—two classes above Kit and known for creating enemies with his fervent Puritanism, his inflexible certainty. Penry was well born enough to know the high-born and stubborn enough to stick out wheresoever he went.

"John Penry," he pronounced, saying the name before he repented his treason. He pushed John Penry's serious countenance out of his mind's eye. "John Penry, I heard, was involved in this conspiracy. He is a Puritan and would rather have another such on the throne."

Poley smiled. "Ah. John Penry, now that's a name. And where does he reside?"

"Bishop's Gate," Kit said. "I heard he came recently from seeing the King of Scots."

"Ah," Poley said. "The King of Scots, now that's interesting." And with a smile that showed teeth but no warmth, he bowed and he said, "We'll talk to Master Penry, then."

He walked out, feline and soundless.

What had Kit done? What had he done?

He remembered Penry's austere, faith-burned countenance.

Not a pleasant man, Master Penry, and often had he upbraided Kit for Kit's late hours, his drunken bouts.

But how earnestly he'd discussed gospel and philosophy. And how quietly he had argued against Kit's arguments, never once denouncing Kit for atheism, though he'd heard more than enough for that.

Kit closed his eyes.

His empty room seemed cold and stark.

It was the room of a plotter, one who would turn on anyone, and whom everyone should fear.

A wolf at bay, his fangs at every throat.

Kit's bile rose at his throat, burning.

Yet he thought of Imp, and what could he do but save all the hope Kit had for the future, and what goodness Kit still believed in?

To save Imp, let all of Kit's goodness burn away. But how many others must be killed in those flames?

Scene 14

⚭

Will's room. Will, who lies on the bed, stirs, obviously waking up. Next to him, ensconced beneath his arm, lies the Lady Silver, fully dressed and asleep.

Will dreamed that Nan lay beside him; dreamed that he was back home, back in his room, safe in the attic of the Henley Street home, in Stratford-upon-Avon.

But as he stirred toward wakening, even before he opened his eyes, he knew it was not Nan's hair that tickled his arm, knew it was not Nan's soft, whispering breath that rose and fell beside his.

The smell of lilac, the smell of the fairykind, hung heavy on his nostrils.

He sat up, with a curse on his lips. With a curse on his lips he looked beside him, to see the still, resting form of the Lady Silver, her hair loose and tangled upon his pillow, her arm spread the width of his narrow bed, her face pale and tired-looking and, in sleep, appearing young and fragile.

"Wake, milady," he said. "Wake." What had he done that the elf would pursue him this way? What had he done that she would follow him, and come to him like this?

Ten years ago, in a night of impetuous insanity, he'd made love to her.

Ten years ago. Since then Will had been faithful to his Nan. And yet the elf followed him; the elf would come to his rooms and try to seduce him.

He groaned as he got up.

Having slept in his shirt, he searched around the room for his pants and doublet, and slipped them on.

He must go to the theater. He must present Henslowe with Marlowe's note.

Well had Will seen how much Marlowe's opinion was respected, how regarded. Surely Henslowe would give Will a part in his play just to please Marlowe.

Thinking this, Will tied his pants in place, and put his doublet on.

Dismal light shone through the dirty diamond-shaped panes of his window, and though it must still be early morning—certainly not afternoon—yet the air felt too hot and too humid.

Plague weather, Will thought, and shook his head, shaking the thought out of his mind. No. He would not think that. He'd not think of that man, so suddenly struck down with unnatural illness.

It was nothing Marlowe had said. Another illness that looked like the plague. There had been no rumor of the plague, no thought of the plague since early spring. Surely it would not come again now.

Fully dressed, Will went to the bed, bent over the Lady Silver, and shook her. "Wake, lady, you must be gone. This is senseless. This is foolish. I am not yours and you not mine."

The thought that this fair lady was also the king of elves made Will angrier.

What was Quicksilver doing? What was Quicksilver playing at? If there was danger, why was Quicksilver here, leaving his hill unprotected? And if there was no danger, why was he here?

Oh, curse the creature, the mutable magical creature that no mortal could understand, no mortal hold.

Looking at her, Will could have wanted her, Will could have loved her. Again as in that night, so long ago, Will felt the enchantment of the creature, the magic of the woodland, the spell of the shaded glen that no man knew and no man could conquer.

His gaze traveled her soft skin and dwelt on the graceful form of her. Oh, to touch such treasure. To dwell in such palaces.

Nan had never been that perfect. Nan had never been that full of charm. Nor had any mortal woman. Ever. No queen's majesty rivaled the pearly perfection of Silver's skin, the unfathomable depth of her eyes.

And yet, looking on Silver, Will saw, as if with double vision, Quicksilver's broad shoulders, his taller form, the waist that narrowed from the muscular chest, the arms accustomed to fighting, the hands large enough and strong enough to ply a sword as it should be plied.

Again Will reached, again his hand touched the bare shoulder above the ruffled dress. Again, he shook it.

"Wake up, lady, curse it all. Your seduction is not going to work. I have one wife only, and she's alive."

Her shoulder felt hot to the touch and silky smooth, and she looked, in her sleep, vulnerable and almost transparent, like a feverish child who struggles through the night from breath to breath, while his trembling parent stands vigil.

And this, Will knew, had to be glamour and disguise, for these creatures were neither soft nor vulnerable.

For a moment Will hesitated.

Silver looked so tired. As though she'd been doing battle. And she had said something about the Hunter and

Sylvanus, the same things Will had heard in—and barely remembered from—his odd dream.

But it couldn't be true. Furious at himself, Will poured water into his cracked ceramic basin where it sat, atop the trunk at the bottom of the bed. He washed hands and face with scrupulous care. He pulled his hair back and ran his fingers through it.

He cast another resentful look at Silver. She couldn't have been telling the truth and well did Will know that the only reason this seductress would have come to London would be to lose Will to his marriage vows, to lose Will to his own conscience.

He knew that her still looking like Silver in her sleep was deliberate, malicious.

Will remembered well enough that this creature, when asleep, reverted to his primary form, his male form. But Quicksilver would not have moved Will thus.

Will pulled his gloves on, and stepped toward the bed.

Yet, after two steps, he stopped, and stared at her sleeping form. He felt as if his fingers still burned with the touch of her skin.

He did not trust himself to touch her again.

And she looked so tired, so forlorn. If he touched her again, he would long to console her.

If Will touched her, he would be her lover, enslaved by her, like people in the stories old men told taken forever into the bowels of Fairyland, into the heart of illusion and away from the sane world.

Away from the world where Will had three children and a wife he loved, and a job waiting for him at The Rose, if only he would take it.

He took a deep breath. Mentally, he said goodbye to Silver and her enchantment, and walked out the door and down his steep staircase and onto the road below, to meet his destiny in the theater.

But there, in the midmorning bustle of street vendors and apprentices hurrying away to dinner at the nearest tavern, and forges and small factories working in the tiny, ramshackle hovels and huts of Shoreditch, *there,* he found the broad gate to the enclosed precinct of The Rose closed, and nailed shut.

The paper glued to it was already curling in the hot sun, the sticky, humid air.

The writing on paper began with "By the order of the Bishop of Winchester," and went on to say that the theater had been closed for fear of the "great and common plague" ravaging London anew.

Will's fingers touched Marlowe's note within his sleeve. Useless now. Will's stomach hurt and growled with hunger.

Blinking back tears that sprang, unbidden, to his eyes, he turned around.

Another hour without food and he would lose consciousness. How long from there to death?

He'd never seen anyone die of hunger. No one had died of hunger in Stratford in living memory.

He was like the prodigal son who'd left his father's plentiful table to pasture swine in a foreign land and crave in vain the husks which the swine did eat.

Who had told him he could be a poet? Who had told him to come to London?

On that thought, he heard a cheerful voice, with a cultivated Cambridge accent. "Holla, Will. Will Shakeshaft."

He turned.

A smiling Kit Marlowe walked toward Will, cutting through the dusty, dark-dressed crowds of Southwark like a ray of sunshine through grimy glass.

Marlowe wore a bright sky-blue doublet, figure-molding blue stockings, fine velvet breeches, and his beautiful gloves and boots.

And he grinned like a man who has eaten enough and has money in his pocket.

He clapped Will on the back familiarly, and cast a casual, uninterested glance at the door of the theater. "Closed. Oh, the luck. Never mind. We'll find you something else. Let me buy you dinner."

Will would have followed Marlowe into the very mouth of hell on that promise.

Scene 15

❧

An Elizabethan tavern, furnished with long pine tables and benches that have seen better days. The walls are dark with the soot of torches, yet more torches burn in the metallic holders that protrude from the walls. Their burning smoke smells of rancid bacon grease, and it mingles with the smell of mutton and pork from the broad cooking fire. Men, most of them in the workaday dark clothes of laborers, crowd shoulder to shoulder at the vast tables, and eat meat. No natural light penetrates beyond the immediate area around the door. Will and Kit enter, and Kit, assuredly, leads them to two open spaces, side by side at a table near the broad fireplace, around which five cooks labor over the carcasses of dead pigs and cows and sheep.

As they entered the tavern, Kit glanced at Will, taking in Will's swollen eyes, his pale face, his whole look like that of a man condemned to die an ill death on the gallows.

At the thought Kit shivered, thinking that he, himself, might very well end up being the one who would die such a death.

No. Better turn in Will. And look at the hapless fool, in his old doublet and with no money. Kit would warrant that the man hadn't eaten in more than a day.

What good was he doing? None, losing time and money and happiness in London.

And as for Will's poetry, Kit still winced at the thought of it.

No. No. Will was, at any rate, doomed. That much bad luck could not be fought. Kit might as well help Will to a quick end.

He escorted Will to the empty broad bench at a table by the fireplace. Will sat down beside Kit.

Almost immediately, the wench came. Kit knew she would. He was a customer here and well known for his liberal purse. Besides, this middle-aged woman hadn't yet given up on attaining Kit's love. And Kit's purse, too.

What fools women were.

Feeling superior, he gave the faded blonde, with her much-mended shirt, her pale, reddish-looking brown kirtle, orders for two full dinners of mutton and bread.

When the plates came, filled with steaming portions of boiled mutton and large pieces of bread, Kit allowed Will to eat a little first, to fill his mouth.

The silence in which Will greeted his food, his haste in eating, the gratitude in his voice as he turned to Kit and said, "I am not able to pay you, Master Marlowe," all of it gave Kit a measure of the man's hunger, all of it convinced Kit that Will was doomed.

Doomed, doomed, before Kit ever stepped into his life, before Kit had need of Will as the moving piece in the plot that would save Imp and restore Kit to the world of honest men.

If Will were a conspirator, he was a poorly paid one.

"Pay?" Kit asked. "Pay? Why, good Shakestick. It is a matter of courtesy, almost a matter of duty, for a poet to feed another. Other professions have leagues and guilds. Tinkers and weavers and even players, all have someone to resort to when their luck runs out, but not poets. When I came into town, I was like you, starving and poor." For a moment, in his mind rose the image of the despair he'd felt when he'd been forced to pay for his lodging in South-wark with his presence in his landlady's bed.

Who would know that such despair would lead to Imp? Still smiling, Kit took a piece of his meat upon his knife, and tore a bit of his bread. "I'll feed you now and some-day, mayhap, you'll feed another starving poet."

Will shook his head. Stuffing the stale, dry bread in his mouth as it were manna of the gods, he shook his head. "Nay. I'll be gone come morning. Gone back to Strat-ford." He paused in his eating for a moment, then said, "Mayhap I can send you the money to pay for the meal then. If I don't starve on the road."

The bread felt drier and even less appetizing in Mar-lowe's mouth. No. Will couldn't go to the country. . . . Or more likely starve on the way.

Kit needed Will. Penry—he thought with a pang of his sometime colleague—Penry would not hold the question-ers that long.

Soon the torturer would find out that though Penry was a heretic, he had no such knowledge as Kit had claimed for him.

And yet—perhaps Penry did.

But Kit dismissed such hope out of hand. Life had never, in her kindness, handed Kit any favors.

Everything Kit had achieved had been hard won, step by step and inch by inch, like a climber working his way up a narrow slope by the strength of his frayed nails, his skinned hands.

No.

Kit needed Will Shakespeare in London, near Elizabeth's court.

He needed to weave a web of deceit and conspiracy around Will. He must make Will seem like an archvillain, part and parcel of that rolling machinery of conspiracy that was London.

Then the maw of the secret service would swallow Will alone, and let Imp and Kit go free.

Then would Kit be able to consider whether to marry Madeleine or just take Imp and go with him somewhere— France, or Italy, or another country where Kit Marlowe could start anew.

Looking at Will Shakespeare devouring his food with well-mannered hunger, Kit thought all this, and lies came to his tongue in facile speech. "You're a poet, Will. I can't allow you to go back to Stratford or wherever it was, and there pasture your father's cows or run your butcher shop. Stay in London."

"Not a butcher shop." Will looked at him, his forehead wrinkled. "There is no theater in London," he said. He held a slice of mutton, dripping greasy water, above his plate on the tip of his dagger. The grease dripped on Will's dingy lace cuff and stained his gloves. "There is no employment for poets in London now."

Kit looked away. He smiled. Funny how, if you allowed them, people had a way of playing into your hands and establishing just what you wished them to establish. He'd wanted to give Will connections to the Essex field, so that he could hold Essex hostage on this poet's incrimination, just as Raleigh was being held hostage by Kit's involvement.

And here was Will, obligingly asking if there was some other way a poet could earn a living in London.

"You could follow my own example," Kit said, and seeing a combative look in Will's eye, added, "I don't mean the theater. I mean, lately I have got the patronage and the very great favor of my lord Thomas Walsingham. These young noblemen like long poems that speak of some ancient theme, something that evokes learning like Greece and Rome and yet describes a pleasing couple engaging in that which pleasing couples do." He caught Will's amazed eye and grinned. "And then the nobleman gives the poet coin and keeps him in style, in exchange for the poet's writing one or two lines of dedication, extolling the nobleman's great learning and generosity."

Kit grinned at Will, till his face felt like it would crack. "These noblemen will have their pet hounds and their pet peacocks and their pet poets, perforce."

Will looked back.

He had yellow-brown eyes, golden and clear as a hunting bird's eye.

Eyes like that, Kit thought, made a man feel discovered and seen-through, as though he wore a glass-front window that Will Shakespeare could penetrate with his intellect.

Never having been transparent, not even to himself, Kit Marlowe very much hoped he was not transparent to Will either.

"I don't know any noblemen," Will said.

The game was played as Kit had anticipated.

Step on step, as if in a game of chess, did Will Shakespeare fall into Marlowe's trap and, without cunning, put his head in the noose.

Why, then, did Marlowe's stomach hurt and why did Marlowe feel as though a great, nameless doom hung suspended over his own head?

Was he growing a conscience? Oh, Kit could not afford a conscience now.

"There's Southampton. Henry Wriosthesley, third earl of the name. He's young. He's vain. He fancies himself a patron of the arts. I was mid-courting his patronage when

Walsingham—an old friend—succeeded to his family's title and offered me his own." Kit pushed away the plate which he'd scarcely touched. "Here, I vouchsafe that if you offer Southampton a long poem on such an heroic theme as lovers parted or united." He did his best to leer at Will's amazed expression. "I warrant if you do that, he will give you his kind patronage and enough money to remain in London."

He would, too, if Kit could make enough rumors fly ahead of Will, of Will's ease with a sentence and the way his words could set the blood aboiling.

And Kit could do that, having enough acquaintances and even well-disposed friends amid the servants and retainers, the hangers-on at Southampton House.

"Here," he said. "Here. I know there's a party at Southampton House today." There was a party at Southampton's house every day. And Southampton was a devotee of Essex, as close to him—many said—as man could be.

Kit lifted his hand and gestured to the serving wench, mimicking the action of writing midair.

The serving wench hurried over, carrying ink horn, paper, and ink well. She lay it all upon the grease-stained table in front of Kit, and Kit grinned, and handed her a couple pence as a thank-you.

"I am known here," he told Will, seeing Will's amazed stare.

"Would that I were known thus," Will said. "Would that I were known to need pen and ink anywhere."

Kit elbowed him gently and grinned. The thought crossed his mind that he looked like his own father with his guild friends in the tavern, late at night. Kit had never had friends like that, never experienced the supportive, quiet security of male friendship.

One brief moment of intense desire, intense love, with the elf so long ago, and since then the whole world had gone drab and grey-looking so that nothing mattered, nothing. And human affection, human friendship even, also was taken to mean nothing.

"There will be a time," he told Will. "There will be a time when you will find your reputation as a poet flying ahead of you." Dipping the pen in the ink, Kit wrote rapidly. What he wrote didn't so much matter, as long as it identified the bearer as Will Shakespeare. Before Will ever got to Southampton House, Kit must lay the groundwork that would make Will's name known there.

He would do that, promptly, as soon as Will was gone.

For now he wrote an introduction, and he sealed it with the wax brought to him by the wench.

Handing the paper to Will, Kit felt as though he were handing the country man a death sentence, sealed and ready to be delivered by the condemned man himself.

Not that it would be that easy.

Will must still say, in that august company, things that would incriminate him—best if they would incriminate Southampton also and, through Southampton, Southampton's protector, Essex.

"Make sure you deliver that to Gildenstern," Kit said. "He is the Lord Southampton's secretary and he knows me passing well. He will admit you to his lordship's presence."

Will ducked his head, while he slipped the paper into his sleeve. "I thank you, Master Marlowe. I thank you as I cannot express. Why you'd take so much trouble with such as I . . ."

Kit smiled magnanimously and patted him on the sleeve, but looked away, looked into the far distance, finding that Will's easy gratitude made even hardened Kit feel guilty.

He'd thought his conscience more jaded. He'd thought himself harsher. He turned away from Will and said,

"Well, and well. It is what I can do. And call me Kit. Aren't we much of an age and aren't we in the same profession?"

Will gave him a quick, amazed glance, as though shocked at hearing himself admitted to the lofty company of Kit's own status.

Before he could pour forth more thanks that would further make Kit feel like a two-faced Judas, Kit spoke. "So, tell me of yourself. Your tongue proclaims you from Warwickshire and you mentioned Stratford, a fine market town, if I remember. You said your father was a merchant there . . . did you not?"

"A glover," Will said. "A glover."

Kit felt a sudden pang, identifying with Will more than he wished.

A glover was much like a cobbler, a skilled worker with a small workshop. He could well imagine that Will, like himself, had grown up with the smell of tanning hides, the cutting of the hides, the fashioning of them, and aspiring to poetry the whole while. He made a face. "Ah, the smell of tanning leather, the suede, the fine chervil."

Will looked up surprised and smiled, the first genuine smile that Kit had seen from him. He'd finished his food, picked the ribs of the lamb clean, and now held his tankard of ale within the clasp of his two hands as if warmth came from the ale to his hands.

Noticing the tankard mostly empty, Kit gestured for the wench to refill it. "My own father was a cobbler," he said. Something he'd not admitted to strangers in a very long time. Bad enough how they'd taunted him with his origins at Cambridge.

The wench refilled Will's tankard and topped off Kit's.

The food here was passable, but the ale, sweet and tangy, was worth coming in for, worth whatever the price.

Kit drank it, savoring it. "So you have no great relatives

either, no one with power and money, that would justify your aspirations as a poet?" he asked.

Kit had no hope. Chances were that Will didn't have, even at a remove, the sort of relatives that would be involved in any court intrigues.

Though rural families were peppered through with gentility, as full of noble relatives, as sprinkled with bastards of lords and royal retainers, as a rabbit peppered with shot—yet, Will Shakespeare would be the one who had none.

Again and again, life would make Kit find his own way, do everything on his own.

Nothing would be free, nothing freely handed to him.

Will shrugged, the movement straining the worn-out fabric of his doublet and showing the shirt beneath. "No. My mother comes from gentry. Local gentry. The Ardens." He drank his tankard dry. "Robert d'Ardennes, her ancestor, owned all the land thereabouts and the wide forest in it."

Kit again gestured for the wench, and leaned forward, waiting for Will to say more, waiting for Will to reveal more of these Ardens. Local gentry were good. Local gentry often placed maids in the Queen's court, or married them to soldierly lords who were much at court.

"But they're Catholics," Will said as soon as the wench, having refilled his tankard, walked away. "Recusants. One of them was even involved in the Babington plot. We . . ." He shrugged. "We would not associate ourselves with them. My father is a good Protestant." He made a face and looked as if he would bite his tongue as he added, "He was an alderman, when I was very young."

Kit grinned, finding in this again a resonance of his own life, one he'd not expected to find with this provincial clod. "My father was a constable," he said. And grinned. "I mock you not. Marry, a provincial constable, full of his own importance and misapprehended words, who thought being called an ass was high praise, and often used words too large for his mouth, sentences whose meaning he didn't know."

Kit remembered the last time he'd met his father in that capacity, the last time he'd met his father. "He arrested me, once. When someone attacked me and a friend, and my friend killed one of the attackers."

Kit remembered his father's brutality when questioning Kit, and how he'd preached on dishonor and shame. Kit could no further worm his way into Will's confidence. Not tonight. The Ardens and whatever connection they might have had to the Babington plot would suffice. Suffice to put a veneer of truth on Kit's contriving of Will's guilt.

He looked at Will, sidelong, "And here in London, where the theater is, friend, Will. Who have you met who might help you?" He grinned and again plied his elbow conspiratorially against Will's ribs. "A man like you and alone. Any great dame taken you in for her leeman?"

Will's eyes opened in surprise. "Oh, no," he said in shock. "Oh, no." A dark red tide flowed up his neck to his ruddy cheeks, making them ruddier. "Oh, no. I am a married man, you see, and I do love my wife, my Nan in Stratford. We have two daughters and a son." Suddenly, Will's golden eyes lit up as though a sun shone inside his very soul. "My son is seven. He's the smartest, most devilish little scamp you ever wish to see."

In Kit's mind, Imp's image formed. Imp, whom he'd scared away with harsh words, Imp, the most devilish little scamp who'd ever lived.

Tears filled Kit's eyes, distorting his view of the tavern, his view of the assembled men eating and drinking.

Will was like him. Just like him. The son of an artisan who craved fame and fortune such as fate didn't hand to those lowly born.

Turning Will Shakespeare in would be too much like turning himself in.

Kit grasped his tankard with eager hands, drank down its contents with an unquenchable thirst that ale itself would not cure. He longed for friendship such as even his father had enjoyed. He longed for love such as natural humans couldn't give. He longed for a life as Imp's father, a life he would never have.

He drank and he drank till his head swam. He ordered more mutton and more ale. For a few hours, he'd pretend he was a common man, sitting beside his friend in a common tavern.

A few hours later, maudlin and lost, Kit heard Will singing softly. "When that I was and a little tiny boy, with hey, ho, the wind and the rain," he sang, his voice picking up strength. "A foolish thing was but a toy, for the rain, it raineth every day."

The tavern was almost empty by then, save for a snoring drunk and a man who tapped his mug to the tune.

Will lifted his eyebrows and his mug, daring Kit to pick up his challenge and improvise the next verse.

The wenches grinned at them.

Kit smiled, bemused.

As a little boy, he'd watched his father and his father's friends play this game. But he'd been a quiet child, apart from the euphoria, the socializing of such convivial evenings. And later, later he'd been a learned child, who intimidated his father and his father's friends.

Now, at long last, in the maturity of his years, he was being included in a game men played with their tavern friends. He grinned broadly. Only Will Shakespeare would dare do this with someone of Kit Marlowe's jaded reputation.

Grinning, Kit picked up the tune in the voice that had made him the star of Canterbury choir—a clear, resounding voice, if made lower by age and manhood—"But when I came to man's estate, with hey, ho, the wind and the rain, 'gainst knaves and thieves men shut their gate, for the rain, it raineth every day."

Will raised an eyebrow and smiled, as though asking if that was the best Kit could do. Kit chuckled.

"But when I came, alas! to wive, with hey, ho, the wind and the rain, by swaggering could I never thrive, for the rain, it raineth every day," Will sang.

Kit picked it up before the last line had died in the still air that smelled of ale and smoke. "But when I came unto my beds, with hey, ho, the wind and the rain." He grinned at Will, and lifted his ale mug in silent salutation. "With toss-pots still had drunken heads, for the rain, it raineth every day."

Will laughed at that, and Kit laughed in return.

For a moment, in the glow of the ale, Kit relaxed and thought this was what having friends felt like and how he would like to be friends with Will.

Kit could picture many meetings like this. They'd dine and drink, walk together, and talk. Kit could improve Will's mind and Will's writing. They could discuss poetry, and Kit could learn the easy joys of undemanding friendship that required neither secret nor betrayal.

It was only a moment.

At the tavern's door, they clasped hands and clapped each other on the shoulders.

But when they left the ale house, the cold wind sobered Kit, and watching Will retreat down the street in unsteady steps, Kit asked himself whether Will would be going home, home to his great lady.

Would Will not already be involved in intrigues of his own? Was Will not playing a game of his own?

Perhaps Will worked for Poley. Perhaps . . .

In the dreary world Kit inhabited, too much warmth was

as threatening as too much aloofness. Will was too open, too warm, too easygoing. Too good to be true.

"Kit?"

Kit looked down. Imp stood beside him, looking up, his eyes fearful as they'd never before been, his pale skin marked by the trail of tears. Had the child cried, then, at Kit's rebuke?

Kit wished to undo each of those marks, take back the words that had hurt Imp.

He looked down. He smiled.

"Well met, Imp. Well met." He grinned. "Is Lord Morality come to chide me for my shortcomings?"

As he spoke, he looked to the west, where the sun set in a glory as red as spilled blood behind the tall, dark wood buildings of London.

Kit must go to Southampton House and finish laying the trap for Will, before Will came with his note, to Lord Southampton this evening.

Kit must make sure that one or more of Southampton's servants praised Will's poetry before then, so that the gullible lord would fall for it, would give Will his patronage without even having heard Will's poetry.

And yet, Kit wished he could know if Will was meeting with his high-born woman. . . . Or with Poley.

The wind clearing the fog from his mind, Kit took Imp's hand in his own and walked down the street, measuring his steps with the child's. "Listen, I need your help, Imp. I'm sorry I spoke to you so fiercely this morning, but that man who visited me wasn't a good man. He was a wolf man, gross and evil, and I didn't want him to think I loved you, for then he would . . . He would hurt you to hurt me."

Imp looked up and blinked, his grey eyes looking again older and more understanding than they should—as old and understanding as Kit's mother's eyes. And as weary.

"You're doing something dangerous, aren't you? Mother says—"

Oh, no more of Madeleine's maxims. Kit squeezed Imp's hand hard and looked away from Imp's searching eyes. "Look, it is dangerous but I must do it, and once I'm done, then we will be safe, we will all be safe, and mayhap I'll even marry your mother and be your father."

"You mean it?" Imp asked, his voice full of a strange joy.

"Aye, if she'd have me."

"Oh, she'd have you well enough. She sometimes looks at you that way."

"That way?" Kit asked. He picked the child up and held him, and looked into the veiled gray eyes which were so intent and yet revealed nothing of the emotions behind that little, peaked oval face.

Were Kit's own eyes that unreflective? No wonder men didn't often offer him friendship.

And perhaps, he thought, remembering Will's unsuspecting friendship, Will's trustingly offered confidence, perhaps those men were right. If Will's friendship, thus proffered, was true, how foolish and how dangerous.

"What do you know of the way a woman looks on a man, Lord Curious?"

Imp shrugged, and looked away. "I've seen it," he said.

"Well, and right. But you must stop following me," Kit said. "Besides, I'll need your good services, milord, if you wish to gain the boon of such a distinguished father." He winked at the child, who giggled back.

"What do you want me to do, Kit?"

"I want you to go to Hog's Lane in Shoreditch. Did you see the man who was just with me?"

"What?" Imp asked. "The one with the head like a polished dome?"

"Right," Kit said, and smiled at the image. "Yes. Would

you go to Shoreditch? He lodges above Bonefoy Hatters, and I wish you to spy him out, and find when he leaves, when he comes. And report to me any visitor he has. Would you do that, Imp?"

Imp nodded.

Kit set him down and watched his streetwise, London-bred son lose himself amid the crowds of Southwark.

How could Kit feel such trembling anxiety for such a self-sufficient creature? And yet he did.

As for him, Kit must go to Southampton House and lay the trap that would catch his hare.

Scene 16

❦

*Kit's lodgings. The door is open and Madeleine, in a
dark cap, and dark, prim clothes, stands in the doorway
facing the splendorous Lady Silver. Humble apprentices
and workmen walking by give Silver curious glances.*

"Milady, I'm sure I know not." Madeleine Courcy
tightened her lips in a disapproving, ponderous
frown.

Silver knew she should be here as Quicksilver. Silver's
splendor and her looks were bound to offend Madam
Courcy. But that morning her body had taken Quicksilver's shape only reluctantly, and had flickered back to
Silver instantly.

Silver held both her hands demurely in front of her, the
fingers entwined.

They stood in front of the good wife's house, a ramshackle building whose door opened onto an immaculate
hall strewn with fresh rushes.

Silver piped in her most innocuous honeyed voice,
"This is about my husband, good wife, I'm sure you understand that. He frequents places where he should not go,
and finds his pleasures elsewhere. I can no more control

him than control the moon above, the inconstant moon
that waxes and wanes with every changing day. But I must
know. For my ease I must know."

Silver squeezed what she hoped were convincing tears
from her metallic-colored eyes.

To be honest, she *did* need to know.

Searching the dark trail of Sylvanus's power, of Sylvanus's tainted soul, she'd followed it to this unassuming
house in Southwark. "Lives a woman here?" she asked,
looking demurely toward the upper windows. Glazed, as
she would not expect in such a poor place, and clean, too,
shining in the scant light of early evening. "Lives a
woman here with whom my lord might be consorting?"

She had heard in the neighborhood that Madam Courcy
ran a boarding house, and it might well happen that one
of her guests was the deposed King of Fairyland.

Silver must find the dark creature and return everything
to the way it was before Quicksilver's unwitting sin had
released it.

Madam Courcy twisted her mouth into an expression
of distaste, as she followed Silver's eyes to the high, lead-
paned windows. "No woman lives here. I have only one
lodger now and he has been with me for long enough. His
name is Christopher Marlowe. He is a man of unrighteous
living." She looked at Silver. "Should your husband have
been visiting him, it would bode nothing but ill for your
husband, aye, and your home also."

Kit Marlowe. Silver gasped at the name. Kit Marlowe,
again.

She thought she detected something like a glimmer of
amusement in Madeleine's eye, and heard Madeleine's
lightly accented voice, "Ah, but I see you know him, the
villain. Then you know well enough what it means for
your husband to be seen visiting him, no?"

"Has a man with dark hair, and a dark beard, and wearing dark clothes also been here?" she asked. "Has anyone asked for him whom you're not accustomed to seeing?"

Madeleine shrugged. "People ask for him every day that I don't know and have never seen." She looked away from Silver and spat daintily onto the muddy ground of the alley. "Master Marlowe is a spy, an assassin, and other things that even though true, I wouldn't say for a true lady shouldn't speak of that."

A spy? An assassin?

Possible. That was often the way with mortals loved by elves.

After the love of fairykind, the love of human paled, and the human must seek his excitement in other ways: in theater and politics, in crime and high charity. Some became monsters and some saints, according to the bend and dint of that one soul.

But one thing happened to one and all.

Every man touched by Fairyland—and every woman, too—became more vulnerable to the supernatural in the world, to the other things that traveled through the world of mortals, unnoticed by most, disregarded by others.

Pixies that flew in the motes of light, and fairies in woodland glades late at night, became as visible to those people as the twigs and sticks of everyday reality.

It was belief that did it, and not some ointment as old people would say was rubbed on the eyes of the captives in Fairyland. It was only that those who'd once believed in faerie could never again ignore it.

And those who saw more were also more vulnerable to the things that went unseen by others.

Silver sucked in breath as she realized that the only common link between the unfortunate Nick and Kit was their having been touched by fairykind.

Was that, then, the only indication of peril?

But then, what about Will, Will who had been Silver's,

Will who had been loved by fairykind? Loved with a love hotter than that of Fairyland's normal run?

"Where did Kit—Master Marlowe—go? Know you that?" Silver asked.

The woman shook her head. Her suspicious look had returned. "He could be here or there. More than likely whoring in some tavern."

Whoring in some tavern, he would be safe. Even Sylvanus couldn't cut out a human from amid a crowd and claim him in public.

But Will. . . . Where was Will? Was he, likewise, safe from Sylvanus?

Silver wrinkled her brow in thought, and clenched her hands on the fine silvery fabric of her dress. If Kit was vulnerable to Sylvanus, then so was Will.

And where would Will be at this hour, with the sun going down and the creatures of the night becoming more powerful than they were in daylight?

She must find him.

Silver thanked Madam Courcy and, giving her two coins from the store of old gold coins that Silver carried about with her—the store scavenged from old lost treasures that men had forgotten—Silver bowed and walked away fast.

When far away enough that she'd be lost to Madeleine's sight within the crowd of apprentices and artisans hurrying home for supper, Silver ducked into an alleyway.

There, she winked out of existence.

She materialized again in Will's room.

Scene 17

ⵒⴾⵒ

Will's bedroom. Will is in the middle of changing his clothes. He has his hose and shirt on, and is inspecting his doublet by the insufficient light of a small taper set on his table.

Will thought that his doublet looked well enough. His best suit, purchased ten years ago at Will's wedding, it had developed weaker spots and places where the nap had not worn so well. But all in all, it looked well enough.

Nan had mended it, once or twice, with her large, uneven stitches. Will smiled at the stitches, which were so characteristic of his wife.

An excellent woman, was Nan, but always more adept at fishing and walking through the woods, at digging in the garden, and even at cooking, than at the daintier arts of womanhood.

When she'd been a young girl, Nan had often escaped a house ruled over by an unsympathetic stepmother and several large, bossy brothers to wander the Forest of Arden till she came to know all its paths. Will smiled, remembering the young, tomboyish Nan.

He started slipping his doublet on when Silver materialized beside him in the still, shadowy air.

Will's heart skipped a beat.

He'd thought himself well rid of her.

When he'd returned from the tavern, feeling the glowing warmth of his unexpected and much-needed meal, he'd found his house empty, no Silver in sight.

He'd been relieved. He'd thought the elf had finally desisted of seduction, finally given up on whatever deranged lust and wanton craving had brought her to London.

Instead, here she was again.

Will stepped back away from her. "Milady. I didn't expect to see you again."

She didn't seem to hear him. Her bosom, overspilling from the tight confines of its lacy nest, rose and fell rapidly, as if animated by some uncontrollable passion.

"I had to tell you," she said. As she spoke, she stepped closer, and held each of his arms in one of her long, white hands.

Her hands felt so hot that, even through his doublet, he feared they would burn his arms.

He tried to step back, but found the wall behind himself, found himself surrounded by her lilac perfume.

He could go no farther.

"Lady," he said, and turned his face away.

She moved her face closer. She pulled his face forward to look at him earnestly, with her large, silver eyes. "I must tell you, Will Shakespeare, that you're in danger. Those who've once been touched by the fairy realm always crave fairy love and as such—"

Will slid away from her and, diving under her arm, made away. "Lady, for Jesu sake, forebear. I crave nothing. It is you who seem to have uncontrollable cravings."

She looked surprised, offended, as if he'd slapped her.

Her dainty foot in its silver slipper stomped hard. The dusty rushes on the floor crumbled. "My cravings do not matter. It is those who've been touched by Fairyland, you see, who forever crave excitement. Almost always in their souls there remains an unquenchable thirst, like a hole that swallows normal human emotion and normal intercourse and that . . ."

Will had ceased listening to her. Her voice faded out of his ears as he looked at his doublet, where she had held him.

The force of her holding him, the force of his pulling away, had left several tears in the fabric.

Will could not go see an earl attired in this way. Oh, curse the elf and his-her mutable needs and his-her annoying demands.

Opening his clothing trunk, which was in the main empty, Will rummaged inside for a needle and wool thread. He knew that Nan had packed him some, when he'd left Stratford. If he could only find it.

He turned over his possessions, two shirts and some spare, much-worn stockings.

"Will Shakespeare, are you listening to me?" Silver asked, and grabbed him by the sleeve once again.

Will straightened. His long-simmering acceptance of her needling was at an end. "No, my lady. No. I hear you not. And you will not entice me with your charms, no matter how you try. So cease already." His gaze persisted, nonetheless, in visiting the milky-white mounds of her bosom. "I have to mend my doublet so I can go and see the Earl of Southampton. Kit Marlowe has arranged for me to be introduced to the earl."

"Kit Marlowe?" It came as a shriek, and the Lady Silver stomped her foot harder than ever. Dry dust of rushes rose from the floor. "The wolf has gone to search for Kit Marlowe. The dog is for him, Sylvanus is. Can't you see the danger? Can't you see he'll come for you next?"

Will was tired. Silver spoke in riddles and, even now, held on to Will, leaned into him, her warm bosom against his shirt, soft and resilient against his arm.

If she persisted, he would hold her. He would take her in his arms and he would hold her, and then he'd be as unable to stop as he'd been ten years ago.

And what would he tell his Nan when he returned? How would he explain, once again, violating their sacred bond, their joint sacrament? Or could he lie to Nan? Deny this ever happened?

No, Will couldn't countenance it.

He pushed Silver away. He fought free of her. He spoke in fast and breathless words. "Kit Marlowe has arranged for the Earl of Southampton to hear my poetry."

He picked up the note from Kit and waved it around, before stuffing it into his doublet sleeve. The small tears on the sleeve would have to do. He would have to hug the shadows and stay in the darker portions of the room. Unlikely, anyway, that he would get invited to the high table, being only a poet and an unknown one.

"But Will, you must understand, you're vulnerable to magic now. You—" She had her hands on her waist, her black hair undone and wild with her fury. Her silver eyes blazed in anger.

She had never looked so seductive.

He scurried away from her, backward, opened his door, and escaped to the tiny perch atop the staircase that led to his room. "I understand, my lady, that it is likely that Kit Marlowe's good will would mean more to me than all your magic."

He started down the stairs, holding fast to the tilting banister.

She leaned down. "It's Sylvanus, you fool, Sylvanus you have to fear. Sylvanus, remember that. There are legends that elves, and creatures like elves, who've forfeited their material bodies can possess the bodies of humans, claim them for their own. And humans marked with the Fairyland touch are more vulnerable. . . ."

Will was almost at the bottom of the stairs. He looked up and yelled, "A pox on your Fairyland touch. I want no part of it."

Such was his furious despair that only afterward did he think that doubtless he'd wakened his landlord and that doubtless in the morning he'd be accountable for keeping company with a well-dressed lady definitely not his wife.

At that moment he was conscious only of Silver, more beautiful than ever in her wild ire, stomping her foot atop the tiny perch in front of Will's lodging.

That image stayed with him while he hurried to the bridge and to Southampton's house on the other side of the river.

It took all his willpower to keep walking.

Scene 18

✧

*The fairy palace. Ariel leans over an elf lord who lies in
a bed in a small—if still sumptuous by mortal stan-
dards—room. She looks worried, worn out, and her white
dress for once seems to leech color out of her drained
cheeks. The elf lord looks near death. In the doorway,
an ill-looking Malachite gazes in.*

"How bad is it, milady?" Malachite asked.

Ariel heard the words, and knew their meaning,
but she could no more than shake her head in response.

She felt her patient's cool forehead, bathed in chilly
sweat.

The small, confined room smelled of this sweat. The
smell of death.

The elf was a changeling, Lord Geode, but he'd been
high in Quicksilver's favor and powerful enough. Now,
his power burned around him as it left him, with the waning flame of Fairyland's spreading blight.

How to cure such an ill? How to prevent this stalking
death that, day by day, moment by moment, robbed Fairyland of its bright lords, its fair ladies?

Two more days, and would the blight stalk higher in

the ranks, to Ariel? Or to Quicksilver's uncle, noble Varg-mar?

And what could Ariel do to stop it?

Despair burnt within her, high like a well-fed lamp.

"He was the eldest changeling in the hill," Malachite said. "Placed the highest of all changelings when I was a child, and he looked after us and made sure we were happy."

Malachite's voice, hesitating and small, dipped and wavered as his strength failed him and emotion overcame him. "Faith. I'll be next."

Ariel took Geode's pulse to find it faded and light, a whisper of life against encroaching death.

The waning of magic hurt all. Ariel could sense it, like a damping of power, like a dimming of light and life, coursing throughout the hill like an illness. But it did not affect the elves born to the hill so much as it did the changelings.

Natural-born elves had stronger power.

Would the killer blight stalk them thus, through the ranks, up the power scale of Fairyland?

And how to stop it? Would Quicksilver's return stop it?

Ariel couldn't tell. She'd cast her net and scried upon water and upon pure crystal mined from within the deepest mountain.

She'd found nothing.

Less than nothing—a black and forbidding nothingness, as if a great wall barred her way, a great will, stronger than her own.

And she feared, with a dread she dared not fully face, that this will was the will of Quicksilver, her errant lord.

Was he taking his joy in London, as Silver or Quick-silver, or both? Was that what brought this blight to his people?

Oh, cared he not if they lived or died?

She reached for his mind, as she held the dead-seeming hand of Geode.

Nothingness answered her call. Nothing.

"Oh," she said. "It seems to be that my lord cares not for me." She spoke in a whisper, and felt tears tremble beneath her voice. "It seems my lord cares nothing for the hill, nothing for any of us. How can he be lost to all this, Malachite? He is your milk-brother. He is my husband. Yet because of a disagreement will he forget all this, the multivaried bonds that tie him to this hill? Oh, he'll forget crown and shame and all, for the sake of that human whom he'll pursue."

"Lady—" Malachite started.

On the bed, Geode's power flared in a little explosion as magic left the body no longer able to contain it.

Geode's body changed.

It shrank, shriveled. The long, blond hair turned whiter than the sheets upon which it lay, then fell, all in a breath, leaving the scalp beneath bare like wintry earth. The perfect face, with its small nose, its mobile lips, wrinkled and crinkled and seemed to collapse in on itself.

Ariel let go of the arm that, still living, still warm in her hand, had turned skeleton thin, its skin like paper.

She said, "Oh," as she watched this rapid semblance of human aging.

She could say no more.

Malachite sobbed.

Where Lord Geode had lain, the shriveled yellow creature took a breath that looked as though it would blow away what remained of him, and shuddered as life left him.

On the bed remained nothing but a pile of earth—that dust from which mortals were fashioned, as elves were from fire—that dust to which men returned upon death.

"Oh," Ariel said, and rubbed her palms upon her white dress.

Malachite drew in a deep, sobbing breath. "Oh, lady. Oh. He was a hundred, and now is reverted to what he would be had the essence of Elvenland never infused him. He was a hundred and now he's dust."

Ariel turned around in time to see Malachite sink to his knees. "And I am sixty, the Lord Quicksilver's very age, born the same day.

"If my magic vanishes, where will I be? In second childishness, and mere oblivion, sans teeth, sans eyes, sans taste, sans everything."

While Ariel stared at him, her lips bereft of any consolation, Malachite approached her, on his knees, arms raised as if to the highest worship. "Oh, lady. Lady, marry me." He crept closer.

She stood, amazed, unable to respond.

"Only you leave him, and marry me. Make me king of the hill and thus possessor of everyone's magic with that great honor. And in that honor will my honor bask, and that power will protect mine."

The lean face, the intent green eyes, turned up to Ariel with an intensity not to be vouchsafed. "Only do that, milady, and the two of us, King and Queen of Fairyland, and for once whole, will lend the mending hand to this affliction. Then won't the lord's absence matter."

Looking at Malachite's face, remembering the horror of the thing on the bed and knowing that half of Malachite's treason hailed from desperation, yet Ariel bridled at it, and felt a shiver climb along her spine. "You would do that?" she asked. "You would do that and thus dispossess and kill your lord?"

"Oh, not kill him. Not kill him." Reaching for the hem of her gown, he held it in his hands like a holy relic, and looking up at her with panic fear, he said, "Oh, lady, he's elf born. His life is not at stake. It is our lives he risks with his folly. Not his."

Ariel's mind chided and complained that Malachite was right, that it was Quicksilver's base lust that undid them all.

But in her heart, in her faithful heart, Ariel loved Quicksilver still and she couldn't believe that ill of him, her lord.

Hadn't she loved Quicksilver ever since they were elven children, growing up in the palace? Hadn't she trusted him through his wild youth and come to fruition of their love as maturity molded Quicksilver into a man at last?

And how could she betray him now, even if . . .

No, Quicksilver couldn't have betrayed her. She suspected it yet couldn't fully believe it.

Something else must have taken him away. . . . Something.

She shook her head.

She stepped back away from Malachite. "I have no proof that my lord plays me false," she said. "I have no proof and I am his true wife."

Mad despair burned in Malachite's pale features and a madness was called to battle in his gaze.

Malachite got up. He stared at her with fever-bright green eyes. He swallowed.

"Oh, I'm sure he plays you false now and then, and always has. I remember his father." He met Ariel's shocked look with sudden sobriety. "Wish you for proof?"

"Proof of what?" she asked, all amazed. "Of what accuse you my lord?"

Malachite's Adam's apple bobbed up and down. "If it's proof you want, then proof you shall have. Would you actually wish to see him topped?" He shook his head. "No, it matters not. Some proof you shall have before the night is through. And then will you marry me and we shall cleanse this hill."

Malachite was mad, burned insane by his fear. Tears that shone in his eyes, but did not fall, made his gaze hard and cutting like a blade.

He walked down the hallway and Ariel was left alone with her doubts. She wouldn't think that Quicksilver had left her to satisfy his base lust. But then, why would Quicksilver have left else?

And oh, what damned hours told she over, who doted yet doubted, feared yet strongly loved.

Scene 19

❧

Kit walks by the riverside, having just disembarked from a ferry from Southampton House. The riverside is deserted on that side, bordered by dark warehouses and empty or at least darkened houses and shops, not a few of which are boarded and bear the plague seal, warning passersby to keep away. Kit, wrapped in a dark cloak, starts to make his way inward when a child approaches.

"Kit," Imp yelled as he ran on the darkened riverside wharf filled with the stench of fish, its streets slippery with carelessly discarded entrails. "Kit."

Just returned from Southampton House, Kit had been all immersed in the trap he had built. But seeing Imp, he forgot it all.

He looked at the small running figure and for a moment felt a pang.

What kind of father encouraged his son to be out of doors at these hours when who knew what doom might overtake him?

Yet, he reminded himself, Imp would not be kept indoors, not even by his ever-vigilant and severe mother.

Kit reached out his arms, and caught the child and

picked him up, and lifted him, and shook him with mock violence. "Now, you scamp, now, you rotter, what are you doing abroad at this hour and tramping where no honest soul ever sets foot?"

Imp giggled. "You told me to watch for a visitor to the bald man," he said between giggles, his voice distorted by his being shaken. "And he has one. Now the bald man is gone, but the visitor remains. And I knew you would be coming from the ferry for, pray, you said you were going to Earl So-and-so's house, and that would mean the ferry and the other side of the river."

"You're a good scamp," Kit said, and shook Imp again lightly. "A smart rogue, and with two more like you, you would take over the country and rule it like three Caesars in a new triumvirate." He smiled, but his heart was not in it. Gently, he set Imp down, and bent over him, to talk to him. "You go home now, boy, go to your mother, eat your supper, and go to bed."

Imp blinked up at him. "And you?"

"I'll go look in on this man's visitor, and then to bed anon. Who is the visitor?"

"A fine lady in a silver dress, with hair as dark as coal and skin as pale as moonlight," Imp said.

Kit nodded.

The woman.

She existed, for Imp had seen her. And before his plot proceeded any further, Kit must make sure that this woman would not protect Will Shakespeare.

He must verify that Will was indeed friendless, indeed bereft of courtly favor, indeed safe to set up as a sacrificial lamb.

"Now you run home," he said, and ruffled the boy's hair.

"Will you come home anon?" Imp asked.

Kit nodded.

"And will you tell me a story when you do?"

Kit nodded. He ruffled the child's hair again, and the boy was gone, running down the street.

Kit turned his steps toward Shoreditch, up the narrow, muddy road where Will Shakespeare lived, up to where a light shone on the highest window of the otherwise darkened house.

An odd light, not like the light of any earthly tapers, but a shine diffused and glowing throughout the entire space at once, a shine like a million fireflies, captured and held within that room.

Kit had seen that light once.

It was the light of Fairyland.

His heart beating at his throat, his hands trembling, his mind protesting with desperate certainty that such a thing could not be, that it happened not, that elven ladies—or lords—didn't haunt squalid rental rooms in London, Kit hurried forward.

He grasped the slippery banister of the staircase and he climbed, step on step. Had it been the stair to paradise, he would have been no more eager.

Kit knocked at the door and heard an exclamation from inside.

Though yet he could see nothing, standing on that tiny platform outside the scabrous door, he fancied he smelled, all around him, the smell of lilac, intoxicating him like the best wine.

And something like a voice from his heart whispered that the Lady Silver loved him. Aye, and so did Lord Quicksilver. His elf love had come back to Kit.

The door opened.

Silver stood there, the elf's female form, her black hair falling unfettered down her back, every strand seemingly charmed into place. And her broad silver skirt had been slashed to display a diaphanous white fabric beneath, which revealed, in its transparency, the length of Silver's white legs. That inner gown that, beneath her bodice, cloaked her arms in long sleeves was yet so molding, so transparent, that he could see all of her revealed, save for the narrow waist hid beneath the silver bodice. And that mattered little as her breasts, rounded and pale like twin moons rising above a silver sea, were more than half exposed, lifting with her every deeply drawn breath that matched Kit's own aching, slow, painful breaths, and played a dancing tune to Kit's mad, beating heart.

"Kit," she said, her voice little more than a breath, taken by the wind as soon as it was pronounced. "After all this time! Kit."

He touched her hand. In touching it, she trembled.

Love deeply grounded hardly is dissembled. These lovers parled by the touch of hands. True love is mute, and oft amazed stands.

Thus, while dumb signs their silent hearts entangled, the air with sparks of living fire spangled.

Kit's breath, drawn, brought him her perfume. Her perfume swelled his heart in further breath. Not knowing why, nor how, nor when, they closed the door behind them and, still no more touching than their hands met, stumbled inside the dim, shabby room.

"I thought you away," she said, her voice still rushed and wind-driven, as if passion pushed breath and hurried it through her soft red lips. "I thought—"

He touched her lips with his, not so much kissing her as a pilgrim acknowledging his reaching the shrine of his desire. "Away?"

"Away from London. In Lord Thomas Walsingham's estate. Scagmore. I thought you living there and away, and safe, from all the madness that might come."

Kit, his ears love-stopped, heard no more than that she'd informed herself of his place of residence, and known, known with certainty where he should be at this time. That was enough. That was plenty.

He'd never thought she'd have allowed a stray thought to venture his way, and here she was, confessing that she knew his current estate.

He kissed and kissed, and again he kissed, those lips of whose taste he'd dreamed, those lips like liquor that no mortal vine could ever equal.

With his love he assayed her, till in his twining arms he locked her fast, and then he wooed with kisses and, at last, her on the bed he lay, and tumbling upon the mattress, he often strayed beyond the bonds of shame, being bold.

And craving, joint craving ignited, that which, lonely, might have stayed itself for eternity. It ruled them and held sway.

The mattress protested beneath them, the bed shrieked and complained like the much-abused thing it was.

Silver said, "Stay."

She cried, "Forebear."

But all and all were taken as enticements aimed at making his trespass sweeter.

Kit, surrounded by the lilac smell of faerie kind, her taste on his tongue, the smoothness of her skin traveling like alcohol through his own skin into his veins to intoxicate his brain, thought to die and knew he lived, and knowing he lived knew he died of bliss.

Why did he love this creature and no other?

Why this elf, this fleeting being of moonlight and shadows and deep forest? Why this creature, neither man nor woman—neither and both—and not a mortal chained by the thrall of time? Why was it this creature he must love, in both its bewildering aspects and thus trespass beyond the boundaries of human love?

Why love here, not elsewhere?

Why one especially does the heart affect, of two gold ingots, like in each respect?

No more was there an answer to this riddle than to Kit's heart-pounding, driving need.

The reason for it all, no man knows. Let it suffice that what we behold is censured by our eyes. Where both deliberate, love is slight.

Who ever loved, that loved not at first sight?

Scene 20

❧

Will walks in front of the grand houses on the expensive shore of the Thames toward a particular grand house— the town house of the Earl of Southampton. Two iron gates stand open to a small quay, and past that, broad marble stairs disappear into the green shade of a large garden. At the quay someone in rich livery—presumably a footman—waits. He steps forward.

Will's legs hurt.

He'd had to cross the Thames by the bridge, as he lacked a penny to pay the ferryman.

In front of Southampton's garden gate—seven feet tall and twice that much wide, of wrought iron worked in fantastic shapes—Will put his hand inside his sleeve and touched the paper Kit had given him. Here was his safe-guard, here his passport, to that life of ease and fame that he wanted. Here his way to send money back home, to make enough money for Hamnet to attend the inns of the court, or some college, enough money for Judith and Susannah, both, to marry well, enough money to make Nan into the lady she didn't wish to be. . . . But enough surely to get Nan a kitchen wench or two, and let her rest and lose some of those wrinkles that marred her face.

Will walked down a long path that bisected a garden, with millenary trees on either side and flowers that dizzied the air with fragrance.

A part of Will felt amazed that he dared be here; him, Will Shakespeare, the son of the Stratford glover.

But he had to go in and pluck fortune up by her few, thin feathers, did he not?

Just at that moment, in the dark of night, something moved and a voice said, "Good Shakespeare, I can help you."

The voice resembled Marlowe's and Will turned on his heel and faced the place whence the sound came.

He stared at a face, surrounded by dark, curly hair, tipped with a well-trimmed black beard. Dark eyes laughed at him.

"You need better clothes," the creature said.

Will was sure it was a creature, not a human, because a thick smell of lilac, almost too heavy, almost gagging, filled his nose. "And shoes, and you must look better, if you wish to get the patronage of the lord."

It had taken Will a moment, but in that moment he recognized the face and the look, the expression, the voice.

It was Sylvanus, once King of Fairyland, Quicksilver's deposed brother.

The last time Will had seen this creature, it had stolen Will's wife, and bid fair to keep her a prisoner in Fairyland.

Through Will's mind, in a tumbled confusion, came that impression, and Quicksilver's warnings about Sylvanus.

Will backed away from the dark creature, and he said, "No. I'll have nothing from you."

A carriage went by him, in a rumble of horses' hooves, and voices of merry youths singing merry songs.

Some clots of earth splattered onto Will's suit, and he brushed them off despairingly.

By the torches on either side of the carriage, Will saw there was no one close by, certainly not Sylvanus.

He took a deep breath and shook his head. He was scaring himself with nothing. His contact with Fairyland was indeed driving him crazy, but it was Silver herself who ensured his madness.

To be one of those youth in the carriage, born to wealth and fortune and all that was good, oh, what he would not give.

But Will had been born to a failing business, to a medium station in life in a small town.

He turned a curve in the path and saw the house before him: a massive stone building, looming against the moonlight sky, its every window displaying a taper or a lantern and making bright heavens dark with its riches.

Will fingered the note inside his sleeve anew.

At the top of the steps, a footman blocked his path.

"Your business, master—?" he said, looking at Will with a gaze that implied that Will might have as much business here as a cow in a palace—or perhaps less.

Will handed the man his note, his hands trembling.

The servant received it and looked at the address: from Kit Marlowe to the most High and Honorable Henry Wriostheley, Earl of Southampton. With raised eyebrows, the man appraised Will again, from the top of his domed, balding forehead, to his ill-shod feet, and something very much like puzzlement lit his gaze.

Will could almost read in the man's eyes how unlikely an acquaintance Will was for the glittering Marlowe circle.

But after a long while, the man nodded. "Follow me, please."

He took Will into a vast, glimmering salon, and through

it, into a narrow hallway, and through this again, into another salon.

From somewhere came the sound of music and men's
laughter.

Another servant appeared, barring their way, and Will's
guide into these secluded regions whispered something to
this new man, as if it were of great import, and handed
him the paper.

Reading the address, the man raised his eyebrows and
gave Will a puzzled look. Then, with a nod and a wave
of the hand, he indicated that Will should follow.

He opened gilded doors, and again passed Will onto a
fellow servitor's care.

That way they went, seeming to circle the palace, past
magnificent rooms and statues such as Will had only read
about—statues of heros and statues of nymphs and gods
made to resemble carvings of Greek antiquity.

Along the gleaming marble hallways and through halls
plated with leaf of gold, farther into Southampton House
they went until, at long last, they fetched to a door, from
beyond which male laughter rang clear.

By this time, Will's legs were trembling, and the but-
terflies in Will's stomach had risen to a fever pitch, flying
up his throat and making him feel nauseous.

The servitor lowered a massive, golden carved handle
and a heavy oak door flew open.

Within opened a smaller room—smaller than the ones
they'd crossed—and filled with minuscule tables that tot-
tered on thin golden legs.

On these tables games were laid. Backgammon and dice
and other games for which Will lacked names. At each
table sat several men.

Servants circled, mute and stone-faced amid this babel,
carrying trays with drinks and dainties, which the gamers
quaffed and devoured without ever once losing the thread

of their betting, the elation of victory, the disappointment
of loss.

Youths pushed money back and forth upon the tables,
as the turn of fortune brought forth a lucky win or a das-
tardly loss.

More money than Will had seen in any single room, in
his whole lifetime, now winked and shone at him from
every corner.

For this much money one could buy a house in Stratford, aye, even buy New Place, the best and most spacious, the grandest house in Stratford, whose possessor
was assured of a pew close up by the altar to listen to the
service at the church.

This much money, even half the money in this room,
would assure Will of his highest ambitions—of a better
house for his family, servants to help Nan, an education
for Hamnet, and even money to purchase himself a device
and become a gentleman.

He watched, fascinated, as the glimmering coins passed
around, tossed from one to the other of the careless young
men, with no more than a mock expression of disgust, a
mock sound of indignation.

So absorbed was Will in this contemplation, he didn't
notice that the servant stopped by one of the tables, looking pointedly back at Will.

"Ah, Shakespeare," someone said. From the table near
which the footman stood, a young man rose, holding Kit
Marlowe's elegantly penned note in his hand.

For a moment, still dazed, Will thought that this person
was Quicksilver.

There was the same finely sculpted face, the same high
bridged nose, the expressive eyes, the gold-spun hair
combed over the left shoulder to the waist over a velvet
suit of dark blue.

But Will knew that this was a human, younger and,

perforce, less perfect than the lord of Fairyland.

This resemblance disquieted Will, who had just left the female form of Quicksilver in his room, after being unable to rid himself of her.

More disquieting yet was the way the lord gazed eagerly at Will and extended both hands to him. "Welcome, Master Shakespeare. Welcome. I've heard from my servants, all around, that you are the next great poet. A very sweet swan of the Avon."

Will felt his face heat, as his cheeks colored. This had to be a lie, for who in London knew of his poetry?

Uncomfortable, he bowed and murmured something, even he knew not what.

And Southampton laughed, and gestured for a chair to be brought forth and placed next to his, and when it was, he sat and waited for Will to sit. "You are too modest, I know you are," he said. "A rare quality in an accomplished poet."

Will felt uncomfortable and hot in his worn suit.

He noted how everyone's gazes fell on him. In some of those stares he fancied he saw something less than bonhomie.

"Kit says you intend to write a long poem on a worthy subject," Southampton said, and as he spoke, his long-fingered hand tossed the die upon the polished dark wood table. He looked at the result and watched, with a small smile, while other gamers heaped coin upon the table in front of him. "Would you tell us what the subject would be, Master Shakespeare?"

"I intended it to be . . ." Will raked his brains and came up only with Marlowe's suggestion that this be about a famous couple and much be made of their embrace. Out of this confusion, he murmured, his voice catching, "Venus and Adonis, your lordship."

Southampton, who'd been counting the money, turned

and looked at Will. "Indeed? You mean it so?"

He placed all the money again forward, indicating a new bet. "And when might we expect this masterpiece?" The hand that held the die and rolled them displayed as many rings upon it as fingers could hold—ruby and diamond and sapphire—so many rings, any one of which would have given Will more than he could expect to earn his life long even if all his dreams came true.

"I do not know, your lordship, for I lack the wherewithal to write it. I'm at the end of my stipend and must find other work."

"Indeed?" Southampton asked, without turning, as he supervised the other men's handing over of the money they'd bet.

Southampton raised his hand and gestured.

A servant appeared, carrying a small sack. Into the sack, Southampton's careless, bejeweled hand scooped his win for the night. At a glimpse, Will counted over ten pounds.

The earl grinned at Will. "Poets should have the money to write poetry. Take this and write about Venus and Adonis. And mind you, compose me a pretty dedication." He grinned at Will, looking, in the grinning, more mischievous and more like elven spawn.

Breathless, still expecting all this bounty to melt like elven gold, Will held the purse. "Milord," he said. "The love I bear your lordship—"

"Oh, take it, take it," Southampton said. "It is a trifle. Only, mind the dedication."

He turned his back and forgot Will. But the other people in the room did not.

Servants, as though wakening to his presence, plied Will with honey cakes and cheris sack.

Unused to any drink stronger than small ale, Will drank the sack with relish and soon felt the dizziness that often comes with unaccustomed indulgence.

Around him conversations swirled, on matters of importance and state, on the pressing matters of the realm.

"But she is old," one of the younger men said, "Gloriana is."

And before Will recovered from realizing it was the Queen they spoke of, in such a careless tone, the same cultivated, measured cadences, sounded again, "Why, I hear she has grown so suspicious, like old women will, that she holds an old rusted sword in her room, and thrusts it into the arras cloth in the evening before she lies abed, to ensure no assassins hide beneath the tapestry."

The rest of the room tittered.

It seemed to Will, dizzied by the wine and made sluggish by the unaccustomed pastries, as if too many eyes turned in his direction, to observe his reaction to that story.

He strived to show nothing. He was an honest burgher, a faithful subject, and it did not become him to mock royalty.

But later in the evening, a languid, black-eyed dandy approached him. "And what think you of the Queen's age, and lack of heir, Master Shakespeare?"

Someone else, a creature with a sharp face, who looked somewhat like a fox, pressed close in. "Pray tell us," he said. "We long to hear the opinion of the intellectual elite."

Will, caught with a pastry in his mouth, choked, the taste suddenly sweet-cloying upon his tongue. "I think King James of Scotland will inherit," he said. "When our Queen is gone to her reward and that no one will be the worse."

"Oh," a sharp, high-voiced creature to the left of him said. "You think then that King James will be better?"

Will knew not what to say, but someone else behind him attested, "Well, he is a man, and younger than the old woman. Why, it is said that, as in the days of her youth, she roams the streets of London, in disguise as a common gentlewoman, listening to the opinion of the people, for she's convinced her councilmen deceive her."

Will had scarce absorbed this when someone else asked, "What think you of that, Master Shakespeare?"

"I think that, if it's true, then it's a great folly."

Will felt very hot and had reached that stage of light intoxication when every voice appeared to come from a long way off. "Anyone could kill her in the streets, late of a night, and leave the kingdom in chaos till an heir prevailed."

In the silence that followed that comment, several people in the room traded dark glances. Will wondered what it meant. Had he said something wrong?

No, to his unfocused eyes it appeared more as though these people traded secret glances of satisfaction.

He could understand none of it, and he endured, attempting patience until, later in the night, he could run out through the sweeter, fresh perfumed gardens and hasten home thereby.

Scene 21

༺ঙ৩༻

*Will's bedroom, late at night. The candle stands on the
writing table, half consumed. The bed lies in some disarray, the cheap blanket thrown to the floor, the covers
rumpled. Kit's clothes lie scattered around the dusty
wooden floor. Kit himself sits on the bed, looking dazed
and lost, like a man who's endured a blow to the head
and hasn't fully recovered. In his male aspect, fully
dressed, his hair perfectly coiffed down his left shoulder,
Quicksilver paces the room. The moon, circled with red,
sends her light through the window, adding a blood-
tinged cast to the scene.*

"Come and lie down," Kit said. "Why did you change
aspect, even as I slept for no more than a moment?
I can't have closed my eyes for longer than a gathered
breath. What can have disturbed you so in such a short
while?" He blinked uncomprehending eyes at the elf.

"Come and be sweet, come and be mine again. Come
and lie down." And with what enticement he could muster,
Kit patted the rumpled bed beside him.

But Quicksilver only glanced at Kit, as if in that space
that Kit had closed his eyes and opened them again,

Quicksilver had forgotten Kit's name and visage and the joy of their erstwhile embraces.

How Quicksilver frowned, and how his countenance changed, moment by moment, like a motley moon.

Staring at him, Kit couldn't help thinking that the change between male and female was a small thing and this changeableness, from smile to frown, from hesitant hope to utter despair, from love to scorn, the greater change.

Nor could Kit, despite his wishing to hold on to what had just happened and the recent memory of the elf's kind welcome, help remembering the last time he'd been dismissed by this creature, and in what manner.

He stared, and waited for the ax to fall and hoped it mightn't, and craved yet more of what had failed to evoke satiety, however greatly enjoyed.

"Quicksilver?" he said at long last. Not a call, so much as plaintive questioning. "Quicksilver, if you so wish to be, I love you as I love Lady Silver. Only be mine again. . . ."

The elf stopped in his pacing. Red moonlight bronzing his golden hair, he turned to face Kit, but what he said were not so much words as something that sounded like a fragment of lost poetry. "The expense of spirit in a waste of shame, 'tis lust in action."

Kit shivered as sweat cooled upon his body.

He reached for the blanket that he and the elf had tossed to the floor earlier, in their exertions, and pulled it over himself. Caught on the edge of the bed, the cover would only come up at an odd angle, hiding Kit's legs and little more. Not enough to stop the chill that climbed his body.

Once before had this elf dismissed him. Once before, had Quicksilver, in his most foreboding mood, barred Kit from touching Silver.

It was as though this creature were not one and the same

with his lady love, but someone else—a tyrant brother or a harsh father—bent and determined to keep her under lock and key.

And yet, Kit recognized Silver's gesture in the hand that Quicksilver lifted to the air and then let fall in a swoop. And those hands were the same, oh, different sizes and yet the same—they were so white, and long and more perfectly shaped than mortal hands.

Kit wanted those hands and their touch, the magical entrancement that came with elven love. He didn't care in what form he got it—Silver's or Quicksilver's well-loved shapes—so long as he was touched by burning elven love and thus attained that state where he was purged of mortal dross, and reached the heavens with an immortal madness. "Come to bed," he said, aware that he whined. "Come to bed."

Quicksilver looked at Kit—an opaque look. Who could read those moss green eyes? Were Quicksilver human, Kit might have ventured to guess at pity and sorrow, and perhaps a touch of affection, a hint of remorse, a brief lament over lost pleasures, flying fleetingly across that gaze.

But Quicksilver was not human and all these emotions flashed in his countenance, one after the other, like shapes within the golden flames of a blazing fire. They darkened the glow a moment, then were gone. Behind them remained only a blank slate, a diamond perfection, a face etched by eternal fire and eternal ice, and not created or doomed by human love.

"No, Kit," Quicksilver said.

Bending in a fluid movement, the elf gathered up clothes where they lay—Kit's discarded hose, his breeches, his fine lawn shirt, his well-cut boots—and with cold efficiency, set them on the bed. "You must dress," he said. "And go."

Kit couldn't believe he'd heard right. Even before,

when Quicksilver had dismissed Kit, he'd never been this curt. "But why?" Kit asked. "In whose name should I leave now?"

"In mine." Quicksilver's moss green eyes seemingly turned one shade darker, and the soft mouth, so well suited to pleasant smiles, and pleasanter sporting, shrank upon itself and closed more firmly, before opening to say, "In mine. It was a mistake all, and I do regret it. It was only my loneliness and Silver's loneliness, these many years. Or maybe—" The perfect face flinched in momentary pain, then smoothed itself out. "Ah. It matters not. What matters is that you must go, Kit. I bring danger on you. Nothing better than danger."

Kit opened his mouth, closed it, opened it again. He knew he looked like a fish, newly pulled from water and drowning in the air.

Quicksilver stood by the window, looking out.

Faint sounds of that nightlife reached Kit. As from a long distance off came a bawd's high, insane laughter, and a horse's mad gallop, and someone singing a bawdy drinking song.

Oh, to be out there and know nothing better. Oh, to be in the real life of true, mortal men. To smell the reek of urine and vomit and human sweat that pervaded these streets nightly, and not to long for the scent of lilac that came from the elves, nor for their immaculate, light-filled world, or the luxuriating of their touch.

Blinded by tears, Kit reached for his hose. With trembling hands, he pulled them on. Standing, he slid his breeches on and fastened them.

"Is all my hope turned to this hell of grief?" he asked aloud, in bitter, querulous tones born of his pain on behalf of that poor Kit who still seemed to Kit's confused emotions to be someone else, some poor, deluded fool he hardly knew. "On seeing you after all these years, I thought, fool that I am, that you remembered me, that you had cared, cared enough to know where I lived and what I did after that cursed day when you pushed me, ice cold, from your sight."

Kit fastened his shirt whichever way, then pulled his doublet on and started buttoning it, noticing halfway through that the button was in the wrong hole, and that the doublet pulled askew on his body, rising at a tilted angle at his neck, and protruding oddly below his waist.

It didn't matter. Nothing mattered.

"If it was not for me that you came to London, for whom, then?" Despite Kit's best efforts, his voice echoed shrill, like a fishwife's asking her man for an account of his time and ill-spent affections. "Is it for Will Shakelance?"

Quicksilver answered not, turned not.

Kit forced himself to laugh, a hollow laughter that seemed to rake his throat like a pestilent cough. "Surely not Will, the very married burgher of Stratford. He'll never make it, you know? Not in London. Not in the theater. He could, I suppose, make it as a wool merchant in London. But for a playwright, he lacks the fire, the verb, and the glory that could play well upon a stage.

"Will is like all other country boys and will spend his meager money upon London for a few years, only to go back home to his wife and die, many years hence, prosperous and bitter, talking ever of how great his plays were that London has forgotten." Kit's voice lost force as he spoke, till his very last words came out as little more than a whisper supported only by bitterness and bile. Because halfway through, Kit had realized how he envied those young men who, indeed, had something to go back to in the country.

"Is it Will you love?" he asked.

Quicksilver, his back turned, spoke as if from a long

distance off. "I am no longer a prince, Kit, nor a youth. I've come of age within my own sphere. In my own race I'm a king, and within my estate there are duties and ranks and obligations, as there are in mortal life. I've a kingdom to run, and I have a wife. To my wife I owe what I promised her and that already sullied by . . . But no, it's not your fault."

Quicksilver turned and set a hand on Kit's arm, only to withdraw it, too quickly. "It's not your fault. It is mine. I did remember you, Kit. Much too well. Memory entangled in my speeding heart and led us both to trip." He glanced at the bed, then at Kit.

"But I promised my wife there would be no others—as mortals do promise at their weddings—and all I can do now is hope she forgives my transgression. I have a duty to her. As for what brought me to London . . . A darker errand than I intend to tell you about, Kit. An errand bound with kingdom and elven breed and the safety of both spheres. Indeed, you are in danger while you are near me." While speaking, Quicksilver looked down and, as if his gestures were disengaged from his voice, frowned at Kit's doublet.

Unbuttoning it with nimble fingers, he buttoned it again, the proper way, and patted it into place, like an adult straightening a child's attire.

Looking up at Kit's face, Quicksilver started a smile that reverted to an intent frown. "Go, you fool, go, before you force me to commit I don't know what madness." His hand caressed Kit's face in a fleeting, soft touch. "Go before the forces that I came to do battle with smell you out and come for you."

Kit felt a surge of hope. He raised his eyebrows. Quicksilver wished to protect Kit. Did not that mean that the elf still cared?

He straightened himself, anxious, eager, ready to die if

needed to keep his tenuous hold on this worshiped creature's heart. "I'll fight beside you, if that is needed," he said. "I'm not afraid of anything that comes for you. I'm not a child any longer, Quicksilver, I have worked for the secret service. I have fought, I am not afraid of a fight or of killing or dying. I have—"

But Quicksilver shook his head. "It is the stain of what you have done, your betrayals, your compromises, that makes you all the more vulnerable to this attack. Go, Kit. And don't come near me again."

The elf marched to the door and opened it wide to the too-real night outside, with its smells of sweat and vomit, of wine, and frail humanity.

Kit walked down the steps, a brittle imitation of his normal smile plastered on his face, his eyes blurring everything through the lens of tears.

His love had turned to a lump of ice within him.

Oh, that he could reach the cruel elf and with ready hand tear that heart of stone from that soft chest.

Oh, that he could hurt Silver as she'd hurt him and bring Quicksilver to reckoning with the passion he so carelessly ignited.

"Master Marlowe," said a voice behind him. "I've been looking for you."

A smell of lilacs filled Kit's nose, but it was a slightly *off* smell of lilacs, a smell of flowers that, having fallen to earth during a wet day, rotted and perished on the muddy ground.

A mingle of Silver's smell and London's, Kit thought, as he turned around to see a tall, dark-haired gentleman with a perfect, well-sculpted beard and ringlets of dark hair falling to his shoulders.

Something about the man's stealthy look, something to his appearance of having hidden long in darkened rooms, gave Kit the feeling that this was a secret service man, like Poley.

"Yes," Kit said. "What do you wish of me?"

The man smiled, revealing sharp teeth almost like fangs. "No, Master Marlowe. What do *you* wish of *me*?" Advancing, he put an arm through Marlowe's arm and, with his arm in Marlowe's, walked forth like the dearest of friends. "I believe you've been offered an offense?"

"Offense, I?" So many of them crowded at Kit's tongue that he knew not what to say. There were the beatings of his uncaring father, the sneers of better-born boys at Cambridge, and now this light, uncaring dismissal from Quicksilver.

Oh, that Kit had enough tears and he would cry his sorrow in volume to drown the salty sea.

"Come see the whipping of the blind bear," a tavern crier screamed, just to the left of Kit. "See the blood run down his hoary back. A most droll show."

"The offense done to you by a certain poet—and by an elven lady?" the gentleman asked, leaning close.

Kit's arm that the gentleman held felt ice cold.

The stranger smiled. "Be not amazed. It is a gift I have of seeing the future."

"The future?" Kit asked.

"Even so," the man said, and smiled broader. "The future where we avenge ourselves upon them."

Them. Silver and Quicksilver and Will, whom the elf preferred to Kit.

Kit would get revenge on Will soon enough. If Kit went to the gallows, then would Will precede him. But Silver, beautiful Silver, would go on laughing and living her immortal life, caring not where he was or what had happened to him.

"Card games and dice, try your luck within." A street

urchin grabbed Kit's sleeve, while pointing at the dim interior of a tavern.

Kit wrenched his arm away and narrowed his eyes at the stranger. "Who are you?" he asked.

"My name is Sylvanus. I am an elf, like the lady who offended you," the creature said. "And powerful enough to take your revenge. Wish you for revenge, sir?"

Kit hesitated for only a minute, but his need for quenching his grief was unmistakable. The fire in his heart would answer only to the lady's sorrowful tears.

For the moment he was lost to all—his love of Imp, his hope for the future. All was drowned in his need to bring the elf down. "Yes," he said, his voice just above a whisper. "Yes, I do."

"Oh, I knew we were kindred spirits," the elf said, and led Kit insensibly away from the heavily traveled street they walked, and down an alley, to a less populated part of town.

Scene 22

❧

Will's room. Quicksilver, in his male aspect, paces back and forth in the narrow space.

Quicksilver still trembled and still felt as if a nameless fear traveled upon his limbs and knocked nonstop at the door to his reason.

Even as Quicksilver, as king of elves and possessed of all his power, he felt the sick-thoughted predominance of Silver in him.

It was Silver who cast her eye upon the bed, and smiled with remembering sweetness at the creases and folds.

And it was Silver's thought that Marlowe had been still sweet after these many years, and twice as eager. Quicksilver, instead, dwelt on Kit's unquestioning acceptance of both his aspects. No one else, not even fair Ariel, accepted him thus.

He sighed at the thought of Kit's gentle, vulnerable love, that love too willingly given.

He'd thought his heart would break when he'd turned Kit away. And he could not explain his motives to the wounded mortal.

The human would never understand. But Quicksilver

had broken his heart's bond and rendered useless his carefully planned redemption.

He'd meant to kill Sylvanus and thereby to stop him from taking human life in London, or to control Sylvanus and return him to what he'd been before Quicksilver mistakenly freed him.

Instead, Quicksilver found himself turning into Silver and seducing a human to whom he'd already done much wrong.

But how? How had Silver overpowered Quicksilver's will? Had Quicksilver not always been the dominant aspect? Would Silver now be it? And would Quicksilver remain but the pale reflection of the Dark Lady's glory?

He shivered and crossed his arms upon his chest, and in doing so realized that the arms he crossed were rounded and white and bare, and that the chest upon which they crossed had lost its muscular tautness, and displayed, instead, the voluptuous curves, the rising mounds of Silver's lace-encased breasts.

Silver stomped her foot as tears came to her eyes.

Oh, vile, insufferable submission. Would the king of elves then be this way, forever imprisoned in a woman's body?

This change in body without Quicksilver's meaning it was like the change of sea when the tide shifted, like all things obeying onto a season, like a human body pending onto death, like the shifts and motions in the power of elves.

This thought brought Silver up short.

Around Quicksilver's feminine aspect so unwillingly assumed, currents blew, which made Silver tremble with their intensity.

A weather vane creature, Silver and Quicksilver had ever shifted and turned, locked in an endless, adversarial dance—now one won power, now the other.

Only now a shift in the prevailing wind, a permanent breeze blowing, from the shores of femininity made the dance one-sided.

And a disturbance like that . . . It had never happened, in Quicksilver's long life, nor in the history of his race, which he felt like a second memory.

He thought of the Hunter's being injured. That, too, had never happened in elven memory.

Oh, were the beliefs of the first elves true? Had those first elves, those brutish ancestors little better than short-lived humans hiding within their caves, known about the universe more than civilized Quicksilver with his power and glory?

Was it true that there were two elements for each thing in the universe? That the all was composed of two elements, male and female, the two interwoven seamlessly?

Was Quicksilver's obvious duality only more glaring than that of other creatures, but no more unusual?

And was the Hunter, then truly, as primitive elven religion had made him, one of the three parts of the male element?

And had the feminine element reacted to the injury of the Hunter by becoming overpowering?

But no. That made no sense. For the feminine element was not unfettered, nor could it subsist long without its counterpart, and in its brutish, primeval wisdom, it would know that.

Silver shook her head and sighed, and then trembled, as someone knocked on the door.

Opening the door, she found a little man, wizened and old, and looking much like one of the underbrush gnomes, who sometimes, for a grand holiday, visited Quicksilver's court.

Yet Silver's pulse sped at the sight of the creature. It was a male.

She shook her head and said, with a roughened, hasty voice, "What do you wish?"

The man opened his mouth wide and looked at her, and looked down at the road below, immersed in respectable late-night silence, then looked at her again. "I was seeking Master Will Shakespeare, ma'am, if you may. I brought him this letter from his wife, in Stratford. The first courier having died, I took the letter over." His sly, narrowed eyes made Silver think that this man believed her Will's fancy bit, and that Will was betraying Nan with her.

Yet even that knowing expression made Silver's heart race, her pulse speed, and made her pause, enthralled, at the man's balding head, his staring, motionless eyes.

The part of Silver that remained rational thrust her hand forward, and made her say, "Give me that letter."

The man shook his head, looked at the ground. "You're a fine lady, but as my name is Christopher Sly, and I'm a tinker from Burton Heath, when I do a bit of a favor for a neighbor, it is customary to receive . . ."

Silver thought of what he would like to receive, while Quicksilver, subdued, submerged within Silver's mind, roared inaudibly with anger at the man's daring.

Even Silver knew, though her baser instincts told her otherwise, that she did not truly desire this man, that what she felt was a mere result from a changing pattern in the world of archetypes.

The female side of things, Silver suddenly realized, was strengthening and growing—not in triumph, but more as skin thickens when it heals after a cut, to protect the body against further injury.

And that meant—what?—that Sylvanus intended greater harm? Did he threaten the female aspects as well as the Hunter? Was his intent, then, more than drinking the life force of humans?

More than possessing them? Toying with them? Did Sylvanus mean to take over the world?

Oh, indeed, Silver had a lot to atone for.

Blindly she thrust her hand into her sleeve and pulled out the purse of coins that she'd brought with her for such necessities.

She handed the old man a golden coin, sporting the effigy of a forgotten king, and to his bumbling thanks, for only answer, she stretched her hand.

The letter was set into her hand, sealed. She set it on the lopsided, peeling table that served Will for a desk.

Slamming the door shut, without seeing nor caring if the man outside was startled, she backed onto the bed and sat down.

She knew, without fully knowing how she knew, what Sylvanus's plan was. Within her mind the older memory of elves, and her own, feverish emotions, had congealed, and she liked not the shape of this scrying of hers. For she was sure that Sylvanus meant to take over the universe, to replace the very fabric of reality with his own essence—to be sole master, sole owner, sole god of all.

Fear trembled along her every limb and she thought the world was dying and Silver with it.

Scene 23

❧

Kit Marlowe walks along increasingly narrowing streets, with a dark-haired, darkly clothed man who seems to become transparently ethereal when moonlight shines upon him.

Kit was scared.

He didn't know what this creature beside him was. But he felt a fear, a panic, a scared, shying distrust of it. It was an animal fear, all skittering and hiding and small paws hurrying away from danger.

Now looking at him this way and now that, it seemed to him that Sylvanus was a man, or an elf of ethereal beauty, or only something dark and twisted, with long fangs, and sharp lupine hunger etched on every feature.

Kit had calmed. His temper, so inflamed by Quicksilver's turning him out so bluntly, had cooled.

"I fear . . ." he said, and let the words hang, midair, not knowing how to explain what he feared. For indeed his fears crowded around him, many and clamorous, like dogs around a hunted hare.

Kit feared the man beside him, and he feared the depths of his own anger, the enthusiasms of his own sudden and dangerous passions.

He'd been thrown in prison twice for brawling. On less
provocation than he'd received from Silver.

He still felt the injury of his dismissal, and with it, a
muted, roaring anger. An anger that scared him.

Kit realized he'd been ever cleft in twain: the scholar,
calm and impenetrable, above the world with curious eyebrow cocked at human follies—and the enraged, betrayed,
mocked cobbler's son that moved through the night, his
dagger out, seeking revenge on those who'd done him
wrong.

He cast a look at the man—the creature—beside him.
The elf's arm weighed like cold, dead iron in Kit's.

The creaturé turned his perfect face and smiled at Kit,
showing teeth that were just a little too long, a little too
sharp.

But more than the teeth, what scared Kit was the hunger
in the eyes that regarded him.

"I'll get your revenge for you," the elf said, and he
smiled. His tongue appeared, sharp and pink between his
teeth—the lolling tongue of a dog.

Kit thought of what Imp had said, of the man with the
face of a wolf. He looked at Sylvanus with new eyes. Had
this been it? Kit felt his heart race.

Was this the creature who had sought him at home?
And for what purpose?

He tried to pull away from the arm that encircled his,
and the arm's grasp tightened.

What had Kit done? What? What had he agreed to when
admitting he wished for revenge on Silver?

"All *that* I *will* do, and yet more," Sylvanus said, his
voice as gentle as a spring breeze. "All that I will do, and
yet I'll grant that Kit Marlowe will not squander his life,
that he shall not give up breath and heart for the heartless
elf, the foolish peasant."

The gentle wind carried a smell with it, a heavy, gagging stench. Kit felt as if the elf's voice had a physical presence that rubbed against his leg like a large dog.

Kit looked down, but where he thought there would be a dog, he saw only a darker patch of night, as if a concentration of darkness. The darkness crept up, like a miasma, and engulfed the shape of Sylvanus, making the elf look as if he'd emerged, half formed, from overarching dark.

What was this creature?

Kit pulled away, but the strong, cold arm would not let him go.

Kit thought of Imp. He thought of Will and his easy friendship, in the tavern, the day before. Those thoughts were rays of light in the gathering dark.

But Imp was threatened and Will must be sacrificed to Kit's and Imp's safety.

Kit felt trapped in one of those dreams where one wishes to stand up but can't, the dream wrapping around him tightly, like a suffocating blanket.

Like a swimmer amid overpowering waves, crossing the broad arm of a perilous sea, Kit, wave on wave, saw his death near, and felt the abyss rob him of his very breath and life.

Kit thought of Imp and plunged headlong toward the promise of air and life, even should that air prove stale, that life fickle.

They were now in a part of town where no living thing walked. Houses, many houses, were marked with the seal of the plague that had so suddenly returned to ravage the city.

"Who are you?" he asked the elf, while the air around them grew very still, filled with the smell of the grave and of rotting flesh. "What are you?"

An apprentice, clad all in black, walked by on the other side of the street.

Kit struggled to cry for help, but he could not form the words. And if he found words, what could he say? That the gentleman at his arm was molesting him? Kit Marlowe, a grown man, who'd survived a rough and secretive life of London for so many years, would now ask for help from an adolescent?

The apprentice walked past. He gave Kit a sidelong glance over his shoulder, then with an obvious stare at the tavern sign above Kit's head, shrugged his shoulders.

And perhaps I'm drunk, Kit thought. *Or perhaps dreaming without sleeping.*

But what dream of his had ever smelled so foul?

Laughter, unmistakably male in its low accents, and yet laden with soft, flowing promise, echoed all around Kit, seemingly wrapping him in coils of the mind. The creature grasped Kit's arms with both hands. His fingers looked like claws and felt like crushing bonds.

"Who are you?" Kit asked again.

"I am that which can grant you your heart's desire," a male voice said, soft and slow. "Your desire of revenge and love and life, and everything you ever wanted.

"Only take me in, give me asylum, and shall your brow be crowned with a poet's crown, and future generations will compare their meager efforts to your greater worthiness. And all your enemies will be destroyed and you shall reign, effortless and fair."

Kit cleared his throat against the foul stench that surrounded him. He did not know why his heart beat such a disordered dance within his chest.

This was all a dream. It had to be a dream.

Did he not stand in a Southwark street, looking on mundane facades of wooden buildings, and watching apprentices walk by? Was the morning breeze not cold upon his skin? Did his clothes not feel clammy with his own sweat?

Was he not in the world of real things, the world of the living?

By asylum, the elf could not mean more than for Kit to hide him for a time.

And yet, the elf offered to have all of Kit's enemies destroyed. . . .

Kit thought of Poley and of the dark coils of the secret service. He thought of them threatening Imp. Oh, to see them laid low and Imp free. "How do I know you can do this? Who are you?"

"I told you, I'm Sylvanus. I was once King of Fairyland."

"How do I know that you speak true?"

The elf laughed. "Because I know your future, Master Marlowe. Aye, and your past, too. Your future is to reign upon all earth. As for the past—did you not once stand in an ancient grove of trees, in a garden in your own home town, when you beheld Lady Silver? Aye, and when you rushed to her embraces, and submitted to those of Quicksilver, too?"

Upon all earth? It was insanity. As for the rest, Kit's throat closed. How could this creature know the secrets Kit had told no one in all these years?

This dream knew too much and was too mocking. This dream knew about Quicksilver? If a dream of his own, it was a foul dream that lifted the scab off the not-yet healed injury and exposed Kit's own heart to the cold and bitter bite of memory. And if it came from elsewhere, this creature knew too much, human or elf.

It seemed to Kit that a blanket of darkness enclosed him, a warm fog that obscured his vision.

Darker flecks floated in this black haze, like black diamond dust tossed in the wind. And a voice came from it.

"You must share my life and I yours, and in that life

will you gain immortality, so that not only will your poems be remembered through the centuries, but you'll be there to hear the praise and reap the accolades."

The blanket tightened around him, keeping the cold breeze out. A different scent than the smell of rotting flesh surrounded Kit, again a smell not unlike that smell of lilac that he associated with Quicksilver and Silver, but grown overpowering, so as to become rank, cloying, like flowers arrayed around a funereal urn. "This I'll do for you and more, if you take me in and give asylum to my high and lofty purpose. Rulers of the world, we'll conjoined be, if only you keep me within your heart and mind. You rule humankind, and I Fairyland."

"Fairyland?" Marlowe asked, the one word costing him all the accumulated breath he'd gathered, while the blanket coiled and coalesced around him. The creature had said he was King of Fairyland before, but how could that be, when Quicksilver had made the same claim? Did Fairyland have many countries? Many kings? "Where in Fairyland?"

"From Fairyland I hail," the thing said. "From the hill within the Arden Woods. And there I ruled, before that demon, that low shape changer, Quicksilver, took my place, and with cold, unloving hand, thrust me from my race to die."

"Quicksilver? Quicksilver banished you?" Kit asked. In his own mind was the image of Quicksilver, the fair youth in all his noble splendor turning Kit away from his love, and from his true lady's bed.

"Banished?" A bitter laugh echoed on the heels of the word, and the darkness coalesced, so that over Kit's shoulder, Sylvanus reappeared, this time much taller than Kit, and better formed for war, with broad shoulders and powerful arms so that, beside him, Kit felt like a child, less than half grown.

Kit made as if to move away, but a hand grabbed him around his middle, a powerful arm held him immobile. "The vermin had no right to banish me, nor to punish me, nor did he have power to do so. I was his king and he a foolish boy, playing with his mortals and his maidens. Yet, like the snake, well nurtured to the bosom, did he despoil me of kingdom and of country, and send me wandering the desolate darkness, with no one and nothing to sustain me. But give me asylum, and together, we'll recover my land, my kingdom entire, and lay the worm in the darkest dungeon that the imagination of man has ever built."

Kit felt he should say that he did not wish to see Silver harmed—nay, nor Quicksilver either, harsher though he was—nor did he wish their enchanted life brought low.

Yet she should be punished, and Quicksilver, too, for their wanton disregard of Kit's love. But no more than a rebuke, a soft rejoinder.

Just as he thought this, another thought intervened, that Quicksilver had cast him from his bosom and from Silver's warm favors.

Twice.

Into that thought wrapped the memory of disordered sheets and warm bed, of the soft, silken body beneath his own. He sighed and bit his lips, and didn't say anything, did not defend his erstwhile love, nor attempt to turn away condemnation from that fair head.

In that moment this other elf was upon him, seemingly still blanket-shaped and yet human-formed, his hands everywhere, and prying upon Kit's breast, his thighs and every limb, and up again, and close beside him pressed, and talked of love.

Gasping for breath, scared and giddy and confused, knowing what he'd allowed Quicksilver but not ever truly craved from mortal, Kit made reply. "You are deceived, I am no woman, I."

The elf smiled at that and said, "It is no love such as human love I crave, but the fair use of your fair body that we will become one and the other and both interchangeable."

Too late, Kit thought to run. Too late he thought that if it were so, if this creature were to have use of his body—whatever that use meant—Kit, the weaker, would lose his body, aye, and his soul, too, and all that went with life.

What good was life, if just a semblance, if Kit seemingly would walk and talk, but another creature use his mind and limbs?

He ran, pushing his feet hard against the dusty ground.

The elf ran with him, the darkness clinging around Kit's cold limbs. Laughter, immortal laughter, stopped Kit's ears.

Kit ran and ran, in disordered running, till each breath made bid to burst his lungs, and upon each breath he thought it would be his last.

Then in a dark place, far away from the awakening street where he had started, his legs gave out. He fell down. His knees bent, bringing him to his knees upon a muddy street, wet with slops and smelly discards.

Kit's eyes stung from sweat. Blinking, he looked around, and saw that all the houses here, once taverns and bawdy houses, were blocked, the board nailed across their doors, the seal of the Queen upon the board and a warning that here reigned the plague.

Kit Marlowe made as if to rise again, but his knees wouldn't support him.

Kneeling like a penitent on the muddy street, he heard the elf laugh and felt a touch, upon his whole body at once, like a million wanton hands seeking to explore his skin, to know his every pore, and trying to possess him and have him and win him as never human lover could have done.

He tried to shrug away from this feel, too intimate and knowing to be pleasurable, but found nowhere to turn since it was everywhere, and his legs would not allow him to rise.

Trembling, he knelt and wished that he would die, or else that he would, instantly, be consigned to the raw attentions of the torturers Poley had threatened him with, torturers which, not feeling this soft, would yet be kinder.

The myriad hands seemed to sink deeper and, through his clothes, touch his very skin.

Then the touch turned burning, hot, intemperate, and sank lower and deeper into Kit's being, so it seemed to have captured not inconsequential flesh, but his very soul.

Like a bird trembling between the hands that would crush it, Kit sought to escape, but couldn't. What lay inside could not be escaped.

With a fearful burning upon his every limb, he collapsed to the muddy street and thought that he'd sealed a hellish bargain.

But something in him laughed, something pushed, like a rider will set spurs to a sluggish horse, something whispered within his brain, "You will rise and do my work now. Morning is nigh, and from now on, must you spend all night awake and doing my will, if we are to achieve our revenge over our mutual enemy."

Scene 24

❦

Will's room. Silver has made an attempt at straightening the disordered bed and paces, back and forth, her dainty silver slippers ticking a fast rhythm on the floor. Now and then her long, white fingers tug at her neckline, pushing it ever lower, to reveal more of her white, rounded breasts, as if she were too hot to bear the contact of the creamy lace. Will opens the door and steps in.

Will opened the door to his room, his head still swimming with confused elation.

The Earl of Southampton had given him money—given money to Will Shakespeare, the boy from Stratford, the provincial that no one believed could be a poet. The earl had given him money to write a long poem.

Will felt drunk without drinking, tingling with excitement and trembling with fear at his own daring.

This one evening Will had been treated like a poet, accepted into the highest circles of nobility by the power of his mind, the strength of his learning. Why, the gentlemen with the earl had asked Will's opinion on politics and religion and important, weighty matters, and they'd listened to his words as if he held a secret to knowledge they could but guess at.

On this wave of triumph, he opened his door, on this wave of triumph he stepped into his room, to be engulfed in Silver's arms, enveloped by the cloying lilac perfume of fairykind.

"Milady," Will said.

Silver's skin burned, like the skin of a feverish child, and her arms around Will scorched like brands pulled from a blazing fire. Her breasts pushed against his chest, so that he could feel them even through his doublet and his shirt.

"Milady," he said. He could say no more. Her lips, hot, searched for his with the blind eagerness of a child's.

For a moment her lips touched his. For a moment their mouths joined, and he breathed in the taste of her—like wine, newly bottled, full of spirit and bursting with life.

He thought of Nan. Nan in Stratford. Nan patiently waiting for Will beside their hearth. Nan, who should hear of Will's triumph. Nan, who deserved not to have her husband betray her with an elf—something not human, something beautiful but also cold and distant like stars twinkling in the velvet of the night sky.

His hands lifted and rested on Silver's shoulders, and pushed away at her till she stepped back. Looking dazed, she tried to approach and kiss him again.

He wiped his mouth on the back of his hand, wiping the taste of new wine from his lips, and pushed away harder.

Silver lost her balance, with his too-rough shove, and stepped back, till she stood against the bed and looked at him with wide, unfocused eyes. The eyes of a drunkard.

"Milady," he said again. "Milady, you forget yourself."

Silver opened her mouth. She took a step toward him, then a step back. Her hands trembled, and her body, too, giving the impression of a great struggle, as if she were two people, one rushing eagerly toward him, the other

holding back, pulling back. Like an eager horse being restrained by a severe trainer, like a chained bear struggling
against the chains to reach the dogs that wound him.

A mewling sound came through those parted red lips.
A sound of complaint. "I don't wish . . ." Silver said, her
voice low and rough. Quicksilver's voice. "I don't wish
to do this. It is the universe-ordering thought, the elements
and images through which elves and humans perceive the
universe. It's all disturbed. The female element—the triple
goddess, the eternal trinity, maiden and mother and
crone—feels threatened. And like a person preparing for
a blow, it increases its strength, it rules all, trying to appear powerful, trying to . . ." Silver's mouth opened and
closed, her body trembled.

Will thought of his dream, his odd dream. He thought
of the maiden, the matron, and the crone.

He shook his head. He did not wish to think about it.

He wanted nothing to do with the slippery world of the
supernatural. He wanted his solid home, his commonsense
wife, his profitable career, his coat of arms. He wanted
his son to attend a well-regarded college.

His hand within his sleeve touched and felt the solidity
of the leather purse he'd got, the metal coins within. He
took a deep breath. The world of reality called him, the
world of coin and work and family. The faerie world was
delusion, a mad dance of nonsense that permeated reality
yet didn't impinge upon it.

He walked toward his bed, intending to put the purse
beneath the mattress.

Silver cut his advance.

Her trembling hands stretched toward his shoulders, her
chest rose and fell in fast, eager breaths—reaching
breaths, imploring breaths, demanding breaths. Her lips
parted, promising a heaven within—the taste of fresh
wine, the caresses of her searching tongue.

Will looked at her lips and at her rising and falling breasts, and heard his own voice come small and strangled from a throat that felt suddenly tight. "Madam," he said. "Madam, you forget yourself. I am married, and so is Quicksilver."

As he spoke, he stepped backward, toward his desk, hoping nothing was in his way.

If he fell and she touched him once more, it would all be up.

Will might resist temptation while looking at Silver, but resisting temptation under the touch of those long, knowing fingers—resisting temptation then would take a less lively saint than Will could ever hope to be, a saint of plaster and painted wood like those the papists venerated.

He smelled Silver's heady scent and felt as though his very blood responded to it, flowing through his veins in a heat of fire and air, demanding action where honor dictated restraint.

She stepped forward, as he stepped back. Her tongue flicked over her half-parted lips. Yet the words that came through those lips were Quicksilver's, steady and rational, spoken in Quicksilver's rough, preoccupied voice. "There is some way, Will, that my brother is threatening the female element. He holds one of its aspects hostage, or he will soon kill one of them. And the only way I can think for him to hurt them, the only way that would require a human body, is sympathetic magic, which is a magic stronger in humans than in elves."

Will blinked. He couldn't think of Quicksilver's words, while desire for Silver's offered body assailed him so. He stepped back, and back and back, and stared at the lovely, unfocused silver eyes, and asked, his own voice too low and gruff, "Sympathetic magic?"

Silver smiled as she gained space, and through her smiling lips Quicksilver's voice said, "Yes, like when you make a doll to figure a man and upon that doll perform the magic with which you wish to influence the living creature. Thus by affecting a symbol of one of the female aspects, Sylvanus will wound the deity itself, and wound femininity throughout the land, as he's already injured maleness."

Will hit his writing table behind him, and felt it totter, and turned around, and reached with hasty hands for the trembling candle, and rescued it just in time, before it overturned and its flame caught the papers strewn about.

In that fatal moment Silver caught him, and her soft, rounded arms surrounded him, her soft, rounded breasts pressed against his back.

In that moment he felt her breath hot against his neck, as she parted his curls, and kissed him beneath his ear and whispered into it, in Quicksilver's hard and clear voice, "But what would be strong enough to prefigure the female prototypes with which humans and elves have imbued the immense and indifferent universe? Something strong enough to represent at least one of them?"

More soft kisses.

Will trembled as one with the ague, and tried to keep from turning around, from putting his arms around that willing body. He would not meet Silver's kisses with his own eager lips, he would not let the elf show Will the decadent, exciting ways of elven love.

He tried to tell himself that the thing embracing him was not even human and not even whole. Quicksilver spoke through Silver's mouth. How fractured had this strange creature become? How much did Silver desire Will?

Or was it Quicksilver, lord of elves, who tormented Will thus, attempting to entrap him with Silver's favors?

Staying still, staying turned away from Silver's love,

took all the power of Will's mind, all the strength of his heart.

And through the fever of his struggle, through the sweat that sprang at his neckline and ran down his back in hot rivulets, through the veil of pleasure at Silver's soft kisses, Will heard Quicksilver's voice. "Will, do you have a female deity in your society? A female priestess? A vestal virgin?"

Will thought of the virgin that the papists had worshiped and shook his head, "No, that was the papists, that was . . ." He could speak no more.

In his thoughts, he saw the image of the virgin that his mother had kept hidden in the attic, the chaste image of plaster, painted white, the female form swathed in mantels and voluminous dress.

In his mind, the image divested itself of mantels and cloth, and appeared naked, triumphant. Her form was Silver's—the large breasts, the tiny waist, the flare of hips—beautiful and tempting and clad only in silky white skin.

Silver's perfume enveloped him like a heady dream, and saliva gathered in his mouth, as though he were a child longing for some tempting confection.

Silver's arms, reaching around him, unbuttoned his doublet and reached beneath—hot, hot through the flimsy, worn-down material of his shirt.

Will thought of Nan, but he was like a man drowning and reaching for a shadow. He had no more power to fight off Silver than a drowning man to beat back the raging waves.

"Milady," he said, his voice strangled. "Milady, please."

Was he pleading for her to leave him alone, or was he pleading for the full satisfaction of the desire she aroused?

He didn't know. He couldn't say. His blood ran like a mad spark of fatuous fire along the taut strings of his nerves.

Her hands had found their way beneath his shirt. Her long fingers struggled, blind, with the fastening to his breeches.

He flinched from the heat of her fingers and yet wanted her touch, wanted to feel her whole body burning his, cleansing from him his rough human stuff, replacing it whole with the pure, purged metal of elvenkind.

"Milady," he said again, in a begging tone.

And Silver's laughter, her clearest laugh, which he hadn't heard in ten years, echoed triumphant in his ears.

His thought subsided beneath currents of desire, his hands groped the stuff on the table.

Suddenly, beneath his hand, clear, hard, he felt something that shouldn't be there.

It felt like sealing wax. It had that rigidity, that round shape.

Will opened his eyes, lifted his hand, looked down.

On the table was a folded letter, sealed with a round, rough blob of red wax—with no impression of a ring.

The outside address—he read it as if through a fog, while Silver's hands, which had finally triumphed with the tie of his breeches, ventured beyond, beneath, more intimately. The outside address on the letter read: *To Master Will Shakespeare, from his wife, Anne.*

Nan.

It was like a glass of freezing water poured over Will.

He heard Silver's small protest as he pulled away from her, while, in the same step, he tore Nan's letter open.

Nan had written to him—or rather, Nan had asked someone to write to him. Nan rarely did this. She didn't like to admit that she couldn't write, nor did she enjoy asking someone more literate to write her words. Not unless there were something terribly wrong at home.

Will thought of his father, who was aged and declining inexorably toward the grave.

His breeches, undone, slid down, over his stockings, to puddle around his boots.

But he ignored them and pulled the pages apart, unfolded the cheap paper.

The handwriting was Gilbert's, his younger brother's.

Nan, who could not write, would not have bothered Gilbert, a promising glover apprentice, with anything short of necessity.

Silver, who'd been pushed near the bed, now returned, her hands stretched and open to engulf him.

Will held his arm out, as far as it would go, and kept her at a distance, while he stepped away, hampered by the breeches around his ankles.

Nan's letter was short—as they all were, Nan being a woman of very few words. It said that there had been a fire in Stratford. She said the fire had been odd, starting everywhere at once after a show of fairy lights. Many houses had been consumed, and though the Shakespeare house had not been touched, helping their neighbors had emptied the Shakespeare pantry. The season was bad, food scarce and expensive. If Will could not send some money, Nan could not see how Hamnet could be kept in school, since the fees were so outrageous. She signed herself his loving wife.

His loving wife.

Will felt the weight of the coins in his sleeve, felt the ridicule of his breeches around his ankles. He set Nan's letter on the desk.

He looked at the date. Before Silver had come. Yet Silver had never told him of the fire. Why not?

This being who'd almost seduced Will for the second time had not told Will about this fire that had endangered Will's family.

Will reached for his breeches and pulled them up.

Silver clung to him while he fastened them, and she

tried to find his lips with her blindly searching ones.

He turned his face away. All excitement was gone. All enchantment, all the feel of new wine in his mouth.

Nothing was left but stony cold and dark suspicion.

"Madam," he said, his voice loud enough that Silver stopped her attempts at kissing him. "Madam, what have you done?"

The beautiful silver eyes blinked, close to his, with every appearance of confusion. "Done?" she asked. It was her own voice, not Quicksilver's. Her own voice, small and slight. "Done?"

"The fire in Stratford, why did you not tell me of it?"

She flinched as though slapped. She stepped back, she swallowed hard.

"The fire," she said. "I didn't want you to know." Her long, white hand went to her neck, as if to ease an invisible constriction. And Quicksilver's voice slipped out of the parted lips. "I hoped you'd never find out."

Rage boiled within Will. Silver had hoped Will would never find out. Anne's letter spoke of the fire starting everywhere at once, suddenly, after a show of fairy lights.

Fairy lights. Gorge rose in Will's throat. "Milady, what have you done?" he asked.

Silver laughed. Her eyes wild, she charged toward Will, open arms inviting, bosom rising and falling. "Forget the peasant, Will," she said in the voice of a drunken woman, in the voice of a madwoman. "Forget the peasant and be mine. I need you, I. I've never ceased loving you."

Will met her enthusiasm with his coldness, met her eye, and did not flinch from her desire. But he pushed her away when she would cling, and he would not relent, he would not let her touch him. "You tried to kill my wife, madam. And I love my wife."

Silver stepped back. Her laugh rose higher and higher,

to peels of insane amusement. "Kill your wife? Kill your wife, Will? You think that of me?"

Tears tainted her voice and Quicksilver's voice, the two of them mingling as they came from behind Silver's hand, which covered her mouth.

"Kill your wife? You think me such a villain? Oh, curse you, Will Shakespeare. Why did I think you'd help?" She gathered her arms around herself, as though protecting her body from an invisible wind. "I have other help. I have others who love me better. I'll seek them out."

On those words, suddenly, Silver disappeared, leaving no more than a sparkle of light in the still air of the room.

Standing in his empty room, Will took a deep breath of relief. His trembling eased. He swallowed. He would send Nan some of this coin. Hamnet, his only son, must be kept in school.

At the back of his mind, something wondered where Silver had gone, something worried for Silver. But he wouldn't think about it. Not any more than he would think about the odd dream, about the three Fates, the three creatures who'd given him such an odd mission.

His chances of being a great poet lay with Marlowe, not with Fairyland.

Scene 25

❧

The fairy palace. Elves lean on columns or sag to the floor. Some lie on the floor itself, looking dead—though their chests still rise and fall with breath. Healthy elves kneel by the ill ones, and try to revive them, or just wail their fate. Ariel stands in the middle of the room, her dress torn, tattered, and askew. She looks pale, her lips tremble, and her eyes have that haunted quality of someone who's lived through the end of the world.

Ariel heard the voices around her: the moans of despair, the cries of the afflicted.

And all of it echoed within her head as, "Lady, lady, lady," a cry for help she could not give.

She felt her people's plight and she reached for the reserve of her power, for the fire of power in the hill, to heal the blight.

But the power had waned and burned low: the steady fires had become embers only, beneath a fall of ash. Like a flame beneath a cooling rain, elven power sputtered and burned lower and with a colder light.

The light wouldn't warm, the magical power wouldn't spell, and there was nothing else that Ariel could do to heal her people.

In her despair she'd tried herbs and spells, and hallowed, ancient medicines of elvenkind.

Nothing worked.

The hill power burned ever lower, and more elves died.

At her feet, on the white marble floor, lay Lord Slate, hardly breathing.

Lord Obsydian had died yesterday. Lady Pearl, Obsydian's wife, mourned still even as she herself bent under the blight. Soon there would be no changeling left alive in the hill.

Tears ran down Ariel's cheeks, and her hands twisted at her dress.

"Milady?" a faint voice asked from behind her.

Turning, she saw Malachite standing nearby. His face looked gaunt and pale so that his skin resembled parchment stretched thinly over sharply carved ivory.

From amid the pallor, his eyes burned fiercely like emeralds in which the light caught. "Milady," he said.

Now Malachite would die, Ariel thought, and hurried toward him, supporting him with her arms so that he wouldn't fall.

He let go of the pillar on which he leaned and looked at her, as if from a long way off. "Milady," he repeated, and then his voice dropped, hesitant. "You asked for proof and I have proof."

"Proof of what?" Ariel asked. Then she remembered Malachite's insinuations, his wild plan to marry her.

She'd thought he was ill and raving. He was ill and raving.

Yet he had proof.

Proof of Quicksilver's betrayal?

Was Quicksilver's betrayal, then, causing all this?

But no, *she* raved. It was naught. A mad thing, a glitter of suspicion such as will catch the eye of a babe or the mind of an insane person. It meant nothing.

She would accommodate Malachite's mad humor and deal with him gently, for he was as close as Quicksilver still had to a brother.

Gently, she held Malachite up, feeling as though he, too, might at any minute vanish in a pile of dust, as so many changelings had.

She got him to the relatively deserted hallway before he managed to say, "Here, milady," and hand her a drop of water.

Looking within the drop, Ariel saw Quicksilver, saw him as Silver, smiling on another, a mortal, a young man. And not Will.

This was a redheaded young man, his body twined with Silver's in the rites of love.

It had come to this, then, that Ariel's lord—her lord's other aspect—would be a bawd onto humankind?

He had promised Ariel—promised—upon their wedding day that Ariel would be his only love, lifelong—a promise most uncommon for a marriage between near-immortal beings.

She looked at the image in the water and felt her heart break. Fool she was, she had believed in him.

Opening her hand, she let the water drop roll out of it, roll onto the floor.

Shaking, she turned to Malachite.

"The water . . ." she said. "Silver." She could say no more.

"Two of the small winged ones who remain alive got it. They went to London at my bidding," Malachite said. "And at my bidding did they find milord and take this image. It is a true image. I would have faked it if needed, but this is a true image." He turned to look at her. His hands trembled, and his lips, and though he'd found this proof himself, yet it grieved him, for his eyes filled with tears.

She patted his thin, emaciated arm that so ill fitted the uniform it had once filled.

She never doubted but that it was true, and her heart wandered, parched, a deserted landscape, with no relief in sight.

So it was true that Quicksilver loved her not.

The love she'd sought her life long, the love she'd thought she'd earned ten years ago, that love had been a lie, no truer than illusions spun in a lazy moment.

Oh, curse the day. Curse Ariel with it. Curse all of fairykind with such an inconstant king who, breaking his vow, had broken his realm.

Ariel scant heard Malachite, who pleaded for her hand in marriage, for an alliance that might heal fairykind.

She must find Quicksilver.

Her hands dealt roughly with the soft fabric of her gown. Her mind reached for the power of Fairyland, while she remembered Quicksilver's glittering magical pattern.

But she could no more home in on that strong beacon than she could get the full strength of the hill power.

She felt the darkness of in-between worlds enfold her, and for a moment, she thought she'd be forever stranded in this no-world, this world of shadows and dreams between the fairy world and the human.

The cross between the two spanned the distances of human land through an abyss outside time, and through this abyss elves could move quickly like a dream, between two points in the human world, no matter how far apart.

The instrument they used for this travel looked to elven eyes as a graceful arched bridge, spun of purest light, shining like gold in the dark night.

The elves called it the bridge of air.

Tonight, before Ariel ever set foot on the glittering construction, she noticed that it seemed grey and dimmed, and that it swayed as though on unseen winds that made it appear and disappear into flickering unreality.

Midbridge, in the ascending curve of her journey, she faltered.

Quicksilver's voice echoed in her mind, as if he'd been beside her, as if he'd touched her gown and yelled in her ear, "Betrayed. I am betrayed."

Something dark and cold passed by Ariel, moving fast.

The bridge wavered and splintered.

The pattern of Quicksilver's power vanished from Ariel's mind.

She tried to grab for it, but she could not.

She felt herself plunge through boiling air and freezing loneliness, through screaming silence and pulsing nothing.

Materializing, she saw towering buildings around her, and muddy street underfoot. She smelled the reek of mud and refuse.

Her lord she did not see.

Scene 26

❧

Marlowe's lodgings. On the bed, on his stomach, Marlowe lies. His clothes are tattered, and bloodstained, as is his hair, his hands, and his face.

Before Marlowe awoke, a feeling of heaviness hung upon him, a heaviness such as one feels when illness is imminent, or when, having slept after a great grief, one wakes to find that grief undiminished.

Awakening, opening his aching eyes to the bright light of day that entered through his sparklingly clean windows, Kit smelled a heavy scent of rotted flesh and spoiled meat.

Kit's head pounded with the worst of hangover headaches. His mouth tasted like a midden. Every small movement of his waking body caused untold agony, as though a fiend armed with a sharp dagger worked him over, pushing the tip into his skin, piercing his muscle.

Aching, Kit lay still for a while.

A heaviness rested upon his stomach as though hot lead had been poured down his unsuspecting throat in the night.

He moved not, and he hurt, and hurting, he thought he might as well move.

He pulled himself up on his arms. Hellish pain ran from his wrists to his shoulders. He rolled on his side and lifted himself on his elbow. As he rolled, the cover of his bed came with him, glued by a black substance.

His head pounded and he saw everything as if through a dark veil.

Memories of the night before came in fits and starts, each of them hurting as much as physical movement.

Kit remembered Silver, beautiful Silver, and he remembered their lovemaking, though both mind and heart flinched from the memory as a man will from touching a bruised spot.

After that, his memories became tangled, like a thread that the cat has got at.

There had been . . . an elf? As Kit tried to bring his memories into the light, they shied away farther into shadows and his head pounded to the rhythm of his vain efforts.

Kit sat on his bed and tried to shake his head, but stopped as sharp pain made it feel as if a dagger were worked into his left temple.

Had he got drunk? He might have. He probably had. Yes, no doubt about it. Wine was the best way to drown the sorrows of lost love, and perforce, Kit had used it. And in his cups, what had he done?

He cradled his head in black, sticky hands, and wondered how and with what he'd got himself so befouled. He remembered the mud of the alley, the stickiness of it, but this stickiness was greater than any clay, and it had the heavy smell of the slaughterhouse.

The thought gagged Kit, his throat working against his mind and body to close and stop all thought, all breathing, with overpowering nausea.

He must wash. Whatever it was, he would wash, and it would be gone.

Getting up on unsteady legs, Kit reeled to the wash-basin. His landlady, or Imp, had set a large pitcher full of water on the dresser, beside the metal stand that supported the ceramic washbasin.

Kit poured water into the basin, dipped his hands in it, preparing to splash at his face.

He stopped. The water in the basin, into which he'd dipped his hands, had turned a deep, dark red, like freshly spilled blood.

Kit looked, with wide open eyes at his sleeve, caked with the same black that had been on his hands.

Blood. How had he got himself all over blood?

Had he gone to a bear baiting? To get this fouled, he'd have needed to participate, to climb into the ring with the dogs and tear at the bear with his teeth and hands.

Gagging with nausea, he washed, with his eyes closed. Rushing to the window, he opened it, and threw the blood-ied water out of it, to the outcry of inattentive passersby whose clothes got bespattered.

Had Kit himself got bloodied in this way?

But so much blood. . . .

He poured fresh water into the basin, and again washed his face and hands.

The water ran out, and wrapping himself in a blanket, Kit ran to the door of his room to ask for more.

Upon first touching the iron doorknob, Kit flinched, be-cause the thing felt red-hot, and burned his palm. Why and how had this knob got heated?

He shook his head. No matter. Grabbing his blanket around his fast-blistering hand, Kit used a tip of it to pro-tect his hand as he opened the door.

With the door open, Kit hollered into the cool, dark interior of the house for more water to be brought. While waiting, he paced back and forth the narrow confines of his room.

How could this have happened and what had he done?

The memory ran away from his searching, hiding in the shadows of his mind, whence nothing but evil dreams come to torment unknowing reason.

Imp's small, curious face showed at the turn of the steps, looking up into the hallway and into Kit's eyes. He carried a large pitcher in his hand.

Kit bowed, wondering how fearful his countenance might be, if it were as blanched by fear as his heart was and said, "I thank you, I thank you. I got fearfully spattered. A dog run over by a cart and I was near and suffered the blemish. A dog. A dog. Thank you for the water."

But Imp, setting down the jar, lingered, and watched Kit with wide and worried eye. "Are you well?" he asked, his serious eyes looking like the eyes of Kit's mother watching over him. "Are you well, Kit?" He wrinkled his small nose. "It smells in here."

"A dog," Kit said, not sure what he said. "Go, Imp, go. I must clean myself."

Kit closed the door after Imp, wondering at his not remembering all this blood, wondering at how much he must have drunk the night before.

With a pang of inconsequent guilt, he remembered that he'd never told Imp the story the boy had requested. Where had he been instead?

He removed his clothes and, scooping clear water with his hands, threw it at his face, only to see it fall, again, as crimson as blood.

Looking at his reddened hands still filled him with nausea.

Deep from within the house, he heard steps and noises, and stopped, imagining the constables, come to arrest him for capital murder that he couldn't swear he hadn't committed. Although if he'd murdered someone, perforce the creature had too much blood in him.

He thought he heard a knock upon the door but, listening, heard no more. "Whence is that knocking?" he said, startled upon saying it, and chuckling in his throat, he trembled at the sound.

"How is it with me?" he said. "When every noise appals me? What hands are here?" He lifted his hands from the basin and stared at the red stains in amazement. "Will all great Neptune's ocean wash this blood clean from my hand? No, this my hand will rather the multitudinous seas in incarnadine, making the green one red."

Talking to himself, he knew himself already mad. And with a plot hanging about his neck like a noose and the plot he must create to counteract it, Kit couldn't afford to be insane. He must make madness sane, or else die, and thus end all reeling thought.

The knocking came again, steady, and this time it seemed to Kit that it came from his door.

Not Imp again!

With shaking hands, he reached for the knob. With shaking hands, burning pain making his hand smart, he opened the door.

"Come," he said. "Come and I'll explain."

But neither of the two people who strode through his open door was Imp.

One of them Kit had seen the day before: it was none other than soft-talking, false-dealing Robin Poley. And with him, beside him, was another face that Kit knew well: Ingram Frizer, personal servant to Lord Thomas Walsingham, so recently Kit's own patron.

What could Ingram's presence here mean? Was Lord Walsingham also deserting Kit? Was Walsingham part of the conspiracy to make Kit entrap Sir Walter Raleigh? Did Thomas Walsingham, for whom Kit had written such inspired lines, mean to have his pet poet killed?

With what mind Kit could, with his teeth chattering a

mad dancing tune to his aching brain, Kit tried to think of his cunning plan.

He was going to turn in Will, surely he was, and save himself and Imp, and he would marry Madeleine, and . . .

Poley strode in, dressed in an immaculate cream-colored velvet outfit, and matching suede boots so clean they looked as though they were meant to stride on the very clouds and step on the moon. He held an immaculate glove in a spotless, gloved hand, and smacked it upon his bare hand, as though with contempt. The ruffle on his shirt bobbed. Behind him strode Ingram, his plain face set in square discord, his dark, serviceable wool suit betraying no stain.

"We'd love to hear your explanation, Master Marlowe," Poley said, and raised a brow at the stained water in the smeared basin, at the blood-splattered room, at Marlowe within his blanket.

Together Ingram and Poley wrinkled their noses at the smell in the room. Poley waved his glove in front of his nose, and Ingram twisted his lips as though he would be sick.

Kit stepped back, in his grubby blanket, tripping over his own feet as he backed up. "I thought . . ." He swallowed down the evil taste in his mouth. "I believed . . ." He stopped short of saying he'd believed them, one or both, to be Imp. He did not want to mention Imp, he didn't want to remind them of Imp's existence. He rallied, and managed to stand and square his shoulders, despite the blanket, despite the blood on his hair, despite the smell of carrion in his room. "What should I explain?"

Poley smiled. Walking around the room as though it were a curious exhibit open to the public, like the rooms of Bedlam where the lunatics were displayed for a few coins, Poley looked debonair, controlled, amused. "*Signior* Marlowe, *bon jour!* There's a French salutation to your French slip. You gave us the counterfeit fairly last night."

"The counterfeit?" Marlowe asked, composure gone. "The counterfeit, I?"

How did they think he had fooled them? Had they found that John Penry, poor pious John, knew less of conspiracy than of heresy? "Good morrow to you both. What counterfeit did I give you?"

"You escaped our watch," Ingram said.

Slow, direct Ingram walked right up to Kit and poked a large, sausagelike finger into Kit's chest. "Last night. You gave us the slip."

Poley only smiled. He stood over the basin. "What was here, I wonder?" he said. "It looks like murder, murder most foul. Is it murder, Marlowe? Did you murder someone?"

Marlowe shook his head.

Had he? And if he had, why would he reveal it? The slip? What did Ingram mean? Had they been watching him?

Oh, but if they had, then they knew of his visit to Will's lodgings. How could he convince them that his visit to Will had been in the service of the state, in the service of uncovering conspiracy?

Shaking, Kit wondered if they'd even now arrested Will and put him to the question. If they had, then no chance remained of Kit's making it appear that Will was guilty, no chance of escaping the noose closing around Kit's neck.

Kit shook his head, not knowing at what, and opened his mouth to deny an accusation never made.

Poley sighed. "No use lying to us, you know. We will find the truth. Even if you so cleverly evaded our vigilance yesterday, even if you seemed to vanish into thin air outside that door in Shoreditch, we know you didn't vanish.

You went somewhere. You did something. You'd best tell us what."

He looked directly at Kit with his frank, amiable gaze that was neither.

Kit shook his head again. "I know not what you mean," he said. This, at least, was true.

Poley stepped away from the basin with its red contents. Looking vaguely disgusted, he waved his glove in front of his nose once more.

At the gesture, the glove's perfume, like the smell of a hundred pines, diffused through the room, mingling with the smell of carrion.

"Come, come, Marlowe. We are not fools, though you think us so. All your running and all your lying, the stories of a big conspiracy. There's no conspirator here but you, Marlowe. Let us be well understood."

"But, John Penry . . ." Kit started.

Robin smiled. "Aye. John Penry. The songbird sang a song treasonous enough, of desire for Scottish rule and Puritan control. But no hint of a conspiracy in that song, no hint of a false note. The false note is with you, Marlowe, and you must be made to sing. Tell me, will it take the wheel to draw your song from you?"

Once more, he'd got close enough to Kit that their faces almost touched. Once more he started rounding on Kit, around and around and around. "The wheel stretching your body, breaking your legs, wrenching loose every bone from its appointed socket." Poley smiled and walked around Kit.

Thus, in a display of marvelous beasts from overseas, had Kit Marlowe watched a slick black panther go round and round a dog it meant to eat.

And like the dog, Kit Marlowe turned, trying to keep the panther within the scope of his sight. "I know not what you mean," he said.

"Well, then, I'll speak plainly," Poley said. "For I'm a plain man." He grinned at this, enjoying his own, self-conscious irony. "Let me remind you, then, Master Marlowe, that a paper has been discovered amid your affairs, written in your hand, a paper proclaiming offensive heresies and denying the divinity of our lord and savior, Christ. This paper you wrote while at Cambridge. What say you to this? Who taught you heresy? We have it on good authority that you learned it from a nobleman, even one close to the Queen. Who was it? Name his name and you shall go free. Do not, and you shall sing upon the wheel, even a higher and sweeter song than was ever heard."

Kit sweated. It was back to the paper again, back to the accusations of heresy. Enough to hang him. Enough to burn him.

He couldn't remember such a paper, but it might well have existed. In those days, Kit hadn't yet learned caution.

And if they had that paper, there was no escape.

And yet . . .

"This paper must be old," he said. "And some two years hence, I had a roommate in this very room. Thomas Kyd, who wrote *The Spanish Tragedy*. A loose-living sort of fellow. A theater man."

Before Kit had finished his sentence, before he had finished turning in yet another innocent lamb to the maw of official condemnation, a smirk passed between Poley and Ingram Frizer.

Kit followed that smirk, mutely, feeling his hopes sink with it.

"Thomas Kyd was questioned," Poley said gently. Too gently. "Questioned before we came to you. For it was amid his effects that the damnable paper was first found. And he said it came from you." He seemed to think on this point and ponder it. "But he only turned you in after much wracking, Kit Marlowe. I fear your friend Tom Kyd will never write again. There's one who doesn't turn in his friends lightly. . . ." Poley shook his head, as if at the folly of such loyalty. "As for you, Master Marlowe, you'll come with us. If you wish to put down that ridiculous blanket and—"

Tom Kyd questioned? Poor Tom Kyd, broken at the wheel. Not a genius, never a promising playwright, and yet what a friend he'd not been when they'd shared a room.

And yet, Kit himself had been ready to turn him in.

Guilty for a sin he'd never got to commit, afraid for what was to come, Kit muttered, "But, masters—"

A small creature burst into the room, a fury of whirling fists and kicking legs. "You'll not take him, cowards. Not unless over me."

"Imp," Kit yelled. "Imp, to your mother."

But he might as well have ordered the devil to absolution or the Protestant Queen to the Pope's bosom.

Imp threw himself on Poley, biting and gouging, his small hands scratching at Poley's fine clothes.

Ingram Frizer grabbed Imp by the back of the collar and lifted him from the ground, looking on him as though Imp were a noisome insect.

Imp wrinkled his face in rage, but his lips trembled on the verge of tears.

Kit, thinking only that the child was in danger once more, said very softly, "Go to your mother, Richard, for Jesu' sake."

And as though the unusual exhortation, the unusual name, had scared Imp more than screaming, more than the strange men in Kit's room, Imp's face melted like wax too near a flame.

The wrinkles of anger turned soft. Rage became grief, as tears overflowed the wide grey eyes. The child took a deep breath and sobbed. "They'll take you," he said.

"Aye," Kit said. "And best for all."

To Ingram, in a tired voice that yet betrayed the certainty of being obeyed, Kit said, "Put him down. He's not worth your time. You may have me."

Poley laughed. "Thus is the wiley playwright brought to bay. So easily does his run end. Good Kit, kind Kit will do what we wish for the sake of this cub. Should we take the cub then as surety?"

Kit swallowed. He shook his head. Oh, let Imp go free, and then Kit would do as Kit best pleased.

"No," he said. "No. You need no surety. I'll say what you want me to, or else die."

Ingram put the child down.

Poley waved the child away, "Go," he said. "We know where to find you, should Master Marlowe not behave."

Imp hesitated on his normally fleet feet, turned and stared at Kit, and said, "They're going to take you."

Kit shrugged. He couldn't answer. He felt tears prickle their way beneath his eyelids, felt them tighten a knot at his throat.

And then, as Imp walked slowly away, as Poley and Frizer stood there, he felt something else.

He heard an inner voice, clear, in his mind. "Let me," it said. "This is ridiculous."

And then a dark tide, a dark wave, engulfed Marlowe's mind and took over his thought. From that dark wave, words ensued, spoken by Marlowe's mouth but not, for that, his—or at least not his in any conscious sense.

What was this, then? What was this thing? It was as though another Marlowe lived within Marlowe, another creature within his deepest bosom, a smoother talker to his smooth-talking ways.

He could hear convincing arguments, rolling honeyed, word upon honeyed word from his tongue. They assured

Poley and Frizer of Kit's verity, of his certainty of a conspiracy.

Yet, the words in themselves would not be enough. The
words would not suffice to turn the threat from Kit's door.

But with the words he could feel magic flowing. Magic
sparkling and tangy on the tongue and soft-stinging on the
skin.

Whence came the magic? How had Kit got it? From
his fabled ancestor, Merlin?

And how could he use it thus, so easily?

He told Frizer of the big conspiracy about to be uncov-
ered, and suggested that Frizer, Poley, and a servant of
Milord Essex should all meet at the home of Mistress Elinor Bull, in Deptford.

Kit had no idea why Deptford, nor what he intended to
do at such a meeting that would keep the threat from his
door, keep him out of jail, and keep Imp safe.

Like a lame beggar trailing after a good walker, his
mind limped after his lips, unable to catch up to the wit
of his speech.

The meaning of the words sank in slowly. Kit was not
used to listening to himself speak, even less to having to
think of what he meant. How smooth he sounded, he
thought, how plausible.

How strange this.

Had Kit finally become two? Had his soul, ever divided
between love and hate, violence and beauty, finally
cracked?

He knew not what tale he spun, yet he saw Frizer and
Poley exchanging looks, at least half convinced.

Inside his own mind, Kit Marlowe screamed in despair.
His mouth was not his to control.

He would save his life, that was true. Maybe even Imp's
life in the bargain.

But what would become of Kit's mind?

His reason followed his words, made sound of them. Links fell together in his mind and he second-guessed his own ideas. Elinor Bull, a distant cousin-by-marriage of Queen Elizabeth herself, was not at all wealthy. For adequate compensation, she'd long permitted her house to be used as a safe house by the secret service.

Kit could get all those men there, each of them a servant of a member of the Queen's inner circle.

The Queen herself, who now resided at Greenwich Palace, near enough to Deptford, was known to have grown fearful and suspicious in her old age.

If word of the meeting got to her ears—and Kit had enough acquaintance at court to ensure it would, the Queen would perforce eavesdrop on it. She'd probably send her men to arrest the whole group and let it be sorted out later. In which case, Kit could convince the Queen herself that these men were involved in a plot.

Yes, he'd trust his silver tongue to let him walk out free.

Even better, the Queen, who was said to be suspicious enough to often check such meetings and conspiracies herself, might come by herself to Deptford. In which case, in the confusion, Kit might well walk away free without even the need for being interrogated.

Kit Marlowe's headache was gone. Never had he felt so lucid. Never had he spoken with so facile a tongue.

It was, he thought, as though he'd become a whole new man, one with a magical capacity to manipulate others.

After Poley and Frizer had left, Kit finished washing and dressed himself.

He wrote letters to his acquaintances at court and sent them off by messenger. In each one he hinted at the events to take place in Deptford, and at a plot against the Queen, ensuring he said nothing too clearly.

If he succeeded, not only would the Queen's suspicions

be awakened, but other people's, too. Aye, when he was done, Elinor Bull's house would be creeping with so many spies that none would be safe. None save Kit Marlowe, himself.

He smiled and set about ensuring that Will Shakespeare would be in Deptford, too—one more lamb that must be led to the slaughter for Kit's safety.

And yet Kit, a stranger to half of his own mind, wondered what he was saving and how long before the tear in his soul widened and he went quietly into that good night of oblivion, from which there would be no return.

Scene 27

Will's room. He sits at his table, writing. His hands are covered in ink stains, as is the top of his tottering writing table. The papers in front of him are an unsteady tower, displaying scrawled writing and checks and crosses aplenty. He has pushed back the sleeves of his black doublet. His eyes are circled in dark, bruised rings, and sweat drips from his forehead.

Will paused in his writing and looked up at his reflection, dimly seen as a ghost upon the grimy surface of his window.

His eyes looked back at himself, full of fear.

Fear, he realized, had installed itself at the back of his mind when he wasn't thinking, and from there mocked all his endeavors at poetry.

He surveyed his work, his crossed-out sentences, his poor constructions, his unreliable storytelling.

No, this would not do at all. Will couldn't seem to work poetry and sense into a single piece.

And yet, Will had been given money for this piece in advance. What would happen if he displeased the nobleman who'd so financed him?

Nothing good. Worse yet, Will would see himself without disguise, and know that he truly was no poet, no smooth weaver of words.

And yet Kit Marlowe made it all look so simple.

Perhaps Will should ask Marlowe's help. He'd been so kind so far. Yes, Will thought, he would ask Marlowe.

Will had no more than stood up and started toward his door when someone knocked on it.

With his hand on the latch, Will thought he smelled, through the door, a smell very like Silver's. He hesitated.

The thought of Silver—of how forward, how brazen the elf lady had been—still made Will tighten his fists in anger.

That Silver thought he would be an easy mark. She dared . . . She'd endangered Nan. Oh, the idea galled him.

The knock sounded again, impatient.

It could not be Silver, after all.

Silver would have come in by now, through her magic means.

He opened the door.

Marlowe stood on the precarious perch atop the steep staircase.

"Ah, the man himself," Will said, and smiled at Marlowe's slightly startled expression. "I would have gone see you."

"You would?" Marlowe asked.

He sounded eager, anxious, perhaps a little too eager and anxious. Yet, he smiled smoothly and his grey eyes sparked with humor.

Will could swear that the heavy smell of lilac came from Kit. Was this the new fashion in London? Perfuming oneself like the fairykind?

No, normal people didn't know of the fairykind. Will forced a smile, pushed thoughts of the supernatural world to the back of his mind, and told himself he wasn't worried about Silver.

"Truth is," Marlowe said and grinned, "I need your help, friend Will."

Friend. The great Marlowe had called Will his friend.

On this word, Will forgot his misgivings at Kit's strange smell.

Kit had called Will his friend, and on this friendship, Will dared fund his hopes. Certainly more than on any world of fairy.

"I will gladly help you with whatever you need," he said, and smiled. "Provided you lend me *your* help."

"Surely, you may have it. But I need your help, Will, with attending me to Deptford tomorrow, where I am to pay some creditors a debt I owe them. I would fain have a friend to witness my payment. Would you do it, Will?"

Will looked up. "Gladly," he said, and smiled. As he said it, he thought of all the times he'd been cozened in London, of how easily he'd so often lost money and purse and all.

But surely, he had no reason to fear this from Marlowe. Marlowe had already proved himself Will's friend so many different ways.

Will had been afraid that Kit wanted him to second Kit in a duel or to help him with a rhyme, or something else for which Will was wholly unqualified. But to witness something, Will would do well enough.

His eyes were as keen as the next man's.

"And you wish my help with . . . ?" Kit prompted.

Will sighed. He explained his interview with the Earl of Southampton and how unwarrantedly the earl had thrown money at Will's untested poetical skill.

"I've never tried anything this long before," Will said. "All my poetry has been sonnets, and I find that when it comes to this, I am wholly unprepared.

"No, I was not born under a rhyming planet, nor can I woo fame in festival terms. As for the subject, well . . . Leander the good swimmer, Troilus the first employer of panders, and a whole bookful of these quondam carpet-mangers, whose names yet run smoothly in the even road of a blank verse, why, none of them will do for my verse.

"Marry, I cannot show wit in rhyme; I have tried: I can find out no rhyme to 'lady' but 'baby,' an innocent rhyme; for 'scorn,' 'horn,' a hard rhyme; for 'school,' 'fool,' a babbling rhyme; very ominous endings."

Kit laughed.

He touched Will's arm, and in that touching, Will saw the palm of Marlowe's hand and upon his palm a mass of bubbling blisters and burst blisters that showed raw flesh.

He stared at Kit's hand till Kit looked down at it. Will would swear Kit looked surprised.

But how could a man take such injury and not notice?

Kit grinned at Will, a forced grin that showed all his teeth and made him look, for a second, like a wolf, a carnivorous animal. "Aye, a burn, a burn, 'tis but a burn I got, upon my spit." He grinned, but his grin seemed hollow. A baring of teeth against the world and little else besides.

After Kit had left, that grin haunted Will's thoughts.

How strange it all seemed.

Will had wanted to come to London and be just like Marlowe, and now he wondered if Marlowe was as Marlowe wished to be.

Scene 28

❧

*Tyburn Square, midday. Walking back from Will's, Kit
chances upon an execution. The gibbet is mounted mid-
plaza. Official-looking buildings—their stone facades imposing, hem in a varied crowd of Londoners. Vendors
and sightseers circulate. On the gibbet, a man stands
between two executioners.*

Kit stopped, staring at the gibbet.
He knew the man upon it, the condemned man.
His mind, searching, brought forth a name.
John Penry.
Kit reeled. John Penry had been arrested, of course and
Kit knew he would be put to the question. But—con-
demned?
Around Kit, the crowd milled and swirled. A few souls
watched the gibbet attentively, but most were there to see
and be seen, for a meeting point, for a break in routine.
"An orange, ducks, fresh off the ship from Spain," a
woman in dark garments said. She thrust a golden fruit in
front of Kit's eyes. "A penny, no more."
Kit sidestepped the proffered orange.
His eyes upon Penry, Kit neared the gibbet. The exe-

cutioners were demanding a last speech of the prisoner, last words, a token of repentance.

Kit stared, fascinated.

But for him, Penry wouldn't be here. But for him, Penry might be well, walking the streets, minding his own business.

How he looked, too, how much thinner than he had in his Cambridge days. And his arms hung in an odd way, within their long black sleeves.

Had Penry been broken on the wheel?

Something like remorse tore at Kit's conscience, something like empathy knocked and hit upon his mind, with no more effect than a moth flying at a glass window.

He felt sorry for John Penry, well enough. Yet Imp must be saved.

With that thought he looked up, and chanced to meet Penry's eyes, and in Penry's eyes he saw a hint of recognition, a hint of gratitude.

Gratitude that, of all their Cambridge fellows, Kit had come to see Perry's end? Did Perry think Kit had come to lend him comfort? Oh, Kit wished he could.

Something almost like a smile twisted Penry's pale lips up, and he nodded toward Kit as he said, "God have mercy on us all. I have no more to say. God have mercy on us."

On those words, the executioner kicked Penry's feet out from under him.

Penry fell from the platform that supported the gibbet, and the noose tightened.

A spasm, a gasp, and a body was carrion.

A nearby church bell tolled dolefully.

Kit felt something—breath? life?—fly by. It felt like warm wind, like a sigh.

Old women rushed to the gibbet to collect pieces of hair and bits of nail, to conjure upon.

That pious Penry should be used for black magic beggared the mind.

Disgusted, heartsick, not knowing why he felt so hollow, Kit turned and walked away.

He had been forced to turn Penry in. He had been *forced* to save himself and Imp, and Penry was their only salvation.

But no matter how many times Kit repeated these words to himself as he walked amid the festive crowd, he kept hearing Penry's earnest words, *God have mercy on us all.*

Kit shivered and wished he still believed in a God of whom to ask forgiveness for what he'd had to do.

Scene 29

❧

A narrow Elizabethan alley, dark and murky. It is night-time and only faint lights of candles shine in some windows of the five-story buildings that loom overhead, on either side, obscuring the view of distant stars, the cloud-flecked sky. Through this alley, Kit Marlowe stumbles, looking like a somnambulist.

It was midnight on the clock, and Kit bumbled abroad, not sure where he was, walking the dark alleys in a restless search for something he couldn't understand.

He felt as though some dark core of his soul had control of his body, and he were a horse that the rider impelled on and on, with fierce jabs of spurred boots.

The horse knew not where he went, nor did Kit. Only that he must go on and on, breathless and tired, longing for sleep, longing for rest, but craving . . . craving something he could not explain.

Where was he?

Nothing in the houses around him gave him a hint of his whereabouts. The houses were tall and narrow, not mean looking, and yet not great. The muck underfoot smelled no worse than it did anywhere else.

And yet, muck and mud though it was, it made Kit wish to lie down in it and sleep, he was so tired.

Stumbling he walked.

Thoughts of life as food, of living force, living strength as fodder, streamed through Kit's mind, making him crave—crave life? Or death?

Kit thought of John Penry's shuddering, suspended from the gallows. He trembled and licked his lips.

Impulses and thoughts for which he had no name used his body for their lair.

Ahead, on a low window, a light flourished.

Kit rushed, put his hand against the door trying it.

What would he do if he got in? Why did he wish to get in? Thoughts of biting living flesh, the longing for fresh blood upon his tongue, the need for something else— for the life that fed some power, some weakening strength. His thoughts shocked him before they were even words.

Kit pulled his hand away from the knob. What madness was this? What was happening to him?

"Soft, soft," Kit said. "What light beyond yonder window breaks. Oh, go to sleep whoever you be, maiden or man, or child. Go to sleep, stay safe from such as me."

His words, though whispered, caused a sound behind him—a scuffling sound, like someone faltering.

Kit turned around.

And looked into Poley's well-meaning eyes, Poley's calm, agreeable face.

Poley and Frizer had followed Kit again.

Kit felt no fear, not even anger. Instead he thought of Poley's and Frizer's lives and strength, and craved those lives like men crave food.

Kit craved killing.

Tear, slash, eat, drink the life, Kit's mind cajoled, and Kit recoiled at the thought.

Kit bent his knees, not knowing what he did, and

crouched like an animal about to spring. His hands formed into claws, and as he watched, he swore his nails grew longer.

Something else must be happening to him, something visible in his countenance. Kit's features must have changed, because Poley whispered softly, "Marlowe." And Poley's voice vibrated with trembling fear.

Kit looked up at Poley and bared his teeth, feeling a crazed hunger, a need to kill. His reason screamed at him to stop.

What loss would Poley be? Kit told his reason. *What loss to the world?*

He could not answer. But just then, as he meant to spring, someone else approached, walking stealthily along the narrow dark street.

Someone who'd been following Poley as he'd been following Kit?

This person walked with uncommon majesty, with squared shoulders, a confident stride.

It was a woman dressed in a gentlewoman's attire.

Closer, she hesitated, her commanding walk halted. A beam of moonlight shone up on her features.

Kit saw the face on every coin, the pattern handed out for painters to draw the Queen.

The Queen.

But the woman wore a dress of dark stuff, and her hair was white and not the red of the portraits, and Kit wasn't sure.

Within him the demand for life and strength, the hunger for the fluid substance of breath that had consumed Kit's inner core, now changed.

It changed to a snickering joy, a happy smugness.

Kill the Queen, the something whispered. *And the game will be won.*

Kit screamed at his own thought, a muffled, strangled scream.

The woman stopped, staring at him.

She screamed at whatever she glimpsed in Kit's features. Something within Kit sniggered.

The Queen blanched. Her hand at her throat, she stepped back. Poley half moved forward, and made as if to talk to her.

Kit stared Poley in the eye. Poley stepped back, against the wall, actually paling in his fright.

The Queen turned and ran unsteadily down the street, tottering on high heels.

Yet, Kit recoiled, sweat beading on his skin. The fight within him was similar to the fight within a starved man who wishes to fast.

Part of him wished to kill Elizabeth, wished to kill her more than he wished to draw the next breath.

Yet Kit knew what would happen if Elizabeth died here, without descendants, with no appointed successor.

The many pretenders to the throne, from Spain and France, Scotland and principiates in Germany, would fight it out for England's Crown. When they were done, there wouldn't be two villages in the country that would be together, belonging to the same lord.

Whence this dark need to kill her, then? Whence this craving?

His own impulse scared him. He arrested his movement with overwhelming willpower.

Scared of himself and his darkest urgings, Kit Marlowe stepped back, and back and back.

Poley, across the alley from Kit, made a strangled cry, and took to his heels as Elizabeth had, running down the alley with scarcely more grace than the aged Queen.

Kit stepped back farther. Everything in him clamored for pursuit of this strange prey.

Tear, slash, eat, drink the life.

One more breath and Kit would give in to his urges.

Horrified, he took another step back.

With a clang, he fetched up against the broad iron gate of a private backyard. The gate felt red-hot against his flesh.

Kit screamed.

His hands and his neck, unprotected, burned, as though they touched fire.

Even through Kit's velvet suit, his lawn shirt, heat shot in continuous, searing waves.

Kit lacked the strength to move away.

The metal in the iron gate burned him like pitchforks heated by a thousand fiends in the deepest hell.

Blue light burned all around Kit, as the pain leeched away his strength and power to think.

Kit screamed as the pain shot through his every limb.

Slowly, he fell to knees that could no longer support him.

Contact with the iron gate broke.

His pain still lingering, his strength drained, he rolled on the muddy ground, screaming his torment.

When he came to an exhausted, trembling stop, covered in the foetid mud of the alley, he was soaked in sweat and weak, and his heart thumped within his chest like a prisoner begging for release.

Yet his brain was clearer than it had been in a long time.

Kit thought how strange it was that he'd wanted to kill the Queen. How strange the thought that had crossed his mind that he'd set such a careful trap for her in Deptford, and she'd just walked into him in this muddy alley.

He hadn't set a trap for the Queen, had he?

How foolish the Queen of England. How foolish the woman who'd been so cunning and intelligent in her youth. How could she go walking alone in the dark, where anyone might kill her?

Where Kit might have killed her.

Kit didn't mean to kill the Queen, did he?

He blinked drops of sweat from his eyes.

Poley and the Queen were nowhere in sight.

And Kit had finally fractured, he thought, finally become cleft in twain. The spy prone to secret violence and the poet enamored of beauty were now truly two, two souls fighting within the one narrow body.

"I'm for Bedlam," Kit whispered, picking himself up from the muddy ground and surveying the damage to his suit with despair.

Yet little by little, at the back of his mind, the hunger for life resumed, stronger, harder, beating with horrific insistence against Kit's reason.

He must have life. He must have living force. He must kill.

Tear, slash, eat, drink the life.

"Kit?" a small shadow asked from a doorway two doors down. The little shadow detached itself from the building, revealing a child with auburn hair, wearing a fine blue velvet suit.

His eyes widened in surprise and shock at Kit's appearance. He looked up into Kit's eyes.

"Kit?"

Scene 30

❦

Ariel walks, dazed, along the same streets where Kit has been. Her eyes are sunk within dark circles brought on by sleeplessness, her dress rent, her whole countenance pale and pinched. She walks with a staggering, limping gait. She looks as she is, a fairy princess lost in an all-too-mortal world.

Never so weary, never so in woe. Ariel's legs could not keep pace with her desires, and longing for her absent lord tore at her heart.

She dragged her feet, which hurt, unaccustomed as they were to walking this long.

Under the moon of Elvenland, the bright sun of mortals, she'd sought for Quicksilver all over bustling, heartless London.

Her aching, blistered feet, her muddied dress, stood as mute witnesses to her travails.

She'd labored in vain.

She'd braved the unaccustomed smell of refuse in her nostrils, the shrieks of children, the barking of dogs, the grunting of pigs—all of them feral, all of them uncontrolled. She'd seen executions and duels, and rough men had attempted to lay rougher hands on her.

But she'd not found the pattern of power on which she homed, her sovereign lord, King Quicksilver, whom she'd come to seek, whom she'd come to upbraid with righteous anger.

Did he hide from her? Should she not have come looking for him? Did the hill need her more?

And yet without Quicksilver, the hill could not be healed.

Without Quicksilver, Ariel could not be happy.

And she remembered, with icy fear, his cry of *I am betrayed.*

Had that truly been his cry? And if so, what had happened to Quicksilver, to Ariel's brave, loving lord?

Ariel felt tears prickle in her eyes. If he had been attacked, by whom had he been attacked?

Had he been doing battle all this time? Had she been misled as to his intent and actions in London?

Her feet hurt and bled and she wished she could fly, as she was wont to do in Arden's green woods. But the power of the hill, like a distant, vacillating light, would not allow her such strength as would lift her toward the heavens. She must continue crawling, footsore, upon the earth.

If only she could use her scrying power, and look through the surrounding houses for her lord. But no, she could not.

The houses hereabouts contained too much iron, too much cold metal, too much that was poison to the gentle ways of elvenkind.

No, Ariel must go on searching for her lord with her eyes only, on foot and sleepless, through the smelly, dark alleys of London.

Ahead of her, something stirred, a feeling of power much like hill power, a feeling of power much like Quicksilver's.

But this power felt corrupted, dark, blotched with evil and full of unrighteous anger.

Had Ariel then driven her lord to this?

Oh, let it not be so.

Let her find him, unscathed and clean and capable of coming back to the hill. Never again would she complain about Silver. Never again would she, with shrewish voice, tell her lord how much she wished he were a proper man, a proper male elf and not a mad weathervane shape changer.

But as she walked closer, around the tall house ahead of her and into the narrow little alley behind it—so narrow it barely admitted her—she saw the marks of darkness and evil stronger and stronger upon that power that glimmered softly at the end.

She knew the whirls and twists of that light radiating ahead between the two buildings like she knew the lines and etchings on the palm of her own hand.

From the same place, a very small scream emanated, followed by grunts and sounds of pain.

Ariel's elf senses knew what the sounds meant.

Ahead someone died.

Ahead, someone else drank that life.

But only dark creatures fed on death: the Hunter fed on the life of wrongdoers, as did the dogs of the Hunter and other, minor spirits linked still to the darker spirits of antiquity who used to be thus fed.

"Quicksilver," she said.

She walked into the alley.

In front of her was a scene such as she'd never before witnessed, such as took her a while to comprehend.

On the ground lay a small body—it looked like the body of a child. It had been gutted and lay still, obviously dead.

The thing stooping over the child raised a bloodstained face.

It was a human face, yet it looked—for just a moment—as though it possessed a snout and powerful jaws such as hadn't been seen on any creature on earth for millennia.

As it straightened, the snout disappeared, and the man standing in the clearing would have looked normal, and perhaps comely, were not it for the blood dripping from his face, staining his clothes, pasting his hair.

He grinned at Ariel, showing bloodstained teeth.

"Not Quicksilver, milady. That fool is where he should have been consigned by our long-suffering mother at his birth. In Never Land, where, amid the potentials never realized, his magic shall drain away to nothing. He shall trouble us no more."

Though the voice issued from a mortal's mouth, from the bloodstained lips of a man that Ariel had never seen, never met, yet the voice, smooth and honeyed, velvet soft and flowing like fresh water, was well known.

"Sylvanus?" Ariel said, and stepped back, step by step, while her mind reeled.

It couldn't be Sylvanus here, Sylvanus the parricide, Sylvanus the murderer who had killed his parents so he could inherit a throne that rightly belonged to Quicksilver.

It couldn't be Sylvanus.

But the bloodstained creature bowed and chuckled. "At your service, milady. Though you'll soon be at mine, for I have now secured this body you see.

"With it I shall slaughter the maiden, thus unseating the three aspects of the female element through which humans and elves perceive reality. I have already, with your husband's help, dethroned the Hunter, my erstwhile master. I shall soon be the master of creation, and creation's sole arbiter."

He walked toward Ariel with a smile.

Quicksilver was in Never Land? Quicksilver had helped unseat the Hunter? Why should he? Could Ariel trust this creature to tell the truth?

Yet, if he wasn't in Never Land, where was he? And how had Quicksilver helped Sylvanus defeat the Hunter? Had Quicksilver, then, been so lost, so alone, that he must go and find camaraderie with his evil brother?

Sylvanus's new body stepped nearer Ariel. She could smell the blood and gore in his clothes, and face, and hair.

The closeness of pure evil sent a shiver through the queen of elves.

What did he mean to do to her?

Nothing good. That much was sure. Nothing good.

Quickly she raised her hand.

She reached for the weak power of the hill, that burned through her like a dying fire, all embers and smoke. Wishing it stronger, she interposed it, as a flickering shield between her and Sylvanus.

Sylvanus attacked. His raised hand came down, and she heard the crackle of magical power, the fizzle of a transportation spell that didn't work.

If she hadn't shielded, she, too, would be in Never Land. Lost to this earth, lost to any hope of helping Quicksilver.

How had Quicksilver been so surprised by his brother that he hadn't shielded? Did he know this mortal? In the scant light the man's hair looked red and his form and figure reminded Ariel of what she'd seen in a water drop, disporting with the Lady Silver.

Trembling, she called the power of the hill back to her. It burned into her, slow and hesitant, like a light with insufficient fuel, like a candle near its end.

Whatever the blight was that consumed the force and strength, the nobility and fine flower of elfdom, it tapped, too, the force that the elven queen could use for defense.

Her shield would not endure. She would not be able to use it again.

Yet Ariel saw Sylvanus raise his hand.

She would not have the power to shield from him.

In a fright, Ariel turned and ran away, heedless, into the dark night and the labyrinthine alleyways of London.

She ran because she had no power to fight. She was doomed if they met again.

The laughter of the creature behind her told her that Sylvanus knew this as well as she.

Scene 31

ॐ

Kit Marlowe's lodgings. Again, he lies on his bed, on his stomach, and the bed and himself are covered in blood.

Kit Marlowe didn't startle at the way he stuck to the covers, nor at the reek of blood on his nostrils, nor at the dull ache behind his eyes, nor at the feeling that something horrible had happened the night before, something that made the world a black place and his earth a hell.

He woke with a curse upon his lips, and opened his eyes to the dull throb of headache and the grey light of an overcast day coming in through the diamond-shaped panes of his window.

Curse the world and the light and the blood, and his headache, too.

From the street below came the calls of wakening vendors, the hurried footsteps of apprentices and laborers, children's voices raised in high, playful calls.

Kit's head throbbed.

He rolled over slowly, bringing the blanket with him, stuck to him by a dark substance that smelled pungently of blood and that Kit didn't even attempt to tell himself wasn't just that.

He pulled the blanket away from his body—he appeared to have lain abed naked—and amazed himself only with how calm he felt, how collected.

Horror experienced once is horror indeed: marvelous, strange, and terrifying. Horror experienced twice is dim and dull, an occurrence expected if not welcomed.

Thus step by step do humans become used to their own sins.

Thus had he become used to the idea of betraying friends and strangers to the secret service.

He dragged himself up, out of the bed, and set his feet firmly on the floor. His clothes were by the door, in a blood-soaked heap. Another suit ruined.

Walking like a drunkard, or one only half awakened, Kit tripped to his basin, and poured in it the cool clear water from the jar, dipped his hands in it, and watched the water turn red. He realized, with a sob—caught in his throat and suffocating his emotions—that the desperate revulsion of the day before was not gone. It had turned, instead, to an aching despair.

He remembered craving life. He remembered. . . . What had he done?

All this blood, whose was it? Where had it come from?

Some knowledge, some thought, tickled at his mind, but he could no more hold it than a child's hands can hold the fluttering butterfly.

He'd done something horrible. The darker half of his mind had committed what crimes? Oh, better die than live so.

And yet no.

All the things he'd done, to avoid death, and now he'd play the roman fool and fall upon his own dagger?

No. It was useless.

Kit was damned, and he might as well learn to live with his damnation. Indeed, he was not all that unusual. As

he'd written in Faustus, Kit had for some time suspected
that all on earth were in some way damned—Hell was
empty and all the demons were here.

"I am in blood steeped so far that, should I wade no
more, returning were as tedious as go over," he told himself reasonably, while staring at his hands, submerged in
the red liquid in the white porcelain basin. "Strange things
I have in head, that will to hand; which must be acted ere
they may be scanned."

He rinsed his hands with prosaic calm and, opening his
window, poured the bloodied water out.

A man, passing underneath the window, jumped away
and shook his fist at Kit.

What land this England was, what a place this London
that a man might pour blood from his window, early
morning, and draw from it no more censure than if he'd
poured the nightly wastes from his chamberpot?

Bemused, Kit returned the basin atop its stand, and
poured fresh water into it, then cupped his washed hands
with fresh water to wash his face.

It was when his hands touched his face that he remembered clearly.

He remembered John Penry's prayer and his death.

He remembered the dark alley and Poley's face, and the
woman behind him.

Had it really been the Queen?

Marlowe couldn't help remembering her face, and jux-
taposed on his memory of royal portraits, it looked like
the same woman.

He'd long heard that the Queen, mistrusting all, her
mistrust growing as she got older, often personally followed the high personages of the court, spied on them,
and sometimes, attired as a peasant woman—unguarded,
alone—sneaked out of her palaces and her keeps, to listen
to the common people.

But that she'd spy on her own spies . . .

Kit washed his face, and watched the water run red into the basin. He'd almost attacked the Queen of England with his bare hands.

Why? He couldn't even guess. His mind was a foggy mirror that reflected nothing to his questing reason.

His father had been right, then, when he'd told Kit that too much reading would disturb his reason. Kit almost smiled at the thought, and yet indeed, here he was covered in blood and without knowing how.

If he was not insane, then who was?

He finished the water in his jug, opened the door, and called for more.

He hoped Imp would bring it, and not Madeleine. He could not explain to Madeleine how he'd got all bloodied again. Had Imp told his mother about Kit's state the day before?

He heard steps coming down the hallway. Heavy steps. Madeleine's steps.

She came into the room, perfect and immaculate, in her starched apron, her impeccable white cap, and looked at him with raised eyebrows, but said nothing.

The two heavy water jars which she carried she set on the floor beside his washbasin.

"Thank you," Kit said dismissively.

It must be fear, fear of the secret service and their revenge, that drove him insane. Well. After tonight he'd be free and safe.

He must go to Southampton House and gather from his friends anything else Will might have said to incriminate himself. He must go to Will, himself, and attempt to gather more details of his life that could be woven into a plausible conspiracy.

Though Kit couldn't quite forget Penry's death, nor ab-

solve himself of that guilt, yet he must go on. His life—
Imp's life—depended on it.

This work was not so different, after all, he thought, as
he poured fresh water into the basin, from the work of
writing plays about events and people so long gone that
all that remained of them was a vague impression, like
that left by a foot on the river side, and then erased by
the tide.

Now he must weave treason where there was none.
Only those who died in this play would not come back
again for a final song.

He washed his face, and looked up.

Madeleine stood by the door, staring at him.

Her thin lips writhed, and her eyes had a strange, trem-
ulously tearful look.

"Yes?" He kept his voice cold, trying to prevent an
outburst of Madeleine's righteous morality.

Her plump hand searched inside her dark sleeve, and
came out with a handkerchief. She touched it to her eyes.

Oh, not crying, Kit thought. Aloud he said, "Madam, I
am in a great hurry. You must know—"

"It's Richard," Madeleine said.

"Imp?" All plots vanished from Kit's mind. The thought
of Imp brought a flinching inside, as though thoughts and
memories skittered away from a raw wound.

"Imp," Madeleine said, for the first time calling the
child by that name, and taking her handkerchief to her
lips, and covering her mouth with it. From beneath the
handkerchief, she spoke, with a voice that trembled and
fluttered. "Have you . . . have you seen Imp yet today,
Kit?"

Make that two firsts, for his given name hadn't crossed
her lips in many years.

"No. I've not seen him. Is he ill?" Alarmed, Kit advanced toward her, hands extended, meaning to shake sense out of her.

But she backed away from him, step by step, and he remembered his gory condition, and that he was naked.

He backed away from her. "Speak, woman. What has happened to our son?"

Her eyes veiled, she sniffled her righteous sniff, and for a bare breath Kit thought she would chastise him for calling Imp his son.

She did not. Instead, she let out a sob and said, "I've not seen him this morning. His bed is unslept in. And all over London people are talking of animal attacks, of beasts who savage people. And you come home . . . all over blood. I thought . . ."

Now Kit thought, too. His head spun. That feeling of dread, that curious flinching that his mind effected when he pushed the memory of last night to the fore, now seemed ominous.

The need for life force within him. The taste of blood on his tongue.

He had a vague idea of bodies: of apprentices and prostitutes, of incautious people caught out of doors and devoured.

Devoured by Kit?

"Go woman, go," Kit yelled. And in a frenzy that mirrored more than masked his internal strife, he pulled on clothes, blindly, and rushed like a madman out of the house.

Scene 32

❧

A London street market, ending in a copse of trees. Tents flutter in the street. Peasant women display bread and fruit within them. A man walks through advertising pamphlets.

To Will's accustomed eye, the street market in Holly-well Lane looked half-empty, just as the streets between Hog's Lane and there had looked still sleepy and vacant.

It was the plague, making her rounds, Will supposed.

Yet, with it all, there was a sense of excitement in the air. Perhaps a sense of fear.

"A bear, I tell you, a bear," a portly gentleman screamed as Will passed.

Will ducked past the gentleman and his interlocutor, whose conversation he'd obviously interrupted, and walked past bread and fruit uninterested.

His destination was the copse of trees, as it was old enough to, maybe, harbor elvenkind.

Will couldn't believe he was looking for Silver, yet remembering their last conversation, he felt anxious for the sovereign of Elvenland.

He'd gone out and paid his overdue rent early morning and, by means of a pedlar, sent money to Nan.

Now he should be writing, but he couldn't sit still. His anxiety for Silver would not abide.

What she had said about female goddesses and Sylvanus was too close to the half-remembered fragments of Will's own dream. He must find her.

"A fox," an older man, with white whiskers, pontificated. "It will be a fox. With the crops as bad and the weather as perturbed as it's been, foxes must find their rabbits few and far between."

"But a fox maul a human? And to death?" a younger man asked, facing the older.

What did they talk of?

How excited everyone looked, how red of face, how fleet of tongue. And on every tongue, the same words *maul, death, animal, attack.*

Though sparser by half again than usual, people were more animated than ever.

It was the same combination that Will had ever noticed during bad plague years. Despite the boarded doors, the taverns and ale houses emptied by the plague, yet people laughed louder and talked in higher voices.

Will had thought it the bravery of life in the face of death. But maybe it was something else.

And there were those disturbing words. *Maul. Attack. Animal.*

Animal attacks in London?

"Ten people mauled in the night in London," a pamphleteer called, waving papers. "A demon dog roams the city, punishing our sins and eating the entrails of sinners."

Could this have anything to do with Silver?

No.

Now that Silver was gone, now that her presence didn't make itself offensive, her seduction inescapable, Will found it hard to even believe Silver had started a fire.

Silver was malicious and often a prankster. But her pranks were in the manner of a child who played practical jokes upon his elders. She might be irresponsible, and trample, with immortal feet, mortal morality and mortal tradition.

But when had Will known her to be evil and seek the death of mortals? No. Not Silver. Nor Quicksilver either.

And her manner had been so odd, so disconnected— Quicksilver's voice whispering dire warning in Will's ear, even while Silver's body pressed itself on him.

Something was wrong.

As a Sunday child, able to feel what passed beyond the curtain of mundane events that hid the supernatural from other men, Will could feel something wrong, could sense it as a disruption.

Something disturbed time and space alike. Something moved between this world and the elven world. Something . . .

He'd tried to ignore it. He'd still ignore it, if he could.

But something was rotten in London, and Will's intuition whispered to his reason that he should not have turned Silver away, that he should have listened to Silver.

What if Silver were dead now?

But how could she be dead? Silver was immortal or as near it as made no difference.

Will neared the trees, shaking his head.

"A wolf, I tell you, man, it was a wolf," another man shouted. "I caught a glimpse of it, early morning, a grey thing with bristling fur."

"Bahh. Wolf, this far in London. When have you seen a wolf, sirrah? Dog, more like, gone feral," the man's interlocutor argued.

But in Will's mind, an image formed, of a wolf-dog

with a square head, powerful jaws, and a squat, low-slung body.

Sylvanus. Hadn't Silver said something of it?

Will must find Silver. Without thinking, almost without trying, Will followed his instinct to the only place in London where he could imagine an elf hiding.

It was a large abandoned garden.

There, beneath the centenary trees, lovers would go to tryst, poets to write, and youths to practice archery.

Its green shadows hid all, and kept all safe, save sometimes from the stray arrow.

Bending his steps to it, thinking it was the only place in London where Silver might be hid—at least if she were still alive—Will crossed Hollywell Street market and soon found himself at the edge of the trees.

And smelled something soft, sweet—a lilac smell. No such plants grew hereabouts.

He thought of Silver.

Looking through the trees, he saw a glimpse of white, a shape that, from this distance, looked as feminine and imbued with grace as Silver's.

Should he continue? Silver needed him. He knew that as he knew himself alive. Yet, how offensive Silver's behavior had been; how she'd tried to trick him into an affair.

Silver might well have caused the Stratford fire that had almost killed Will's family.

No. Silver would do no gratuitous evil and some reason there must be for her odd almost-seduction.

Approaching the vague white form in the garden, he called out, "Milady?"

The woman who turned to face him looked too slim and blond and too delicate to be Silver.

Will recognized fair Ariel, Quicksilver's indomitable

lady, who'd dared marry and try to tame the King of Fairyland.

"Milady?" Will asked again, his voice rising on a note of his own uncertainty.

That Silver would come to London to seduce him made sense, or at least Silver sense in that Silver—or Quicksilver for that matter—was a cold, magical being never much interested in anything beyond its own good, and its own wishes.

But Ariel? Ariel had ever been better than the other elves, who often resembled immortal spoiled children who went about the world throwing tantrums and flinging their toys about.

Possibly Ariel had come to London in pursuit of her errant husband. Possibly, Will's assessment of Silver's intentions had been right. Possibly, Quicksilver had argued with Ariel, and as a revenge, Silver ran rampant through London, intending to seduce balding poets of dubious genius.

Yes, and possibly the animal attacks were nothing but that—attacks by a bear tired of serving for human amusement and being flogged for human entertainment.

And yet, up and down Will's spine a chill worked, like an icy finger moving and pointing and moving on, an icy finger that forecast other things colder and more terrible than what had already happened.

"Milady?"

Ariel turned. She looked drained and pale, her eyes sunken and dull, and leaking tears. "Who—" She wiped her eyes on the back of her white sleeve that, now that Will thought about it, looked more frayed and far greyer than an elf's sleeve should look. Her mouth formed a slow oh, as her eyes showed signs of recognition. "Nan's husband," she said.

Will, who had been known by worse epithets, bowed and smiled.

Nan herself, who, ten years ago, had spent some time captive in Fairyland, had told Will that of all the multitudinous, changing, possibly evil creatures she had met, Ariel was the best, the most humanlike.

The daughter of a human and a high duke of Fairyland, Ariel was an orphan whose only brother, Pyrite, had been killed ten years ago.

Now Ariel advanced on Will, hands extended, looking as threateningly enthusiastic, as animated of purpose, as Silver. Only her purpose didn't look like seduction, her enthusiasm extended not to Will's body.

Her small pink lips strived to form a smile, against the downward pull of her grief, as she closed the distance between them. "My dear Will," she said. "Have you seen my husband?"

Will blushed, as naturally he would, in remembering how he'd last seen Quicksilver and under which guise.

"Two days ago, milady, two days ago and she ... Silver ... She ..." He floundered, neither his pronouns nor his language equal to telling Ariel what he thought Quicksilver's intent had been, or Quicksilver's purpose, or even why Will had thrown him out. "I asked him to leave, and he did, for I thought his purpose ill," Will said.

At this, Ariel withdrew her hands, and a fresh burst of tears issued from her eyes, fountainlike, while her small foot, in a muck-covered slipper that looked like it had once been mother-of-pearl, stomped the dirt of the garden. "Oh, cursed be this," she said. "Cursed."

Will took a step back, because when elves cursed things, it might very well be more than just an expression of distaste.

But Ariel's cloudy-day eyes lifted toward him, as fresh water issued anew from the wellsprings of her grief. "I

believed so, too, milord, I believed so, too, save that I . . .
Since coming to London I've started to think otherwise,
and then yesterday . . ." On these words and whatever recollection they evoked, tears ran down her face in such a
flood that they drowned out her voice, and make it squeak
with uncertain accents. "I saw Sylvanus in an alley and
he said . . . He said he had sent Quicksilver to Never
Land."

"Never Land?" Will asked.

"A place . . ." Ariel struggled, her lips working to form
words that human language didn't accommodate. "A place
that never was, never will be. A land of shadow. A cold
land. Any elf lost in it will die by his second sunset there,
his energy and magic dissipated beyond recall."

A fresh burst of tears issued from Ariel's pansy blue
eyes.

Will, not believing himself that he was doing this—
encouraging an elf—offered Ariel his arm.

"Milady, you're not well," he said. "If you wish to
come to my quarters, you may rest there." He thought of
his landlord, briefly, as Ariel's hand clasped on his arm,
but then he threw caution to the winds.

Ariel, with her restrained, high neckline, was no more
likely to invite assumptions of her being a harlot, than was
Will himself.

Should the landlord complain, should he ask, Will
would say that Ariel was his widowed sister, come to town
to consult with him on some family business.

Surely, Ariel's crying eyes, swollen with tears, gave the
truth to recent widowhood. Will shivered. He hoped Ariel
wasn't widowed.

Silver was in Never Land? Oh, he should never have
sent her forth, should never have repelled her. Would she
die so soon?

By sunset this day, he thought. But she'd tried to seduce him. Yet she'd warned him also.

And how could Sylvanus catch her unawares? Didn't she know his tricks and accustomed ways?

She'd said she was going to someone who'd help her. She'd said . . .

Will's head reeled with guilt and worry.

Ariel's hand upon his arm felt light, ethereal. The creature looked half alive. Something was indeed wrong, something that extended to Fairyland.

"How can Sylvanus be free, though?" he asked Ariel. "Was he not in thrall to the Hunter?"

Ariel shook her head, then nodded. "Aye, he was, and aye, how he came to be free I know not. Only, there was a menace, an alarm, and my lord went to look at it, and my lord returned not." She took her hand from his arm to wipe her tears on the back of her fragile-looking hand. "And Sylvanus says Quicksilver helped free him."

Will fished in his sleeve for his rumpled, clean kerchief and pressed it into her hand.

Ariel took it and wiped her eyes, with an almost impatient gesture. "Ever since Quicksilver left, the hill has been blighted, power draining from it like grain pouring forth from a slit sack." She was quiet a long time. "The servant fairies, the winged ones, have died. Almost all of them. And the changelings. . . ." She spoke in a whisper, a low whisper, for which Will was glad since, all about him, people walked, and there were people who lived in the area they crossed, only two streets away from Will's own lodgings, only too close, and neighborly enough to take an interest in Will's affairs.

Ariel's lips trembled. "Oh, Master Will, you do not know how we suffered."

Her little face—yet oval and pale and perfect—hardened. The lines of her delicate bones became more solid, more square, her little lips firmed into something like a straight line of disapproval.

She swallowed once, as though she swallowed things she wished to say but could not. "I thought it was Quicksilver's absence that did it. I thought . . ." She wiped her eyes, with decisive swipes of his handkerchief. "I know that he was unfaithful, that he disported himself with someone, that he . . . I thought it was that, nothing more, causing the blight in the hill, and I came to London to call my lord to his senses. But midway here, I heard him cry, as if in my mind, *I am betrayed*. And then I could not find him.

"Then, last night, in an alley, I saw Sylvanus, the evil one." Her voice trembled, and her arm also, within his grasp. "And he told me he'd sent Quicksilver to Never Land. And he told me that my husband had helped free Sylvanus from the Hunter and that Sylvanus meant to destroy both male and female elements—the fundamental essences of the universe that compose all that is male and female in both elven and human realms—and in their place weave himself, and thus master and control all."

Male and female elements from which all was woven. Will thought of his odd dream, the three women saying they were that of which all females were made. Was his dream then right? Was his dream more, then, than the foolishness that his mind spun in his sleep?

While Will's mind reeled at the thought, Ariel's small, determined voice went on, "And there was a child, the remains of a child, that this creature—this creature that was Sylvanus and yet not him but a mortal man—had *eaten*. Oh." Fresh tears burst forth, and Ariel covered her eyes in the handkerchief.

A child had been eaten. The animal attacks. The animal must have been a wolf-dog, a creature that Will had seen once, in unhallowed circumstances. In Will's mind, the square muzzle formed, remembered, with its cruel, massive teeth.

Will heard again Quicksilver's words, while Silver's sweet breath tickled his ear. He'd spoken of possession, of elves possessing humans.

So, Sylvanus had possessed someone.

Will thought of his impression that he'd seen the wolf in Southampton's garden. Had he been so near danger, and not known it?

But who could Sylvanus be possessing? And why? Even Quicksilver didn't seem to know that.

They had arrived at the bottom of Will's staircase and clambered up. Atop the narrow platform they squeezed, one against the other, while Will opened his door.

No one on the street below seemed to notice them, Will thought, and his landlord, duly paid from the Earl of Southampton's purse, now seemed less interested in following Will around and pursuing him. Or perhaps Will, his conscience appeased by the payment of his debts, imagined his landlord's prosecution of him less, and disdained to see the man in every shadow.

Inside the room, he led Ariel to the bed, and bade her rest.

As for him, he must find the reason for all these mysteries, and his poor mind was not up to all of it. It would take a genius.

Will thought of Kit Marlowe. Kit Marlowe, worldly Kit Marlowe, might not believe Will. Aye, he might even think Will was insane. But Will had to try. Kit was the only kind person Will had met in London, and kind Kit would have to help Will save human and elf worlds.

Will could always show him Ariel for proof of his words, and thus bid Marlowe believe in the impossible.

Scene 33

❦

The alley where Imp's body lies. It's undisturbed, abandoned in this isolated spot. Kit runs in, looking bedraggled, and drops to his knees on the mud.

The memory of the night past had guided him here, fogged and twisted though it was. He knew he'd gone down one road and then the other, and there it was the alley where he'd walked, the very gate he'd touched.

Though his steps shied away from it, he went into the alley, step by step, each step pushed against the instinct to stop.

His mind slid sideways away from full recollection, yet he knew this mud, these buildings. He remembered the hunger and the need, and the hot blood upon his tongue.

Imp's body lay in the mud that his dried blood had turned glossy black.

The boy might have been asleep, save only for his rent and tattered suit and the undeniable fact that the body had been gutted.

And yet Kit felt nothing. Nothing at all.

He advanced, step on step, sure this was a nightmare, sure it must soon end.

A high, keening scream of someone nearby disturbed him. He wished it would stop and looked around for the screamer.

But his throat hurt, raw and aching, and he realized that he was screaming.

He checked his scream on a deep sigh and in that sigh he heard his own grief and was shocked by it. A half-startled sob followed the sigh. Kit pressed his fist to his half-open mouth, surprised that such a sound should come from it.

He stood over Imp's body and met the sightless gaze of those grey eyes. Imp looked puzzled in death. As if he could not understand this visitation.

Kit's knees went slack. He sank to the mud of the alley. He reached gingerly, and lifted Imp's rigid, cold hand.

Only yesterday the child had come to him. Only yesterday. Kit's mind remembered, with remorseless clarity, Imp standing in this alley, saying, "Kit, you were late coming home. Kit, you promised you'd tell me a story."

And instead, what had Kit given him?

Kit stared, in dim-witted incomprehension, at the dead child. How could Kit have done this? How could he? What evil lurked in him? How dark was that dark side of his soul? How could Kit's nature have separated so—the poet and the spy thus divided?

And how could Imp be caught in Kit's internal struggle?

Only yesterday, the child had been alive, Kit told himself, as though by telling himself this he could turn back the clock and undo the damage. Alive, he'd been and now he was dead, and this transformation was too sudden and too final.

How could such a thing as life be lost forever in such a moment?

He held the cold little hand in both of his, and wished
it warm and moving.

"No, no, no life!" he whispered. "Why should a dog, a
horse, a rat have life, and you no breath at all?"

The glazed grey eyes stared at him but saw him not.

"You'll come no more. Never, never, never, never!"

From outside the alley, just steps away, came the
sounds of the city, the cries of fish sellers, a woman's
high, sweet laughter, a man's hurried steps.

How could life go on like this? How could no one notice that Imp was dead? Kit trembled with the force of the
grief and guilt that rose, battling, within him.

"Howl, howl, howl, howl! O, you are men of stone:
Had I your tongues and eyes, I'd use them so that
heaven's vault should crack," Kit said. "Look, how he
stares at me and all unmeaning. He stares at me as he so
often did, those grey eyes so reproachful and so knowing.
Well did he know and well should he have reproached.
Look what my keeping from the right hand the deeds of
the left has wrought. Look."

Steps had entered the alley and approached.

"Marlowe? Kit?" Will Shakespeare stopped steps away
from Kit. "I heard your voice and I—"

"Oh."

Kit saw Will's worn boots through his tear-distorted
vision, and glanced upward, and up and up and up, at
Will's face.

How Shakespeare had blanched. How shocked he
looked. Or how surprised, as though he thought Kit insane.

And well he might.

"What grief was here?" Will asked hesitantly.

Kit held Imp's hand and caressed it.

"My poor fool is dead. He's gone forever," Kit said. "I

know when one is dead and when one lives. He's dead as earth."

Will's well-meaning face looked like something carved in marble and worn down by time. He looked with horror on the scene before him. "But dead how? How did the child die?"

Kit shook his head. Hot tears ran scalding down his face and his throat tasted bitter with salt.

How had Imp died? How could Kit explain such horror to Will, the good burgher of Stratford-upon-Avon?

"Murder, stem murder, in the direst degree," Kit told Will's impassive face. "All several sins, all used in each degree, throng to the bar, crying all, Guilty! guilty! I shall despair. There is no creature loves me; and if I die, no soul shall pity me: Nay, wherefore should they, since that I myself find in myself no pity to myself?"

"But you'd never have done any such a thing," Will said. "Your guilt is misplaced, your grief distorts all. Who was this child?"

"It is mine only son!" Kit said, and as tears multiplied upon his face, he stroked Imp's blood-soaked hair. "Ah, boy, if any life be left in thee, throw up thine eye! See, see what showers arise, blown with the windy tempest of my heart, upon thy death, that kills mine eye and heart."

"Courage," Will said. "Courage. You'll get other children."

But Kit shook his head. How could he explain to Will that love of elven kind had cleft him from humans, that spying had separated him from reason, that his multitudinous treasons, multiplied, had turned him into this *thing*—this divided *thing*, a half of which had just killed the one love the other had to live for.

Looking up at Will through the distorting veil of tears, Kit wailed, "Oh, can'st thou minister to a mind diseased?"

But Will only shook his head and, practical and kind,

put his hands on Kit's arms, helped him rise. "Get up," he said. "Get up. We must take the body to his mother, must give him Christian burial."

And covering Imp with his doublet, blocking the sight of those piteous open, surprised eyes, Will made as if to pick up the child.

"No," Kit said. "No. I must do it. For he is my son, and the burden no burden."

How strange that now, when it was too late, he could recognize Imp and call him son.

Lifting Imp, Kit felt hot tears roll down his cheeks. "Alack. Poor Madeleine. Harsh she is, but she deserved not such a blow. And I bring her this grief. And yet I love myself. Wherefore? For any good that I myself have done unto myself? O, no! Alas, I rather hate myself for hateful deeds committed by myself! I am a villain: yet I lie. I am not.

"Fool, of thyself speak well: fool, do not flatter. My conscience hath a thousand several tongues, and every tongue brings in a several tale, and every tale condemns me for a villain. Perjury, perjury, in the highest degree."

Will gave him a piteous look, no doubt thinking that Kit raved from his grief.

Kit could not explain it. Oh, yes, it was grief and mourning, but it was guilt, yet stronger than both and well deserved.

Kit had feared so much and dared so much, he'd got involved in so many schemes and deceptions. He'd flaunted his meager knowledge, he'd braved hell itself, in betraying others for his son's sake.

And now, watch how from his own corruption his son's death had bloomed like a rank flower from an abominable stalk.

His gloved hand stroking at Imp's auburn hair, Kit felt his tears renew and spoke louder, as though to drown out the cold, implacable voice within his brain. "O, pity, God, this miserable age! What stratagems, how fell, how butcherly, erroneous, mutinous and unnatural, this deadly age daily doth beget! Oh boy, thy father gave thee life too rashly and hath bereft thee of thy life too soon!"

Grief washed over Kit's mind, bringing with it thoughts and images that might be unconnected, but that in his heart seemed to fit with this most mournful occasion.

Kit remembered his childhood in his father's small workshop: his clumsiness with the leathers and needles, the easy gallop of his mind in school.

He remembered the masters who had praised him, the neighbors who had envied him, the father who had scolded him for daring his mind to stray beneath the bonds of decent piety.

He remembered his scholarship and how hard he'd worked for his masters at Cambridge. He remembered his plays and what acclamation they brought, the recognition and the wild bouts of drinking and discussing poetry with the fashionable youth and other poets in the Mermaid.

And Kit had spied, and Kit had betrayed, and Kit had turned himself from what he was so that like a sleeve made of coarse stuff but lined with satin, he'd turned himself inside out to become something that he was not: a spy and a dandy, a knower of lies, a friend of corrupt aristocracy.

And through all this like a thread of gold in the base stuff of Kit's heart, Imp had run. Imp's innocence, his simple trust.

From the moment of Imp's birth, from the moment that Kit had beheld his own face sculpted small in another soul's possession, Kit had done everything for his son's sake.

The love Kit's father had denied Kit and that natural pride that did stem from having begotten his like and his successor, all that he had invested in Imp's skipping grace, Imp's quick mind, his irreverent wit, his daring ways.

And all for this. Bloodied meat in the mud of an alley. Nothing more.

Carrying the child, he walked slowly across London streets.

His appearance and bloodied face and hands made passersby recoil, but he noticed not.

He would go, like one on penance.

If another had done this, then Kit would have killed the other.

Yet, he himself had done it though he remembered it not, or only as through a glass darkly—the darker, secretive half of him was a murderer—and upon that must Kit take revenge.

At the door to his lodgings he hesitated, delaying the moment of grieving Madeleine, and almost laughed at his own scruples.

How considerate of others he had grown, now that there was so little to consider. He saw Will standing by, Will looking at him. Will had followed him here, and would follow him further.

Will, whom Kit had sought to implicate in his own treasons, in his dark plots. Will, who would have died, as surely as John Penry, to keep Kit and Imp safe.

Only there was nothing to keep safe anymore.

The motor of the world had come to a stop, and in this halt, by the sudden clarity of his grief, Kit realized that there was nothing left anymore, and no reason to tie Will, who was also a father, to the ill-fated coils of his fallen plan.

Kit put his bloodied hand out and surrounded Will's wrist with his cold fingers. "Leave me now, friend, leave me now."

Will said something of which the word "Deptford" emerged.

Remembering his plan and recoiling from it, Kit shook his head. "There's nothing to go to Deptford for now," he said. "Pray, friend, Will, stay away from it. Even if . . . Even if I should, myself, entreat you. Do not go there."

And leaving Will amazed on the doorstep, Kit turned and went in to discharge his fell duty.

Scene 34

❧

Will's room. The fairy queen sits upon the shabby bed, her torn skirt neatly arranged, her muddy shoes demurely together. Will comes in, looking stunned.

"Did you find him?" Ariel asked.

The question took Will by surprise. "Find whom, milady? Whom should I have found?"

"The man to help us," she said. She stood up. "You said you knew someone."

Will sighed. He closed his door slowly. His mind was full of what he had just seen. Too full.

He thought of Kit and the boy. Had Kit ever acknowledged his paternity? Will could not credit that, yet how fully did Kit reap the grief of the child's death.

How dubious the joys of fatherhood. Will's mind returned again and again to his children, Susannah, Judith, and Hamnet, who, in Stratford, might meet an evil fate at any moment and no one know.

"He won't help us," Will told Ariel. "His son has died. I couldn't ask his help now. He's insane with grief."

"His son?" The Queen of Fairyland stopped her pacing and stared at Will.

She trembled. Her eyelids fluttered, as though in the gale of memory. "His child? The child I saw . . . last night?"

Will nodded. "Possibly. It was a boy. If only there would be a way . . ." he said. He knew he spoke nonsense, knew he spoke out of a heart too full and a mind too drained. Yet he spoke. "Could not the magic of Fairyland . . . Couldn't the child live again?"

Ariel shook her head. Tears from her eyes fell down her face. "No, Will. That is beyond my power, beyond Quicksilver's even, even when the hill is at its most powerful. And now . . . And now Quicksilver himself is in Never Land and will be dead before this day is through, his magic drained by nothingness. And once he's dead, not all the magic of Fairyland, and not all my wishing, can get him back. We have limits also, Will."

"Oh, you magical creatures and your limits," Will yelled. He paced back and forth across his room.

Ariel watched him, her eyes wide, looking every wise shocked and alarmed.

He did not know whence his rage came, but he felt angry, an anger without measure. How odd this world, how odd this magic, that magical beings had to ask Will for help and depend on Will's good grace for shelter. How strange that these same beings who turned Will's life upside down and played upon him as upon a fiddle knew not how to save themselves.

"First the Fates, the three women, in my dream, telling me they needed me to save them," he said. "Then Silver coming to me in search of help, though she didn't seem to know what help she needed or why, and now you!" He flung the words at the queen's little drained face, her swimming blue eyes. "What good is magic if you must come to me, poor man that I am, a poor poet, a man without words or power, without magic, or money, or knowledge."

Ariel's mouth hung open. She sought to close it, looked as though she'd speak, but her eyes betrayed fear of Will's sudden rage.

"Oh, speak, tell me what a fool I am, why don't you?" Will said. "Tell me what a fool I am, because I'm not immortal, not one of your charmed circle. Milady, I wouldn't want to be immortal if in all my immortal years I learned so little and were so helpless as to need Will Shakespeare to protect me." He stood in front of her, his hands open as if to denote his impotent rage. "*Will Shakespeare,* forsooth?"

"Three women?" Ariel said. She reached a hand for Will's sleeve and grasped the rough wool between thumb and forefinger, as if she meant to hold him and yet were afraid of his reaction to her touch. "Three women? Pray tell, Will, when did you see three women?"

"In my dream," he said.

His rage left him suddenly, but something else remained. Anger still, at this fairy world, that so enmeshed itself in his world and yet would not help him, and could do no good. An impotent magic it was, a vain enchantment.

"In my dream, I saw three women. They said they were the three aspects of the feminine, part and parcel of all that's female in the universe. That humans had created them—*created* them—from their thoughts and dreams and their mad need to order reality."

In Ariel's eyes, something like hope quickened. Her breath came fast, through half-parted lips. She swallowed, and spoke again in a trickle of voice. "What did they tell you, Will, in your dream?"

"They told me they wanted me to save them," Will cackled. "I, Will Shakespeare, should rescue them from

Sylvanus, who meant to murder them. But lady, it was all a dream, a dream and nothing more." He stopped. Sylvanus was free. Sylvanus had injured the Hunter. Will remembered Quicksilver saying so. Was it only a dream?

"Murder the female element? Yes, Sylvanus spoke of it. I thought it was vain bragging.

"But if they felt it, if they came to you in your dream, then perforce he can truly do it. Will, what else did they say?"

"They said if I rescued them, they would make me the greatest poet ever alive," Will said, his voice drawing out, and drowning itself in empty despair. He made a face.

But Ariel stared at him, serious and solemn. "Then I say it's time you earned your fee, Will," she said. "Sylvanus is abroad and possessed of a human body, which he must be using in some way. Why would Sylvanus need a human body, Will? He could kill well enough without it. The pestilence, alone, that he unleashed upon the world, the blight of power that drained Fairyland, could have decimated half a continent. So, why did Sylvanus need a human body? To kill one of the female aspects, you say, but how?"

In his mind, Will heard Silver babbling about the female elements and sympathetic magic. He could feel Silver's hands upon him, her breath hot and sweet on his ear, and he could hear Quicksilver's urgent, businesslike voice speaking to him.

Will stopped his pacing, faced Ariel. "Milady," he said. "What's sympathetic magic?"

"Oh," Ariel said. "Oh." Her eyes grew big. "It's when you take an object and, prefiguring upon it a person, maim or wound the first object, to hurt the being symbolized. Did the three aspects speak to you of this? You must tell me, Will."

In a panic of anxiety, she grasped at his doublet.

He shook his hand. "No, lady, no. Silver—Quicksilver—told me about this. He told me that Sylvanus must be trying to perform sympathetic magic, and asked if we had a female priestess or a great female figure that could incarnate the female aspects, or one of them."

Ariel's mouth half-opened. "And do you?"

Will took a deep breath. His mind was clearer than it had been with Silver's arms around him, Silver's breath upon his face.

He thought about the maiden, the matron, and the crone.

There was only one woman in all of Britain who could figure one of them: the Virgin Queen worshiped by her subjects as much for her royalty as for her virginity.

"No," he said when he could get breath. "No. It's monstrous."

In his mind he saw the Queen, in her barge on the Thames, gliding regally over the black water, oblivious and impervious to her subjects' sufferings and the plague that ravaged the land.

Who could kill the Queen? Who could get past her bodyguards, her menservants, even her ladies?

But he heard again the conversation he'd heard in Southampton's study, the talk of how the Queen wandered abroad, mistrusting her counselors, spying and cheating on those who should keep her safe.

"It can't be," he said. "It can't be that Sylvanus would mean to kill Queen Elizabeth."

Scene 35

❧

Kit Marlowe's lodgings. He stands alone, still blood-
spattered, in the middle of his room. The bed remains
in disarray, the basin bloodstained. His bloodstained
suit lies crumpled by the door. From beneath the floor-
boards come the sounds of women mourning. Kit holds
his dagger.

"Whether 'tis nobler in the mind to suffer the slings
and arrows of outrageous fortune, or to take arms
against a sea of troubles, and by opposing end them?" Kit
spoke to the empty room, the dagger in his hands, the
bloodied suit. His own voice, little more than a whisper,
startled him.

He tested the dagger tip upon his finger.

He'd thought of this from the moment he'd first found
Imp dead. But the thought hadn't fully bloomed upon his
tired mind until he'd left Imp with his grieving mother
and come here, to his room, to the bloodied suit, the mute
witness of his crime.

If he could no longer control himself, if his body would
wander the night killing even the one dearest to him, then
Kit must die. It was the only way to avenge himself upon
himself.

Feeling the dagger tip, wondering how he would take the pain of its entry into his body, when he could barely stand a cut taken upon shaving, Kit sighed.

For how could he, who had so often written about death and murder and terrible events, in fact, be afraid of death? He who had sent others to the gallows, yet recoiled from an easy end. And why did he? What had he to live for?

He spoke, his words hardly moving the cold fear in his mind. "By my troth, I care not: we owe God a death: I'll never bear a base mind." But he didn't believe in God, and yet, from the darkness of his mind other thoughts issued. He'd murdered, he'd killed, he'd betrayed.

If there were a God—oh, what vengeance would not that God wreak upon Kit after death?

He thought of John Penry. *God have mercy on us all.*

Oh, if Kit only believed upon a merciful God.

But if he tried to picture God, Kit always saw his father, and he could not imagine mercy there.

"To die, to sleep, perchance to dream. Aye, there's the rub for in that sleep of death what dreams may come?" Would he dream of Imp? Or forever be shunned by the beloved shade? Oh, heaven if there was heaven, judge upon Kit's unworthiness for all but eternal torment and damnation.

He shook his head.

Holding his dagger gingerly, he looked at his own reflection in the polished round that served him as a shaving mirror.

What good was earth, when Imp was gone from it? What good living, when the future had died?

It was time Kit should brave the undiscovered country from whose bourne no traveler returns.

If nothing else were earned, at least Kit would not remain upon earth to be guilty of other deaths.

Holding the dagger gingerly, he stretched his neck and took a light swipe across his skin.

The skin parted, a line of blood appeared. Not deep enough to kill, not deep enough to bleed much, in fact not much more than a cut in shaving.

The sting from it protested along Kit's nerves, but he would not listen.

"It will not hurt," he told himself. "Or if it does, I'll scarce be alive to feel it. Cowards die many times before their deaths, the valiant never taste of death but once."

He raised his arm, meaning to bring his dagger down and cut his throat, and let that blood flow freely for whose continued existence so much blood had been shed.

But his hand stayed in midair, suspended, the dagger glinting in reflection upon the polished metal round.

Kit tried to pull it down, but it would not move. He tried to bring the edge of the blade down on his skin, but his arm would not obey him. "What wonder is this?" he asked. "What wonder? Am I such a coward, then, that my own limbs rebel at the thought of death, and won't do the deed?"

He tried harder, his hand barely moving.

In the metal upon the wall, he saw his mouth open, and though he meant not to speak, a voice issued through his lips. "You cannot kill yourself, Master Marlowe, for killing yourself would kill me also. I've been with you through a sunset. We are entwined, enmeshed, so far involved, that your body and my soul are one. And I don't *wish* to die."

For just a moment, Kit thought that it was himself talking, his other half, the dark, secret half that had turned in John Penry, that had killed Imp.

Then he remembered where he'd heard that voice.

The elf in the alley, that night.

Kit looked at his blistered hand and remembered the

burn of the iron gate in that alley. He remembered elves hated iron.

Kit was not an elf. But he was elf-possessed.

Kit's hair rose at the back of his neck as he realized what had happened. The elf had possessed Kit, taken over Kit's limbs.

Kit was a prisoner in his own body.

Scene 36

❦

*Will's room. Ariel and Will stand facing each other, look-
ing shocked, scared.*

"Oh, if only Kit weren't so immersed in grief," Will
said. "If he could speak to me, and understand what
I ask him. He's the only one I know who has acquaintance
at court, and who might tell us which of the courtiers
might be harboring the wolf."

"Kit?" Ariel asked. "Kit Marlowe?"

Will sighed. Even the fairy queen knew Kit Marlowe.
That was fame as a poet. "Do you know him, milady?"
he asked.

Stepping forward, he felt something under his foot,
something soft, quite unlike the rushes that covered his
floor.

"Not know him, no." Ariel shook her head. "But Milord
Quicksilver did. I mean . . ." She blushed.

Will looked away from her, well understanding what
she meant, by the high color of her cheeks. He remembered how he, himself, had *known* Silver, ten years ago,
and felt heat upon his cheeks.

Looking down, to hide his embarrassment, he saw, beneath his feet, a grey object.

Bending down, he picked it up. It was a suede glove, well cut, with fringes upon the wrist and an ink stain on the index finger. Kit Marlowe's glove.

"When Quicksilver was younger and Kit Marlowe . . ." Her blush increased and she lowered her eyes. "And Kit Marlowe also."

Kit Marlowe? Kit Marlowe was Quicksilver's lover? And why not when Will, married and with more reason to abstain had fallen to Silver's charms?

In his mind, Will heard Quicksilver saying that those who'd been touched by Fairyland would be more vulnerable to Sylvanus, but he shook his head. It was an insane thought.

Yet, this glove proved that someone had consorted with Silver in Will's absence. And it proved who it was. Did it not?

He smoothed the glove in his hand.

"You say Kit Marlowe knows people at court?" Ariel asked. "Could he . . . Could he be the one that's been taken over by the wolf?" she asked. "I remember Quicksilver said that Kit was smart and socially adept. Could Kit contrive to kill the Queen?"

Will shook his head. The idea was bizarre. The idea was unbelievable. It was but a dark cobweb of horrible thought stretching tendrils onto sunny reality. "No, no," he said. "A thousand times no. I've known nothing from Kit but kindness." He looked at Ariel, to meet her skeptical gaze. "Milady, his own son was murdered."

"Yes, and how came that child to be with that man, so late at night? Will, what does Marlowe look like?"

Will shrugged. "It cannot be."

"Just tell me, Master Shakespeare, please."

Will shrugged again. Ariel would see it was nothing. She would see it meant nothing. "He's a small man," he said. "Shorter than I. With auburn hair, and an oval face, a small moustache, and grey eyes."

Ariel's gaze sharpened. Her breathing quickened. "He is the one, Master Shakespeare, he is the one." She looked at the glove in Will's hand. "Is that his glove?"

"Why, I believe . . . But how could you know?"

"There's a lingering mind print upon it, one that is not yours. I shall home in on that mind print, and I shall rescue my lord. Even if he's taken over by the wolf, the wolf won't be so powerful in daylight."

She put a dainty finger forward, and touched the glove.

In the next breath she was gone, leaving nothing behind, but only a spark and afterglow in the air.

Will looked at the glove in his hand.

Kit Marlowe, a murderer? The murderer of his own child? The harborer of the wolf? Kit Marlowe plotting to murder the Queen?

Will could not credit it. Kit Marlowe was a good man, the best poet Will had ever heard. And he'd helped Will so, finding him patronage that would allow Will to live.

But Will remembered St. Paul's, and the amusement in Kit's gaze at Will's poetry. Why would Kit help a poet in whose words Kit held so little faith? And who had been those men who took Kit away? And how had Kit got free of them?

He stared at the glove in his hand. It was Kit's glove, indeed. Will remembered the ink stain upon the index finger.

But Kit had never come into this room while Will was here. Once he'd stayed at the door by Will's choice, and once by his own.

So, he must have been here when Will was not. Kit must have been in while Silver was in here alone.

Will remembered Silver saying she was going to someone who would help her. And Silver had come no more. She'd been transported to Never Land.

Will squeezed the glove. If he could not trust Marlowe, whom could Will trust?

Yet Silver had gone to someone she trusted. And found Sylvanus in that guise.

Scene 37

ॐ

Marlowe's room. He holds the dagger in his hand, and looks, amazed, now at the dagger, now at the hand that holds it, and now at his own face, reflected, haggard and shocked-looking, from his mirror.

Kit stared at his reflection, disbelieving.

Was it his imagination that prefigured another's will where his own cowardice prevailed?

Again he tried, with renewed fury, to bring the blade to his waiting throat. His hand moved not. His mind raced.

Was an elf within him, controlling his every thought? Not Kit's own damned soul at all, not his darker half, but something like this, something evil, come from the darker reaches of the under world to plague him.

"Ah no," the voice of the elf spoke through Kit's mouth, in more pedantic accents than Kit had ever used. "Ah no, you won't lay all the blame on me. For it was your own dark soul that called to me, your tainted heart that held me fast.

"Twice, before you, did I try to possess those touched by fairykind. The first died before I'd fully installed myself. He died at the thought of blood, the thought of kill-

ing. The second rebuffed me before ever I got near." Kit's
mouth twisted upward and smiled at him, in a suave, superior way that reminded him of the dark elf in the night.
"But in you I found my match and my mark, and you *will*
serve my turn."

Before Kit's tongue rested, a scream in his own voice
tore through his lips. It surprised him as much as the voice
of the elf, and yet he knew it was his own, his own anger
and injured grief screaming out of his grief-bruised throat.
"Oh monster, oh creature from the abyss, I will avenge
me."

Laughter echoed through Kit's mouth, stopping the
grief there with bitter gall, and smooth words poured out.
"Vengeance? What? Thyself upon thyself? How will you
contrive such, Master Marlowe? When your own hand
plays you false and will not ply your dagger to seek your
death?"

Kit's eyes looked at the mirror, horrified.

"Yet will you do my bidding and attain my goal, like
a good servant who does his master's will." Kit's lips
smiled at his blank, shocked stare in the mirror. "Ah, good
Kit, you shall be tame, a common household Kit. Your
evil called to mine, your darkness bound me to you. You
shall reign with me upon the earth once we have con-
quered. And to that end, we must only kill a Queen. A
Queen ephemeral and passing as is the common run of
mortals. And she is old. We'll be robbing her of a few
years. Nothing much."

Kit thought of the Queen, of his plan of gathering all
warring courtly camps, and the Queen, too, in Deptford.

Had that been the wolf's doing all along? Kit had
thought himself free. Kit had thought it his own clever
plan. He'd thought he'd contrived it to free himself of
Poley.

Oh, how cunning, how marvelous a genius Kit had believed himself, seeking to lure the Queen to Elinor Bull's. How great he'd believed the workings of his mind to be.

And all the time, there had been another, within his mind, spinning his own plans.

If Sylvanus took Kit to Deptford, if Kit allowed himself to be controlled thus far, then would Sylvanus kill the Queen.

And war would rage, bloody, over fields and towns. England would erupt in fighting and blood, should Elizabeth die without an heir.

To the murder of Imp, Kit would add the murder of England.

A frozen terror clasped Kit's heart in a band of icy panic.

Kit didn't know, didn't fully understand, why the elf wished this, but he could see the deaths, many deaths.

All those Kit knew, Will and Tom Kyd, and even cursed Robin Poley, dying side by side in senseless fray.

And Madeleine, and Kit's family too: that uncaring father, Kit's soft-eyed mother, and Kit's three younger sisters, in far-off Canterbury. All would be caught in the maw of the disorder to come.

It would all come through Kit, yet Kit could do nothing to prevent it. Carried like a lamb bound for the slaughter, he would be both victim and sacrificer, see his world destroyed, his present as obliterated as his future had been by Imp's death.

"This is hell," Kit whispered, his lips barely moving. "Nor are we out of it."

Yet what could Kit do? How could Kit prevent it?

He stared at his own wide-open grey eyes that gazed upon him from the mirror.

And in the mirror, he saw a flash.

In that moment, without his thought, without his saying so, Kit's body turned.

The elf's voice returned to his throat, the elf's roar of surprise, of anger erupted from his lips.

"Dare they?" the elf said.

Kit's hand, still raised, dropped his twelve-pence dagger.

It fell, point down, and stuck a-quiver on the floorboards.

Kit's heart sped up. Was this Silver? He couldn't let this elf hurt Silver.

But the elf who'd materialized in the burst of light looked slighter than Silver had ever been, a blond girl-elf, blue-eyed, with a child's wide-eyed innocence, a child's wide-eyed despair.

She stared at Kit with anger and disgust. "Sylvanus," she said.

Grasping her skirt all into her right hand to uncover thin legs in white stockings, she marched forward in broad strides. "Sylvanus. Give me my husband."

She raised her hand also, the mirror image of the gesture Kit's body made.

"Milady," Kit Marlowe said, amazed. "Milady. I have not the pleasure—" And then, before his lips fully closed, before he gathered his dispersed breath, a voice spoke through his lips, a cold, cold voice that chilled him to the soul. "Ariel. Well met. I'll be more than glad to help you along to Quicksilver's company."

Ariel stomped her foot. "You'll not find me as unprepared as Quicksilver," she said. "You will not find me so easy to defeat."

Raising her own hand, she did something, and a shimmer like diffused light from a candle played up and down her pale, slim figure.

"You oppose me with that?" Sylvanus asked through Kit's mouth. "Think you that the waning power of the hill can withstand *my* power? Did I not *show* you otherwise but yesternight?"

"That was the night," Ariel said. "This is the day. And you'll not have such full control of your body under the blessed mortal sun."

Sylvanus laughed. "You're wrong, milady. I fed long and well, and the strength thus gained, on sweet mortal lives, more than compensates for the loss of magic that the day brings."

A tingle ran along Kit's lifted hand.

All of a sudden, Kit realized what that meant. Magic would issue from that hand.

Understanding seared into his mind. This elf had done something to Quicksilver, and would now do it to Ariel, whom Kit deduced to be Quicksilver's wife.

With roaring intensity, Kit awoke within his own body. He threw all his willpower at his hand. With all his strength, he commanded it down.

Down and down and down, by slow, measured inches. He closed it, too, though the tingle continued, running through his arm, up and down.

"Milady, run," he said, forcing his words past the wolf's incensed roar that would have used up all Kit's breath. "Milady, run. Be gone. He has the power to send you somewhere—I know not where, but I know there you'll die."

Ariel shook her head. She looked amazed, hesitated, as if noticing the difference in the voice, but not sure who spoke. "To Never Land, he'll send me, aye, where my lord is, where no elf can survive a second sunset. To Never Land, where my lord is dying." Tears drowned out her blue eyes. She lowered her hand to wipe them.

"You will obey me," Sylvanus's voice screamed through Kit's mouth, and Kit's hand, breaking free of his control, raised itself.

In vain Kit struggled to pull it down. In vain did he try
to regain control of his own body.

The anger of the elf surged through Kit. Kit's hand
lifted. The tingle on Kit's arm was unbearable, a scouring
pain.

"Slave, vassal, vile villain, you will obey me," Sylvanus
roared, and as his hand lifted, a burst of light erupted and
engulfed the blond and fragile fairy queen.

"Oh, help, help, help me," Ariel screamed. "You are
our only hope."

Her voice died away, as if swallowed by a merciless
distance.

When the light flickered down, nothing was there, no
one was in Kit's room, but Kit and the elf that possessed
Kit's body.

The elf let go of Kit's body, then. Kit fell, exhausted,
limp, to the floor.

His face to those rushes so recently stained with bloodied water, Kit realized that he'd been the undoing of Silver
and Quicksilver also, as well as Imp.

Covered in sweat, too tired, too weak to rise, he whispered his grief to mingle with the howls of grief from
below the floor, the female lamentations so loud that they
blocked even all that had passed in this room.

"Twice I've loved, twice," he said. "And both loves
dead by my hand. How this hand smells still of blood. All
the perfumes of Araby will not sweeten this hand again."

But already the elf quickened within Kit and cut Kit's
breath with a chuckle. "Repine later, now you have my
work to do. We have a Queen to kill."

And on those words, Kit's weak body rose from the
floor, and washed itself carefully, and shaved and attired
itself in Kit's remaining clean suit.

Through it all as a man in a nightmare from which he
can't waken, Kit watched himself act, watched his body

perform the routines he'd so often performed, and marveled at his former blindness.

How vile this captivity, how base. He would go to Deptford and destroy the world, in the command of a master he could not disobey. He, Kit Marlowe, who'd never been true to friend or foe before.

He'd do the command of the thing that had slain Imp.

And yet, and yet he would have it otherwise. For it was right and meet he should avenge his son's blood upon the foul being.

Looking at his smooth face in the mirror, the face from which the elf's possession had erased all brand of grief, every wrinkle of care, Kit sighed.

But for his own cowardice, this would never have happened. He should have braved the council's pleasure and by other means confronted the noose encircling him. By means that didn't require sacrificing others. He should have cut loose the noose by means of truth and courage. Else, should he have run.

That many years ago, in Cambridge, he should have refused to turn anyone in. He should have stood his ground. He should have remained clean and loyal and got his money from poetry only.

"A plague on all cowards," he whispered to the uncaring face in the mirror. "A plague, I say, and a vengeance, too!"

He must find a way to defeat the elf. But how could he, when he was but a helpless slave?

Scene 38

❧

Will sits at his table, in his room. Scribbled-on papers litter the floor. Ink blots mar the table top, and a large bluish black block of solid ink sits nearby, waiting to have water added to it, and thus be converted into usable ink. Beside it sits a bag of fine sand, used to dry the ink after writing.

Will sat at his table, his head in his hands.

How was he supposed to write? His words, never plentiful, now came haltingly and slow to his hesitating pen.

The dream he'd had—of the three women and their threats—and Ariel and her suspicions, all danced in his head, a ceaseless, threatening jig.

How could Ariel believe that Kit Marlowe was possessed by Sylvanus? When had Kit done anything less than honorable?

No. Nothing was wrong. Kit had lost his son and mourned for him, and Ariel would soon see the folly of thinking Kit the vessel of the evil elf, Sylvanus.

Will reached for his pen, dipped it in the ink.

The pen hovered over the new blank leaf of paper in front of him.

Venus and Adonis. He must write about Venus and Adonis.

Something, something, rosy-fingered dawn.

His mind almost touched the words he should use, stretching toward them like fingers.

But—if Kit Marlowe didn't harbor the wolf, who did? Surely Sylvanus was still loose, surely dangerous, whomever he'd possessed?

The words vanished from Will's mind, and into it, another voice, another thought poured—clear as words screamed in that very room. *Oh, help, help, help me,* Ariel screamed. *You are our only hope.*

Will stood up, startled. His chair fell with a crash to the floor and splintered into many bits. His ink bottle spilled, pouring blue oblivion over the few words he'd scratched on the page.

Still holding the pen in his hand, Will looked for the fairy queen. Where was she, and why had she screamed?

His heart still racing, he remembered what Ariel had said, about hearing a mind cry from Quicksilver. Was this then it? A mind cry?

Had Ariel been taken then? Taken to the same place as Quicksilver? The place where Quicksilver would soon die?

But that meant Marlowe truly must be guilty. . . . No, it could not mean that.

Will righted his ink bottle, set his pen down in the midst of a pool of spilled blue, and stared at Marlowe's glove, which was fast becoming dyed a deep azure.

Yet Will remembered the fear in Kit's eyes when the two men had flanked him in Paul's.

Kit had gone away with them, and soon after had come to Will with a job offer, with an invitation to dinner, with marks of kindness such as Will could never have anticipated.

And it was not that Kit believed Will to be a great poet. No. Will knew better. Something had changed, but what? Had Kit thought to involve Will in some secret dealing? Will remembered the invitation to Mistress Bull's in Deptford.

And then how Kit had told him not to go there, under any account.

What did it all mean?

Will's hands shook so that he couldn't attempt to write, couldn't attempt even to right the mess on his desk. The puddle of ink had started dripping onto the floor, staining the rushes and the floorboards beneath.

Will wiped his hand on his doublet.

He was their only hope? He?

He supposed that meant Marlowe really was the harborer of the wolf. And if that were the case, what could Will do?

The two sovereigns of Elvenland had gone to face this adversary, and both had lost.

Why should Will go now, after them? Will, who had no knowledge of magic, no power of deception? Will, who until just now had believed fair behavior to bespeak fair thoughts and hadn't realized that a man may smile and smile and be a villain?

Will's heart beat a marching rhythm, but he did not know where to march. He swallowed hard. He must do something. The three old women—aspects of the female element, Ariel had called them—had told him he was their champion. Those shadows of human thought that enformed multidinous reality had chosen him. Silver had come to him for help. He'd failed them all.

But now Ariel herself had asked for his help, and how could he fail her?

Kit had told Will not to go to Deptford. Yet if Kit were

evil, then Will must do the opposite of what Kit had entreated.

Therefore, Will must go to Deptford, go as soon as possible.

Will covered his eyes with his inky hands. To go to Deptford, he must ride, and Will had no horse. He looked toward the mattress that hid his purse.

Will was fast becoming penniless once more.

Groaning, he went to get the money.

Groaning, he thought what a fool he was to be doing this.

When magical might collided, shaking heaven and earth with its clash—what could a mere mortal do?

Scene 39

❧

*Never Land, the in-between worlds—a desolate place
with no taste, no smell, and no feeling save overweening
cold. Shadows appear and disappear, like windblown
clouds, now prefiguring trees, now palaces. None of the
shapes remains in solid reality but it all changes like
shadows of wind-whipped branches. Amid these shadows Ariel walks, her eyes now dry but looking as if they
have dried from crying every tear that could be summoned to their bruised, reddened orbs.*

Where was Quicksilver? Why couldn't she find him
in the mutable landscape of this lost land?

Ariel stumbled on a grey root that momentarily
sprawled across her path. Before she'd regained her feet,
the root vanished.

Oh, what a terrible land, worse than anything that she
could have imagined. How lost she was. How much she
wanted to see her lord. Oh, that Ariel could cry, that her
tears might warm this frozen place and bring a living
ocean to this world of shifting nothingness.

How cold the shifting shapes made her feel. And her
lord had been here almost three days. Lived he yet?

She must find him. She must see his sweet face again and drink the words of his sweet address.

Tattered rags of trees with things like moss or mourning grey cloth hanging from them brushed across Ariel's face, moved by an unfelt wind.

Sometimes, through the shadows of trees and the glimmering of buildings never built, she almost thought she saw Quicksilver. But running forward, through the shadows and the shades, she found him not.

Like a rainbow, forever receding from the reaching hand, so her lord to her straining heart.

Where was he now, for whom her heart longed?

She wanted to apologize for all her misdeeds—for her distrust of him, her assumption that he had left her to disport himself in London.

He'd left to defend Fairyland. He'd done what any noble king would have done. That he'd kept it from her and would not let her help him was no more than the excess of his love and the trembling insufficiency of his self-confidence. Quicksilver had, by virtue of his division, an over sensitivity to what others might think and a tender, overgrown conscience that would not allow him to have others risk themselves in his stead, or take any part of his responsibility, though his shoulders should crack from it.

His infidelity, if it had been such, was probably no more than a symptom of the disturbance in the cosmos, the swaying winds of feminine alarm.

And if not, then it was Ariel's fault, for so wishing Silver out of sight until Silver's desires burst from their bounds and became uncontrollable in their swollen need.

Ariel walked here and there. She wished to call for Quicksilver, but the cold seemed to steal her voice. The cold was everywhere, came from everywhere at once and leached not only heat but life itself from her body.

Thus would death come, she understood, a sad death—a

nothing, a final whimper in a frozen landscape.

The air smelled musty like the grave, like a never-inhabited womb, like all that might have been but never was.

She sighed as she thought that she might have been Quicksilver's loving queen, but had not been such, and in her barren unlove, her love and her royalty belonged, rightly, in this land.

Her foot caught on something. She fell forward and the hands she put forth to save herself from hurt gripped solid shoulders and silky hair, which did not shift upon her holding them.

Quicksilver.

She knelt beside him. He wore white velvet, or perhaps the magical cold of this place had leeched color from his garments. All in white, he lay on his side, curled upon himself, his eyes closed, his blond hair spread out behind him.

For a moment, blinking, Ariel thought him dead and her heart shrank upon itself, clutching upon grief and mourning over the love she'd betrayed and could never right again.

Then Quicksilver stirred. He opened his eyes, and then his mouth, in astonishment at seeing her here.

He stood up. He put his arms out to her. "Milady," he said. "Oh, how I longed to see you. But not here."

"I thought you dead," she said and put a hand out, to assure herself of his living reality. She touched his cold chest that yet moved, in search of breath.

He shook his head, tangling his already tangled silver-blond hair. "No. Sleeping. Trying to preserve what little strength yet remains to me. It is not much and it might not last long." He unfolded himself and looked down on her, his face set and grave and regal.

Never would Quicksilver appear thus disheveled in his

court, never had she seen his face so grave, his moss green eyes so intent.

He had never looked so much like a king.

Standing on tiptoes Ariel offered him her lips, and after a brief hesitation he covered them with his own. His lips were ice cold.

Quicksilver had lingered too long in Never Land.

"Oh, milady," he said as their lips parted. "I bless your presence, but I wish we could have met beneath the sun of mortals." He ran his long, soft hand along her face, as if to ascertain by touch of the truth of all her features.

He looked so grieved at her presence here, yet so relieved at seeing her, that the warring expressions upon his face made him look comical.

Ariel laughed, as she couldn't remember laughing in days—nay, in years.

Quicksilver raised one eyebrow. "Do I look, milady, like a jester?" But he spoke softly, and his mouth still pulled in a smile, as if her mirth amused him. As though her mirth warmed him, in his cold state in this desolate land.

She shook her head. "Not like a jester, no. Never, milord. It's just that I . . . I've just realized I've been a fool."

Both his golden eyebrows went up, arching in perfect, puzzled demirounds. "You mean it not," he said. "Or else, why do you laugh?"

"Because I'm done being a fool, milord, and I only wish . . . I only wish the world weren't coming to an end through my folly." Tears sprang unbidden to her eyes and rolled down her cheeks to meet her smile.

"Your folly?" Quicksilver asked. His voice was distant, a tolling bell of death over hope. "Your folly, milady. Oh, if you knew my folly and what I've done . . ."

"I know your folly," Ariel said. "Or at least most of it. I know somehow you freed Sylvanus. And I know you made love to the human called Kit Marlowe." To his astonishment she started telling what she'd seen, what had happened to precipitate her leaving the palace in such haste.

"And you hate me not?" Quicksilver asked. His face looked even paler than when she'd first seen it, his eyes wide with horror. "Half my people are dead, and you hate me *not*?"

Ariel shook her head and embraced him. How cold he was, how cold, how icy, how impervious to touch. Like snow, new-fallen, or like old ice on a cliff face.

"How can I hate him who is another half of me?" she asked. "Whose folly is, ever, but a reflection of my own?"

She wished she could share with him the heat of her love, the pulse of her life.

But she could not.

"And now we'll die here," Quicksilver said, his voice as cold as his body. "And Sylvanus shall have sway over the world and all in it."

But Ariel touched the marble-cold cheek, the icy hands, the cold, cold lips.

"No. No. We have hope. We have hope still. There's Will Shakespeare free. He'll find a way to set things aright."

But she knew her own voice echoed with doubt, and she saw doubt in Quicksilver's disbelieving look.

Scene 40

❀

A London market, sprawling in all directions from a central point. Chickens and poultry, pigs and all manner of livestock are sold alive and dead, their feet bound or their carcasses swaying in the air. Women display baskets full of fresh-baked bread or farm-grown vegetables. At a corner of the market, horse dealers assemble. And there, Will wanders, with the look of a man who has shopped long and hard and found not what he sought.

To go to Deptford, Will must buy a horse.

But never having done it, he found it heavy going. Every horse he saw looked half-dead or too expensive. Examining a half-dead one, Will sighed.

Kit—and Sylvanus—must be in Deptford by now.

Perforce, Kit had meant to involve Will in Sylvanus's plan, and then, rebelling after his son's death, Kit had entreated Will not to go.

Else, why would Kit have cautioned Will against Kit again begging him to go? Why else, but that he feared the wolf, within his body, would call Will to Deptford again.

But why Deptford? Did Kit mean to kill the Queen there?

Will must stop it. He was the last hope of humans and elves.

"He looks lame," Will said, staring at the nag in front of him, a grey creature of indeterminate age, with patches upon its hide that looked like the discolorations of mold.

"Lame?" the dealer asked, standing beside Will and speaking so loudly that the whole fair would hear. "You insult me so? You say that of my horse? Why, he was only owned by an old parson, who rode him only to his church to preach, on Sundays, and the rest of the time was he kept stabled, and fed the best, and daily taken care of."

Will wrinkled his nose. The beast smelled diseased, too, a pungent, acrid smell. And its lower legs were all covered in mud, though the legs of the other horses in the enclosure were clean.

Will was not so naive that he didn't know the trick of covering a horse's legs in mud to make it look hale and sound, where there might be deformity or injury.

But he'd asked about every other horse in this fair that would serve his turn, and he could not find better—not among those that he could afford with the five pounds remaining in his purse.

At this rate, he'd not make it to Deptford, nor save the magical pillars of the world from their doom. At this rate, the world would be lost to Sylvanus for lack of a horse.

"Master, this horse will do you proud. You'll will him to your grandchildren, yet."

Will ground his teeth. At least the horse hide, he would will to his grandchildren.

Did Will look so much the credulous fool that all felt they must make up outrageous stories and try them on him?

"How much for the horse?" he asked.

The dealer bowed and smirked. "For you, master, for you five pounds."

And for everyone else two pounds? Will wondered if all the prices told him in this fair were like that, many times more than they should be.

Will's grandfather had left twenty pounds in his will and had been considered a reasonably well-off man.

How could a fearful nag cost five pounds? Oh, all these men must be trying to cozen Will. He must look innocent as a mewling babe. No wonder even Marlowe had sought to cozen him.

And for Marlowe—to save Marlowe, to save the elves that Will had never trusted—Will would spend all the money he had left from what Southampton had given him? What would he do then, without the money?

"Will you take him, master?" the horse dealer asked, untying the horse from the post that held it in place—though the horse showed no inclination to roam.

The beast turned pitiful eyes to Will, as though asking for an end to its sufferings.

Will would very much like to see *his* own sufferings end, too.

If he paid for this horse, if he paid now, if he paid the whole five pounds in his leather purse, he'd be back where he was a couple of days ago, with no money to eat, with no money to return to his family in defeat.

No, no. Let Marlowe kill the elves, let Marlowe and Sylvanus take over the world. Let the die be cast and all come out as it would.

What could Will do anyway, unschooled in magic, against such great evil?

Will was a poor prospect for saving the world from a magical creature, a demigod. To own the truth, he couldn't save himself from penury.

Will shook his head at the dealer, and started walking away, amid the crowd.

"Best poultry in London, buy it here," a woman yelled,

waving a live chicken, its feet bound, in front of Will's face.

Will dodged the chicken's beak. The chicken's cackle rang like a trumpet of doom.

What mattered it to Will who ruled the universe—old pagan deities, or Sylvanus, or the God of Christians, or even the uncaring, amoral deities of Marlowe's plays?

Surely Sylvanus couldn't be any more vicious than the blind woman who cut the thread of life.

Yet in his mind, he saw the child, Kit's son.

Whatever Kit might be guilty of, Will couldn't believe he'd committed that murder willingly.

And what creature would force the hand of a father against his own son? Sylvanus had done it. If such a creature ruled the world—no, wove the world anew in its image—who would be safe? What world would this be, but measureless hell?

Will touched the coins in his purse, the coins that would allow him to go back to Stratford and see his son and daughters again.

But how would they be when Will got there? What if in Deptford, in Mistress Bull's house, the final battle were won by the wrong being? What good would it do to Will to ignore it?

Would he not be like those who, in the time of Noah, feasted and drank, married and were given away in marriage, only to be swallowed by the impending flood?

Like Noah, Will was the only man, the only mortal who knew of the cataclysm coming.

And unlike Noah, Will wished to save all of the world.

Pray, how could he do this by hiding in his room and writing?

How could he do that by shying away from people who thought him a fool and allowing them to go on believing him so?

And how could he get to Deptford?

Will took a deep breath, tainted with manure and the smell of spoiled meat.

"Lace," a peddler yelled, walking past, his wears spread across his arm. "Lace such as should grace your lady's petticoats."

His lady back in Stratford needed no lace for her petticoats. But she did need her life, and she did love her children, and by all that was holy, Will would keep *that* for his Nan.

Without even realizing it, he'd turned around. In the horse enclosure, he laid hand not on the fearful nag, but on a better horse, a dappled brown beauty that frisked about with impatient spirits.

"Ah, you came back, master," the dealer said with a smirk.

"Yes, and I'll take this horse, and I'll give you two pounds for it."

"Two pounds wouldn't buy the shoes on this horse. Two pounds? Villain, you would despoil me."

The scream of the horse dealer brought stares from every person around. Will *should* shy away. He felt his face color. He felt the impulse to hide.

He was a provincial here in cosmopolitan London. He must have broken some rule and revealed himself for the fool he was.

Yet, he remembered his Nan, he remembered his children, he remembered the little corpse in the alley, the symbol and sign of all that Sylvanus might do to the unsuspecting world he bid fair to rule.

And though Will didn't fully understand the means and magic involved or all this talk of elements and aspects, he knew that there was another magical reality that twined his and that the two were linked. Through one, Sylvanus could control the other.

Will thought of Sylvanus, who'd bring children to such low ends.

He ground his teeth. "Two pounds," he said, and held on to the horse's rein more firmly.

A few breaths later, having paid three pounds, he rode the horse out of the fair headed for Deptford.

His mind was elated with his victory over the horse dealer, the respect he'd read in the man's eyes at parting.

But now he faced a tougher adversary, one not likely to be impressed with a firm stand.

Scene 41

༄ঙ

Marlowe, in a small room in Deptford, with Robin Poley and Ingram Frizer and a blond dandy known as Nicholas Skeres—a secret service man at Essex's service. The three men sit at a table, playing a game of checkers by fits and starts. Kit reclines on the bed, attempting to look calm.

Through the window came the sound of a horn, calling warning to ships lost in the fog.

Outside, mist, thick as coal soot, wreathed every portion of this port town. The air smelled heavy, with decomposing fish and unburied plague dead.

Kit lay on the bed and trembled.

She'll not come, Kit told himself, forcing deep breaths into his constricted chest. *The Queen will not come. After her narrow escape the other night, she will not be so foolhardy as to risk her life in this small room, in the hands of secret service operatives.*

But he couldn't convince himself of it. The sun was setting. Night neared. The power of the elf grew within Kit. In Kit's veins, in Kit's brain, the elf's hunger pulsed and the chant for *blood, life, blood* echoed through him like a drum.

Sylvanus hungered and Kit could not think of feeding for the creature once more, could not imagine tearing living flesh, killing men, not now that Kit knew what he was doing.

He shook with need to kill, and yet remained still by an effort of the mind.

Would the same veil of forgetfulness come over him now that Kit knew the truth? Or would he have to face the horror open-eyed? Had he only been aware of what had been done to Ariel because it had been daytime and, therefore, the elf had been weaker? Well did Kit remember that elves and fairies reigned in the night as men did during the day.

"Your conspirators come not," Poley said from the table, casting a half-laughing look at Kit.

Kit sighed. He spoke through his teeth, against the veil of blood in his mind, "Please," he said. "I've told you, my mind is disturbed. Arrest me now."

Poley gave Kit a cunning glance, a halfhearted chuckle. "Arrest is too good for you. You'll beg for it if you've led us a merry dance in a fool's paradise."

But his chuckle and his cunning look told Kit that Poley believed in the phantom conspiracy, believed it more than ever. He cast the die again and said, "I believe the hand is mine, that will be your two pence gone, Skeres."

"I'm tired of the game," Ingram Frizer said, pushing the chair away from the table. "I'm tired of waiting." He lumbered across the room to stand by the door to the garden glaring resentfully at Kit now and then.

Kit looked away and trembled. He wished they were all tired of this. He wished they'd arrest him and confine him in a solitary cell, with no one whom he could harm.

Then would the wolf spend his malice in those tight confines, and maybe even starve for lack of the life on which it fed.

Poley threw down his die upon the polished table and half turned, to look at Kit. "What say you, Kit? Your conspiracy takes long enough in showing itself, doesn't it?"

"It is a shy conspiracy," Skeres said mockingly. "A conspiracy that will come out at night only."

Kit sighed. He closed his hands into tight fists. He could almost taste their blood upon his tongue. He could feel their lives pulse, full and vital and energetic as they rushed like a swelling river all around him. He longed, more than anything, to drink his fill of that current.

If only they knew how hard it was for him to keep the elf at bay. And the sun was setting minute by minute. Soon Kit wouldn't be able to hold back anymore. The elf would have all strength and Kit none. Soon this hunger for life and need to kill would hold full control over Kit's body.

Soon—in Never Land—Quicksilver would die.

Tear, slash, eat, drink the life.

But the Queen wouldn't come and soon, soon, even Poley's cunning patience would exhaust itself, and they'd have to take Kit to some dungeon, give him to the tender mercies of some torturer.

How would the dark elf enjoy being tortured?

Oh, Kit wanted that more than anything, even if he had to suffer alongside Sylvanus. For between them, they'd killed the best child, the sweetest imp in the whole world.

Kit stood up, tripping and lurching as he fought against the sanguinary demands of the elf within his body. He tried to pace around the room, to dissipate some of his impotent anger, his painfully coiled feelings. But pacing was too hard when he was not fully master of his body. He fell to the bed once more.

Poley rose from the table, and Frizer and Skeres with

him, their movement rocking the table and scattering the pieces upon the polished wood.

"Think not of escaping," Poley said. "You have an appointment, Master Marlowe, with the questioner."

"Oh, take me now," Marlowe said, extending both his hands. His voice came strangled, through his need and the demands of the elf. "Take me now. Let the torturer do his worst. There's reckoning to be done, and I'm eager to pay."

"What mean you here? What strife is here?" a sharp feminine voice asked from down the hall, and quick, decided steps approached.

Kit turned, lurching, losing his balance.

The Queen of England entered the room.

Oh, Lord, she came unguarded.

Skeres and Poley and Frizer rose, all of them looking scared, guilty, as intelligence men always did when surprised.

Kit's thought suspended, Kit's amusement at the spies' discomfiture halted. Upon that thought another thought came, trailing upon the heels of the first.

The Queen, the Queen. Don't fail me now, vassal. We hold the world within our hands, the power of the ages within our reach.

Kit felt the wolf's power expand and pull, extending tentacles of thought, reaches of feel to every limb of Kit's, to every pore, to Kit's every nerve.

Like a conqueror entering a citadel whose gates have long been broken, thus the dark elf navigated Kit's veins, and sent his orders along them.

Tear, slash, eat, drink the life.

Yet the sun remained up in the sky. *Vassal,* the thing called him, and vassal Kit might be, but Kit didn't wish to kill his Queen.

For all his crimes, all his mad, reeling sins, Kit had

never yet sacrificed a whole country, nor did he wish to do it now.

"No," he said. "No. Run. Run, your majesty, run. Save yourself."

The Queen stared at him exactly as though Kit were a dog turd freshly laid upon an expensive carpet.

"Run?" she said. "Run from whom? Run from where? This is my country, young man, and I rule it. Let rather all evildoers run from me." Thus speaking, she withdrew her hand from behind her back, and showed that in that bony, wrinkled hand she held a massive sword, its edges corroded by rust and eaten by time.

The dark elf roared within Kit, throwing Kit forward.

The Queen flourished her sword. "What treason is this?" she yelled.

Poley, Skeres, and Frizer surged forward, seized Kit, pulled him back, away from the Queen.

But the elf had inhuman strength, inhuman power that flowed now through Kit's muscles. While Kit struggled within his body, seeking to restrain the dark elf, the dark elf, driven by roaring anger, pulled away from the men who restrained him and, against their curses, their exclamations of surprise, jumped at the Queen.

I will kill her, the elf thought, his thoughts sounding trumpet clear in Kit's fogged mind. *I will kill her and through her, with sympathetic magic, will I kill the maiden, the female image that is a component of everyone and everything feminine in both worlds. With the Hunter already wounded, the fabric of the worlds will not withstand the death of the maiden. The stuff of the universe will dissolve within man's minds, leaving all at our mercy. The worlds will be ours. You'll rule mortals, vassal, and I'll rule elves.*

Elf-possessed, Kit's body dove under Elizabeth's sword-wielding arm and, teeth bared, jumped toward the

Queen's neck. Kit's hands held the Queen's arms.

The Queen screamed.

Kit smelled her perfume of camphor and stale roses. His teeth almost closed upon the parchment-dry skin.

And then he stopped.

A man entered the room, behind the Queen, another familiar face—balding forehead, dark curls, and falconlike golden hairs.

In that moment, Kit regained control of his body and stopped, still holding the Queen but not moving.

The elf protested and pounded upon Kit's nerves like a man punching at an unmovable wall.

But all Kit could think, all Kit could feel, was how sorry Will had been at Imp's death. A true friend and, oh, how kind and honest Will had been to Kit, always.

Of all the people in this room, Kit wished Will to remain alive, even more than he wished the Queen to live.

"Oh, Will," Kit said. "Why did you come? Had I not warned you stay away?"

Scene 42

❧

Will stands near the door of the room. Kit holds the Queen, who kicks and screams but whose arms Kit keeps immobile. Skeres and Frizer, at Poley's gestured command, duck around the Queen to flank Will.

Will would swear it looked as though Kit had been going to bite the Queen and then stopped.

What was it, then? Was it the wolf in Kit, going to kill the Queen by the only methods the wolf knew?

But if so, then why had it stopped? And why did Kit look so stricken, and why had he reproached Will for coming?

"I came because I had to," Will said, ignoring the two dark-attired men who flanked him. "I came because you needed help, and because Quicksilver and Ariel needed help, too."

"So Kit had warned you away, had he?" a good-looking blond man said as he advanced, and pulled Kit away from the Queen. "And who are this Ariel, this Quicksilver? They sound like code names to me."

Kit stumbled backward, as though not fully in control of his body.

Kit's face had an intense look of concentration, as
though every muscle were taut, every nerve straining. The
look was familiar, but Will could not place it.

"You can't help me, Will," Kit screamed at Will, ignoring the blond man. His voice was a lost wailing, his
eyes full of dread. "No one can help me for the night will
come soon and then it will all be up."

"I think it is all up now," the good-looking man said.
"I think it is all up now, Marlowe. Who are Quicksilver
and Ariel?" he asked Will. "And what do you know of
the conspiracy to kill the Queen?"

"Who is he?" Will asked Marlowe. He tried to duck
past the Queen's sword, and get near Marlowe, but the
two tall, dark-attired men seized his arms.

What was this? It looked to him as though the knots of
Marlowe's life had all come to a tying point here, all en-
twining and enmeshing with each other. "Who are these
people?"

"You'd have me believe you don't know who we are?
You, who conspire with Marlowe?" the blond man asked.

"Oh, good Will Shakelance, permit me to introduce the
two men besides you. The one on the right is Skeres, the
one on the left is Frizer. And the other gentleman is Poley,
sweet, treacherous Robin Poley, who sends men to the
gallows with a smile." Kit's voice had a mad echo of his
old, amused drawl. "They are secret operatives. Spies.
Spooks."

He could talk, yet he remained immobile, Will thought.
Immobile and strained, every muscle working at remaining still.

Suddenly, the expression on Kit's face made sense—
the poet looked exactly like Will's seven-year-old son,
Hamnet, when he tried to stop breathing, for a tantrum.

He looked like a man controlling the uncontrollable.

Sweat sprang from Will's every pore.

Only Marlowe's willpower stood between them and the unleashed might of the wolf—the might of a supernatural being in full rampage.

"Treason, foul treason," the Queen yelled. She'd brought her sword down, but she glared at each of them in turn. "If these men be spies, they be not mine. I know naught of what they do. No one tells the truth to me, a fragile woman, and yet I am Queen and King enough for this kingdom." She stomped her foot.

Kit's eyes looked wild and he seemed just like Hamnet when he couldn't stop himself from breathing anymore and must suck in living air.

"Kill me," he yelled. "For mercy's sake, Will, if you're my friend, kill me."

Skeres and Frizer and Poley, himself, stared at Kit as though he'd lost his mind.

Will unsheathed his cheap dagger, which he'd never used for more than eating his meat in taverns. Will had never with his own hand killed man or beast, save only a deer once, when he'd been practicing archery. And that he'd regretted enough.

Could he kill Kit? Could he actually plunge the dagger into the beating heart of the greatest poet who'd ever lived?

Faith, Will did not know.

But aye, he would try to kill the wolf.

Even if he must die trying.

Scene 43

❦

The room as before, but seen through Kit's eyes. He stands behind Poley, facing the bewildered-looking Queen and, beyond her, Will and Frizer and Skeres.

"You do not want to die," the elf whispered through Kit's lips. "You do not want to die, Kit Marlowe."

And while Frizer, Skeres, and Poley stared, wide-eyed, the elf went on, speaking persuasively through Kit's mouth, trying to convince Kit's ears.

"Look, look at all you'll have."

Behind Kit's eyes, like an awakening dream, images of food passed, and images of young bodies, young people, female and male, ready to obey his every whim, and images of Kit, crowned, upon a throne.

"If it's the child you lament," the elf said, "you can sire many."

Those words broke the spell. The images disappeared from Kit's eyes, leaving only the image of Imp. Imp, dead in that alley.

Nothing—no one—could ever replace Imp.

How could this creature, this being, so lack feeling and love that it did not even know that one child was not another, that a child could not be replaced?

And such an elf, such a creature, would rule the world?

The arms that had started turning pliable, the legs that Kit had almost yielded control of onto the elf, suddenly became rigid again and locked, with all of Kit's strength, against the elf's desire.

Kit had not wanted to die before. No, God's death, he'd wanted to avenge himself on the elf, he'd been willing to endure torture for that, but in faith, he'd not wanted to die.

He still didn't *want* to die. The elf knew the truth about Kit. Kit loved the world and its joys too much to wish to depart it at twenty-nine.

Yet he would die, he thought. He would die to take out the wolf with him.

He saw Will Shakespeare draw his dagger, a dagger cheap enough that it probably wouldn't pierce a good suit, and Kit wished it would pierce a suit and more, wished it would plunge into his own treacherous heart.

Will jumped straight at Kit.

Skeres and Frizer moved too late.

Kit still remained immobile, holding the elf at bay, but just barely. Like two men, locked in arm wrestling, each just as strong as the other, they each kept the other from moving but could do no more.

And Kit wished that Will would kill him.

But Will stopped, the dagger poised, in front of Kit as though his courage failed him.

"I cannot kill you, Kit, I cannot," Will yelled.

Within Kit the wolf roared, "Nonsense. All this is nonsense."

He raised a hand so suddenly that Kit didn't anticipate it or stop it.

Force flowed through the hand, magical force, the strange tingling sensation that Kit had felt before.

Was the creature sending the Queen to Never Land? Could humans be sent there?

But instead, the wolf seized Kit's mouth and spoke through it, once more. "All of you," he said as energy flowed through his hand. "Kill her."

Poley, Skeres, and Frizer unsheathed their daggers.

Will looked confused.

Kit gathered all his strength. He'd die trying this, but he must shield the Queen with his own body.

Scene 44

✣

The same scene as before, but through Will's eyes. Will stares in horror as the two men beside him advance toward the Queen, daggers unsheathed. Marlowe steps forward, toward the Queen, in a slow walk, like an ill-controlled puppet.

For the oddest moment, for no more than a breath, Will wished to kill the Queen.

It was the voice of the elf, and whatever magical compulsion he'd thrown from his lifted hand.

But Will had been bespelled before, and had endured the spells and lived through them.

Will was a Sunday child, who saw the hidden and felt what no other man could feel. That gave him power for magic perceived is magic halved.

He shook the spell from his back, like a dog shaking water from his fur.

"You may come all, curs," the Queen yelled. "I'll see you all hanging high." She twirled her rusty, edgeless sword with amazing agility, smacking Skeres's, Frizer's, and Poley's daggers from their hands. "I will see you all hanging. I knew what villainy was passing. I knew Cecil hid things from me."

In her triumph she didn't see Frizer snatching Kit's dagger from its sheath and speeding it toward her heart.

It all took the space of a breath.

Thoughts seared through Will's brain like a dream. He couldn't let the Queen die. The whole world depended on her, old and insane though she might be. Order must be preserved. Hamnet must be allowed to grow up. The wolf must be defeated.

As the thoughts flashed, already Will was airborne, leaping.

He jumped in front of the Queen at the same time that Kit, in his lumbering walk, had got close to her.

Not sure if Kit was himself or Sylvanus-controlled, Will gave Kit a shove, seeking to get him out of the way.

In that moment, Frizer lurched forward, and Kit, tripping, fell toward Frizer.

The dagger Frizer held, Kit's own dagger, plunged into Kit's eye.

Blood jetted forth.

Kit dropped to the floor, writhing.

Horrified, blood-spattered, Will stepped back. He thought that he heard Kit's voice whisper "Thank you," but he had to be dead before he even touched the floor, and from his dead lips the wolf screamed.

"Oh, curse the luck and the world and all of you. I will not die alone."

Kit's dead hand rose, and from Kit's still-twitching fingers, magical sparks flew.

Will felt as if a roaring wind sucked him through unbelievable ice and unbearable cold.

Scene 45

ᗧᗧ

Never Land, where Quicksilver and Ariel stand. Of a sudden, in an explosion of light, Kit Marlowe materializes, a dagger through his eye, bleeding profusely—from a certain transparent greyness, it's clear he's a ghost. And Will materializes after Kit, looking bewildered.

Where was Will?

At first Will thought he'd emerged onto a foggy shore, with the roar of the ocean in the distance, and sand swirling in the whistling wind.

Then he blinked and he realized that he stood in a vast forest, the trees towering overhead.

He blinked again, and saw himself in a city, with tall, baublelike, half-transparent palaces rising in all directions.

And through these half-perceived, half-seen structures, Will saw Kit—or was it Kit's ghost?—a pale and wan Ariel and a Quicksilver so transparent, so weak, that he might well be a ghost himself.

"Never Land," Will whispered to himself, remembering the place where Quicksilver had been sent. "I am in *Never Land*." But saying didn't help his bewildered senses to understand the place.

He stepped, half-dazed, toward Quicksilver while Marlowe, smiling softly despite his horrible, bleeding wound and the blood fast congealing on his blue suit, walked toward Will, his mincing step a fair imitation of his stroll at St. Paul's.

"Friend Will," he said. "I must thank you—"

"Will," Quicksilver said. His voice was very faint, very cold, little more than the whisper of the icy wind. "And Kit. What happened to Kit? What woe is here?"

And Ariel said, "Milord, do not speak. Save your energy."

Never Land, Will thought. Which meant that Quicksilver was nearly dead as the sun would now be setting in the mortal world.

A flash of light shone behind them, and the wolf materialized. Transparent, but not so much as Quicksilver, not even so much as Marlowe, it looked dark—dark and massive.

"You are my soul's abhorrence," the wolf growled. Though in canine form, he spoke with human words, words were shaped and built of growls and malice.

The landscape which, for the moment, had settled to gigantic trees with blowing sheets of moss hanging from them, seemed to become darker, whatever light there was being concentrated, caught by the wolf's dark form, his dark core.

"You"—it turned to Kit—"have cost me my body, so hard-earned."

"And you"—the baleful eyes of the beast turned to Will—"it's the second time you cross me, and it shall be the last." The wolf's fur ruffled and his eyes seemed to flash with cold light as his fangs glinted by the pale light of an evanescent palace. "And you . . ." He turned to Quicksilver. "You, traitor spawn of a lowly woodland spirit, you who call yourself my brother, you and your half-changeling woman also shall die. All of you shall die here. All of you at my mercy. For I have more energy than any of you here, and here I shall ensure that you all die."

Will felt as though fear froze him, terror gripped him, panic stopped his breath.

He'd never see Nan again. He'd die here in this land of half-reality and no one would even know where he had gone.

Or why.

Scene 46

☙

*The same scene as previously, but seen through Quick-
silver's eyes. The landscape seems to waver and shift even
more than before, since Quicksilver is dying of weakness
and lack of magic.*

Quicksilver saw fear of death in Will's eyes. Ariel, her
arm around Quicksilver, attempting to support him,
trembled at the wolf's words.

And Kit—Kit was perforce already dead, already a
ghost. Never Land would eat the substance of Kit's spirit
and wholly drain him away. Kit would be no more. No
soul would remain of the great human poet. Kit would
have no ever-after, no life after life such as other humans
were entitled to.

And Quicksilver himself, feeling himself die, could
only think that he couldn't allow that.

He himself was dead. All his mistakes, all he'd done
since taking the crown of the hill, had only justified Sylvanus's belief that he'd bring ruin to all.

Ariel had told Quicksilver of the blight and the deaths
in the hill, and on whom should the blame for those rest,
but on Quicksilver?

Oh, let him die, but let Ariel and Will leave here in peace. And let Kit go free, while his spirit yet existed.

Trembling, but thinking that if the wolf listened to anything, it would be Quicksilver's true submission, Quicksilver shook off Ariel's arm.

He walked halfway to the wolf and knelt down on the shifting ground, now marsh now sandy desert.

How cold the ground. How cold Quicksilver. He gathered his meager force and spoke, his voice scarcely louder than the howling wind. "Brother, the time and case require haste: Look here, I throw my infamy at thee. I will not ruin my father's hill, nor by demanding the crown see my friends dead. Maybe I was never fit to govern the hill. The present seems to confirm it." Quicksilver took his hand to his chest in a show of honesty. Never Land had leeched him so, he could barely feel his own hand.

"I'll no more bend the fatal instruments of war against my brother and my lawful king. Aye, have the kingdom, Sylvanus, return to the hill. Let the hill power cloak you in a new body. And be our king, and I your loyal subject. In witness of which, I bend my knee." He opened his hands, as if to show that he was there, on his knees, and he bent his head in true submission.

Oh, only let Sylvanus believe his submission. Oh, only let the others go.

Behind him, Ariel said, "No, milord. You cannot give the hill to him."

Quicksilver looked over his shoulder. A single look that commanded his loved lady to silence.

The wolf grinned, fangs exposed in a gloating smile. "You beg prettily, brother." The smile broadened and green, glowing saliva dripped from the fangs. "See what fear does. And longing for life."

His life? Quicksilver had never expected to get out of this with his life. "Life? Oh, I long not for life, nor did I ever expect you'd let me live. Only let these three go on whom my heart is set. Let Ariel to the hill, let Will to London, and let Kit go to whatever destiny awaits him, beyond this desolate land, where his spirit will be swallowed by nothingness." He looked back over his shoulder, taking a last look at Kit, Ariel, and Will. "Listen, listen. I am so sorry for my trespass that I here proclaim myself ready to die. Ariel, you must be loyal to my brother, now your king. And Will, you must strive to be a friend to the king of elves. And Kit. . . . Fare thee well, Kit . . . and pardon me. I was wrong and so to my brother I turn my blushing cheeks.

"Pardon me, Sylvanus. Spare them. And take revenge on me as you will." His words were exhausted with his breath. He knelt, and tried to hope.

Silence reigned yet after he had stopped speaking.

The cold, leeching wind howled around them and Quicksilver shivered with it.

Then Sylvanus laughed. His laughter, colder than his voice, visibly curled in coils of darkness around them all. "Brother, you call me? I have no brother, I am like no brother, and this word 'love,' which graybeards call divine, be resident in men like one another and not in me: I am myself alone. And what do you expect with your speech to excite: pity or fear?" The dog snarled and growled and, with bared fangs, approached Quicksilver's kneeling figure, walked around and around him, in sullen menace.

Quicksilver quivered, but made no sound, nor did he change his kneeling, imploring stance. Was it all lost? Even this, his meager hope, that he might die here alone?

"You ask me to spare your loved ones? I, that have neither pity, love, nor fear." More laughter echoed, chillingly, through the air.

"Indeed," the wolf spoke again. "I often heard my

mother say I came into the world with my legs forward. The midwife wonder'd and the women cried 'O, bless us, he is born with teeth!' And so I was; which plainly signified that I should snarl and bite and play the dog."

With a low growl, half-laughter half-menace, the wolf said, "And so I shall. And so you die. All of you."

Quicksilver saw the wolf jump through the air and tried to roll out of the way. But he had not the energy to be quick, and he knew he would die.

And the other three hostages after him.

Scene 47

༄

The same scene, but seen through Kit's one eye.

Kit saw the wolf leap toward the defenseless, kneeling
Quicksilver. If any love remained in Kit's stilled
heart, it was his devotion to the dual sovereign of Elvenland.

He jumped forward, at the same time that Ariel did.

He smiled at Ariel, a flashing smile, and didn't realize
that his injury might make it look like a rictus, until he
saw her answering, startled gaze.

The elf and the human who loved the same being
looked at each other, both with a kind of wonder that the
other should feel the same, then turned their attention to
their beloved who must be protected.

Quicksilver must be saved, and for that he depended on
them now that he was for once too weak to save himself.

Ariel folded herself upon Quicksilver, protecting his
body with hers.

Kit interposed himself between them and the wolf's
snarling menace.

"No," Kit yelled. "No, cur, no, mangy wolf. You shall
not have him. Your crimes end here. I'm not afraid of

you, for I have died already, and a man can die but once."

But even as Kit yelled, the wolf jumped through Kit as though Kit weren't there and set to, growling and snarling, tearing at Ariel's arm that protected Quicksilver's face.

Scene 48

༻✿༺

*Never Land from Will's viewpoint, as he watches the wolf
attack the Queen of Elvenland.*

Will felt frozen with fear, iced with despair.

Watching the wolf bite and tear at Ariel's arms,
listening to her scream, hearing Quicksilver imploring her
to let the wolf at him, listening to Marlowe bemoan his
immateriality, Will thought the wolf would come for him
next.

If Quicksilver's courage wouldn't move the wolf, if Ariel's grace didn't mollify it, if Kit's mad rage was to no
effect, what could Will do that would save him? Save
them all?

Will was a mere mortal, without even the magic that
Ariel must still have, after Never Land had leeched almost
all.

Will was a nothing. A failed poet. An absent father.

The wind of Never Land robbed him of hope and
strength.

And yet an idea formed in his mind. The wolf had taken
human form to do a type of magic. Sympathetic magic.
Will's hand fell to his dagger.

The wolf was not truly alive, and he couldn't be killed, and yet . . .

Holding his dagger, clasping it tight, Will said, "Thou art a dagger of the mind, and will cut through spirit."

The idea was insane, yet the new Will, the Will who had learned to be foolish sometimes and expose himself to ridicule to save himself greater pains, would try this. And what could happen to Will that would be worse than shortening a life expectancy little worth mentioning?

He stepped up behind the wolf, who, absorbed in mauling the Queen of Fairyland, didn't notice the mere mortal.

Will drew his dagger.

"No, Will. He'll go for you," Kit Marlowe whispered, his immaterial form touching Will. "And he can't be killed thus."

But Will raised his dagger and let it fall. The wolf could be killed thus, for it was magic. Sympathetic magic. Will would do the gesture and thus visualize the result and bring it about by the force of his wishing.

The dagger went into the wolf's grey fur.

The wolf howled, letting go of Ariel, and turned his head to try to bite Will, but his fangs wouldn't reach

Black blood poured out over Will's hand.

And Will plunged the dagger again and yet again.

The wolf bayed and writhed.

Will visualized the wolf dead, the force gone out from the dread creature. "Now die, die, die, die, die."

The wolf bayed a last, awful scream, half-human, half-canine, and then collapsed, rolling off the sovereigns of Elvenland.

Ariel stood, shaking, cradling her torn, mangled arm.

Quicksilver stood, quivering, almost wholly transparent.

Marlowe looked at Will amazed, awe in his one remaining eye.

Far in the distance, a Hunter's horn sounded.

Scene 49

Never Land seems to stabilize and freeze in dark, dreary outlines, with towering trees from which hangs moss like winding sheets. From the grey sky marred by wisps of black cloud, the Hunter's dogs, and horse, and the Hunter himself appear.

Strange how one's idea of fear changed.

The first time Will had seen the Hunter, in the forest so many years ago, he'd thought him a dread being, full of majestic menace.

Now, standing amid a magical land that shouldn't—that in a greater sense didn't—exist, his hands tinged with the blood of a magical creature, Will found the Hunter reassuring. The Hunter was something of forest and glade and the more rational world of Fairyland. A lord of justice, justice that could not be averted.

Will sheathed his dagger, and stood beside the corpse of the Hunter's dog, while the dread gigantic horse of shadow galloped down from the sky, and while the pack of the Hunter's dogs approached, growling, threatening, fangs bared, menace in every limb.

Did the Hunter mean to take revenge for his dog?

Will couldn't credit it.

The man who'd been afraid of approaching a theater owner, the man who'd let everyone cozen him and fool him, for once stood his ground, proud and sure of his actions.

The Hunter descended from his horse, and whistled his dogs to heel.

The creatures crowded around him, silent, menacing.

"How so now?" the Hunter asked Will. "How so now, mortal? You dare kill my dog?"

The Hunter's voice was like icy daggers, his eyes—a blue burning within the perfect, immortal features—transfixed Will.

But Will gathered his voice, and threw his head back. "I did what I must do, to protect myself and those who depend on me for protection."

Something like laughter rumbled from the Hunter.

What could laughter mean from such a creature?

"Did you now?" the Hunter asked. "Did you now? Then no more can be asked of you. I, too, do what I do for the same reason." The darkness that was the Hunter's face shifted and changed. Somehow it looked friendly, calmer. "And the dog's death has healed me, and restored the world."

The Hunter looked, Will thought, knowing it was insane, approving and benevolent. "None of you should be in Never Land." He looked at Will, then at the other three. "None of you."

He frowned at Quicksilver and Ariel. "You—you, sovereigns of the ancient hill. For what you've done to me, oh King, you've paid well. Since all is returned to its proper aspect, you'll evade my vengeance. Get thee hence, before you die of it. Both of you will be well as soon as you return to the world of living. All your wounds will be healed. All your power restored." The Hunter's gigantic arm made a gesture, and in the air, glimmering, a bridge of golden light appeared. The other end of it fetched within the golden throne room of Fairyland, for the moment deserted. "Go," the Hunter said, gesturing at Quicksilver and Ariel. "The blight is gone from your hill and evil from the land. Those who died are gone, but those wounded and ill are hereby cured by this restoring of the natural order. Go and reign justly."

Slowly, incredulously, Ariel, still nursing her arm, helped Quicksilver up.

By the bridge, Quicksilver turned to Will and bowed, and smiled, a small, hesitant smile at Kit Marlowe's ghost. "Good night, sweet prince," he said softly. "And flights of angels sing you to thy rest. Forgive me, Kit."

Kit bowed and averted his face, tears sparkling in his one remaining eye.

Slowly, haltingly, Ariel and Quicksilver turned and walked arm in arm across the bridge.

The bridge, the throne room of Fairyland, all remained visible, till Ariel and Quicksilver arrived there and set foot on the pristine marble floor.

Then they turned to look at those left behind.

Quicksilver looked strong, perfect. Ariel's arm was whole. Then the bridge and the view of the Elvenland vanished.

The Hunter said, "Now you, Master Marlowe, to that judgment you've evaded too long." With a wave of his arm, Marlowe also vanished.

"And you, my good Will," the Hunter said. The smile-like something sparked in the Hunter's majestic, thunderous face.

But Will had remembered something.

"Wait, my good lord," he said. "Wait. For in Deptford, in that room, we left three men with the Queen of England."

"And?" the Hunter asked. "What fear you? Fear not. None of them will hurt the Queen—none of them—once the wolf's magic was gone. The Queen has returned to her palace. Her spies have arranged a tale, that says Marlowe was killed in self-defense. The gears of deception shall grind on, and soon everyone will believe the deception." Something like a gigantic sigh escaped the Hunter. "Few men can believe the fantastic and many often prefer more work-a-day lies.

"However, perhaps the Queen will remember you, Master Shakespeare. Perhaps she'll remember you defended her. Who knows what benefit might not come to you thereby?"

The Hunter waved his hand. "Go back to your room, Will, and sleep well. You shall find the money you spent on your horse multiplied, safe beneath your mattress. You have saved the worlds, Will. Now go and be a poet."

Again the rushing wind, this time warm, and Will lay in his bed, wondering if it were not all a dream.

But he got up and found, beneath his mattress, that the lord's purse was full again, fuller than it had ever been, with ancient coins and glittering golden jewels. A thousand pounds, perhaps. A fantastical sum, enough to buy a share in a theater company, if Will should decide to do that.

Epilogue

❧

The primeval forest of Arden, as it once was, with large trees, crowded close. Upon the ground the three spinners sit, working the threads of life. Amid the trees, Marlowe's ghost appears and solidifies.

The three Fates spin beneath the trees of a forest, outside time and space.

"So the king has got his crown," the youngest one says.

"And the queen's web is spun," the middle one says.

"And the traitor's round is done," says the oldest one. She holds in her hand a dark thread, through which a vein of pure gold runs, and holds her scissors poised over it. A sigh makes her tremble. "And yet it is a pity to waste such thread. This stuff is hard to come by in this debased age. And a magic thread thus bequeathed by an ancestor full of power. . . ."

"It is illusion," the middle one said. "Merlin never was."

The younger one fingers the thread. "And yet, here's the gold, here's the vein of truth and the power and the word."

"What would you do with it?" the oldest one asks, lifting her head.

A little ways away, amid the trees, Marlowe's ghost stands, immaterial, and yet possessed of Marlowe's charm as we first saw it—his clothes are impeccably clean and the best cut, and he looks like a man on his way to a fashionable assembly. His ghost has both his eyes, both full of myrth.

A slow smile molds to his lips, and expands, into something like mischievous intent. He walks forward, charming, confident, his mincing step all that could be expected of such a London dandy, a protégé of noblemen, the toast of theatergoers.

"Give the words to the poet," he says. "Let my words live on, even if another must write them. I bequeath my poetry and the power in it to William Shakespeare of Stratford. Let anyone find fault with that."

On those words, the old woman cuts through the thread with her sheers.

Marlowe laughs. A small ghost appears beside his—a child who looks much like Marlowe, and who wears a miniature version of Marlowe's velvet suit.

"Will you tell me a story now, Kit?" the child asks.

"Of course, Imp." Marlowe extends his hand to the small boy, who takes it. "I have eternity to tell you stories." Together, they walk away, growing fainter as they walk.

Marlowe's voice comes from a long ways away. "There was once a King, and he had an only son. . . ."

"Humans," the maiden mutters to herself, and joins the spun gold to a white thread. "The livelong day I'll never understand them. Treacherous as the serpent and kind as the dove, full of bitter hatred and sudden, mild love."

"Humans are as they must be," the matron says. "And we as we are, that from their minds are born and control their fate only in this small degree."

"Everything that was will be again."

"Humans are all that is, and their heart our reign," the crone completes. The thread measured out upon her lap is now white, but through it shines a single strand of pure gold.

Curtain Call

❦

Within the too-solid city of London, in a shabby room in Southwark, close to the playhouses, Will Shakespeare sits and writes. Words flow from his pen, easy and clear.

Even as the sun with purple-colour'd face, he writes, Had ta'en his last leave of the weeping morn, Rose-cheek'd Adonis hied him to the chase; Hunting he loved, but love he laugh'd to scorn;

Sick-thoughted Venus makes amain unto him, And like a bold-faced suitor 'gins to woo him.

Though not sure whence these words came, Will remembered that Marlowe had died, and feared he'd simply inherited the great poet's genius by some magical transference.

He thought of Kit's too-brief life, his squandered genius, the son Kit had never dared own.

As soon as Will finished this poem, as it ever was, Will would go visit Stratford, and see Hamnet and Judith, and Susannah. Aye, and his sweet Nan again.

He smiled at the thought of his wife. She would soon live like a lady, if his money could buy it.

Will wasn't quite sure why, but all of a sudden he knew

he could finish the poem, too. Finish it well, and it would be good.

It would be admired and great, and live through the ages, long after Will himself had died.

In that space, neither asleep nor awake, where sometimes men know truths otherwise unknowable, Will thought he'd got something from Marlowe, some legacy bequeathed with the poet's last breath.

And though Will needed not the money, he'd go on writing. The poetry itself—Marlowe's or his own—called to him. And if it were Marlowe's, it was as well—for when a man's verses could no longer be read nor a man's good wit heard, it struck a man more dead than a great reckoning in a small room.

O utside, in the shabby street of Southwark, life ground on, the bawds went to bed, and the artificers woke and manned their workshops.

The threat of evil and dark death had been lifted from the neck of humanity, where it had rested like a naked sword. The spheres spun on, as they'd been meant to do for eternity.

In his palace the King of Fairyland made ardent love to his joyful wife.

And the one man who'd known about the threat and done what must be done to lift it from the unaware orb of the great world wrote poetry and thought with mingled gratitude and grief of the flawed genius who'd bequeathed him such a rare gift.

Author's Note

∞

In writing *All Night Awake*, I took certain liberties with history, sins of omission and commission which I should confess.

The fire in Stratford-upon-Avon took place three years earlier and not at the time at which I had it happen. It is true, though, that many houses were destroyed and the houses on Henley Street were saved.

And while it is true that the plague tormented London through the summer of 1593, it is not true that it only started then. Rather, it was a continuation of the plague that had—unnaturally—persisted over the winter. And I'm afraid it did not stop, conveniently, when Kit Marlowe died. His death, in fact, was often ascribed to the plague. A fit end—so the Puritans thought—to his riotous living.

Also, although several of Queen Elizabeth's biographers portray her as a borderline paranoid who trusted neither advisors, nor spies, nor even her ladies-in-waiting, yet it is unlikely she ever roamed the streets disguised as a commoner. But the legend of it persists and it was too charming to resist.

I committed what any student of Shakespeare will consider a more serious offense when I postponed to 1593 the poet's arrival in London. This so called "late arrival" theory was extant through the beginning of the twentieth century. However, now we have too much evidence—albeit circumstantial—of his presence in London earlier. And we believe that by 1593 many of his historical plays, *The Merchant of Venice*, and *Titus Andronicus* (the greatest play Marlowe never wrote) were already in existence. I have no excuse for choosing the outmoded theory, save that it served my own work best.

Perhaps my greatest offenses against history pertain to Christopher Marlowe. The worst of these might seem to be that I gave him an entirely spurious son. Imp is my creation and there is no evidence for him. In fact, it might be considered that there is negative evidence. Such an egregious offense as Marlowe's siring of a bastard son would surely have been written about.

Also, what we think we know of Marlowe's sexuality would make the siring of a son highly unlikely. But renaissance sexuality doesn't easily fit into our twenty-first-century mold. From Marlowe's plays alone, it seems hard to deny that he had an interest in "boys" (which in this context doubtless means men). However, what one is interested in and even what one writes about sometimes has precious little to do with one's private life, as any writer can tell you.

On that, as on other issues surrounding Marlowe's life and death—his character, his supposed atheism, his supposed involvement in the secret service—for lack of space to address them all, I refer those interested to Charles Nicholl's excellent (and deserving of more recognition than it has had) *The Reckoning, the Murder of Christopher Marlowe* (Harcourt Brace, 1992).

I'm sure I've done Marlowe as much disservice as most of his other biographers.

Whatever he was as a human being, as a poet he was

great and his death at twenty-nine was an injury done to the English language, a loss of what might have been its greatest riches. So, go forth and read because, to quote Shakespeare, "When a man's verses cannot be understood, nor a man's good wit seconded with the forward child understanding, it strikes a man more dead than a great reckoning in a little room."

On another note—to those who will resent my implication that Will Shakespeare inherited Marlowe's words—fear not. This is not—yet—the last explanation I'll advance. As unable to explain Shakespeare's genius as all others before me, I can do no more than advance all the same theories others have advanced and, by advancing them all preempt them all.

The truth is William Shakespeare's genius is beyond our ken and far beyond our attempts at explanation. On that, I'll let Kit Marlowe have the last word: "The reason for it all, no man knows. Let it suffice that what we behold is censured by our eyes" and by our insufficient imagination . . .

Sarah A. Hoyt
March 2002
Colorado Springs, Colorado

Bibliography

These are some of the books used in researching for *All Night Awake*. I have also resorted again to all the books used to research *Ill Met by Moonlight*, as well as a few others. A more complete bibliographical list will be posted on my website at www.sarahahoyt.com. However, for now, here are the essential ones, in no particular order:

Nicholl, Charles. *The Reckoning, The Murder of Christopher Marlowe*. Harcourt & Brace, 1992.

Haynes, Alan. *The Elizabethan Secret Services*. Sutton Publishing Ltd., 1992.

Rowse, A. L. *Christopher Marlowe: His Life and Work*. Grosset and Dunlap, 1964.

Christopher Marlowe. Edited and introduced by Richard Wilson. Addison Wesley Longman, Ltd., 1999.

Bakeless, John. *Christopher Marlowe*. Haskell House Pub., 1938.

Weir, Alison. *The Life of Elizabeth I*. Ballantine Books, 1998.

Hibbert, Christopher. *The Virgin Queen: Elizabeth I, Genius of the Golden Age*. Perseus Books, 1991.

Salgado, Gamini. *The Elizabethan Underworld*. Sutton Pub. Ltd., 1992.

ILL MET BY MOONLIGHT

The first book in the Shakespearean fantasy trilogy
by

SARAH A. HOYT

The brilliant story of the love that set
William Shakespeare on the path to
greatness—and the enchantment that
would surround him for the rest of his life.

0-441-00983-2

National Bestselling Author

SHARON SHINN

WRAPT IN CRYSTAL   0-441-00714-7
When a planet's religious sects fall victim to a
serial killer, an Interfed agent must immerse himself in a world of stark spirituality to save the
lives of two extraordinary women.

HEART OF GOLD   0-441-00821-6
A classic Romeo and Juliet romance set in a world
far from our own.

SUMMERS AT CASTLE AUBURN
                    0-441-00928-X
"Romantic spice, a dash of faerie, and a pinch of
intrigue...delicious." —*Publishers Weekly*

JENNA STARBORN   0-441-01029-6
"Shinn puts her romantic and graceful turn of
phrase to retelling *Jane Eyre*...[Her] sf take on a
great romantic tale succeeds wildly well."
                            —*Booklist*